University of Plymouth Library

Subject to status this item may be renewed
via your Voyager account

http://voyager.plymouth.ac.uk

Exeter tel: (01392) 475049
Exmouth tel: (01395) 255331
Plymouth tel: (01752) 232323

After Nietzsche

Notes Towards a Philosophy of Ecstasy

Jill Marsden

First published 2002 by
PALGRAVE MACMILLAN
Houndmills, Basingstoke, Hampshire RG21 6XS and
175 Fifth Avenue, New York, N. Y. 10010
Companies and representatives throughout the world

PALGRAVE MACMILLAN is the global academic imprint of the Palgrave Macmillan division of St. Martin's Press, LLC and of Palgrave Macmillan Ltd. Macmillan® is a registered trademark in the United States, United Kingdom and other countries. Palgrave is a registered trademark in the European Union and other countries.

ISBN 0–333–91876–2

This book is printed on paper suitable for recycling and made from fully managed and sustained forest sources.

A catalogue record for this book is available from the British Library.

Library of Congress Cataloging-in-Publication Data

Marsden, Jill, 1964–
    After Nietzsche: notes towards a philosophy of ecstasy / Jill Marsden.
        p. cm. – (Renewing philosophy)
    Includes bibliographical references (p.) and index.
    ISBN 0-333-91876-2 (cloth)
      1. Nietzsche, Friedrich Wilhelm, 1844–1900 – Criticism and interpretation. 2. Nietzsche, Friedrich Wilhelm, 1844–1900. Geburt der Tragèdie. 3. Ecstasy. I. Title. II. Series

    B3318.E37 M27 2002
    193–dc21
                                                                      2002072519

10   9   8   7   6   5   4   3   2   1
11   10   09   08   07   06   05   04   03   02

Printed and bound in Great Britain by
Antony Rowe Ltd, Chippenham and Eastbourne

For Mark Price

Contents

Series Editor's Foreword

That Nietzsche marks a decisive event in the history of philosophy is a statement often made. Rarely however is it given the type of exploration that enables the location of the impact of Nietzsche in relation to subsequent philosophy. If philosophy in the wake of Nietzsche is given new tasks and goals then the nature of them must require a register of a profoundly new kind. That this new kind of exploration rarely breaks through the writings of Nietzsche scholarship can hardly be disputed.

With the work of Jill Marsden we finally have a voice that can locate the register that is required to begin addressing the kind of breakthrough that Nietzsche represents. Here we find a language that is driven, that tests its own sensible possibilities in its own statements, which can elaborate a response to Nietzsche that does not pre-judge the stakes of argumentation against him. Begging the question against Nietzsche is the most common activity in writing on his achievement. The writing here, by contrast, is carried on the wave of joy that Nietzsche would inaugurate. The type of inquiry that is called for in being able to describe sensations cannot be of the same kind as is appropriate to discourse eloquently on the logical properties of statements. Therefore it requires a particular type of voice to make clear what it would be for the body itself to be engaged in writing.

If Jill Marsden in producing a writing of the kind that fits the intervention of Nietzsche into philosophy has done something rare, it is rare in the sense of the exquisite. To write well about the sensible basis of thought should itself invoke qualities of beauty and grace. To fail at this is to risk failing at everything. It is a true delight and pleasure to return from the experience of this text with the feeling that this failure has here been averted.

If there is philosophy that emerges after and because of Nietzsche then this philosophy will have to be located in relation to his legacy. This is also part of the work that Jill Marsden has here performed: setting out this legacy in relation to a set of writers whose possibility emerges through an engagement with the spiritual embodiments that Nietzsche sets out. This requires an elaboration of a philosophy that while not fitting any orthodox definition of 'materialism' or 'idealism' will interpret again the inheritance of both. Across the works of such diverse figures as Deleuze and Irigaray Jill Marsden sets out the conditions for this new type of philosophical exploration, an exploration that is one of clear *renewal*.

The return to engaging with the nature of philosophy in the wake of Nietzsche is to embrace a novel possibility. This renewal of philosophical enquiry in the fire of sensation is one that has been long awaited. It is the hope of the work that the reader will burn in reading. This is a work that cannot be read in propositional form but requires the bodily self to be engaged in reading. I salute those who would read this book in the spirit that it calls for. They will be intrepid, free and dangerous, dare I say that I can see them coming? O my friends, let us learn to be inhuman.

GARY BANHAM

Preface

This book is about the emergence of rapture in thought, an inquiry into what it enables us to think. In a particularly exquisite formulation, Nietzsche suggests that life consecrates itself in ecstasy, that it is in the highest and most illustrious human joys that 'existence celebrates its own transfiguration' (*WP* 1051). This glorious sense of exaltation also necessarily involves annihilation since joys so blisteringly intense cannot help but devastate as they delight. This is not to suggest that ecstasy is an inherently destructive force, nor that it can only be understood in terms of the states it exceeds. Indeed, this work will be concerned with ecstasy as a *productive* dynamic, one which philosophy can enter and pursue. Identified in classical antiquity with transcendence, it has long been acknowledged that philosophy is a subtle intoxicant yet the 'love of wisdom' is perhaps fated to transcend the very source of its ardour. This is why, despite its transitive formulation, a philosophy *of* ecstasy will find rapture an elusive 'object' of inquiry. Nevertheless, that ecstasy is a *feeling of life* which generates thought is an intoxicating proposition and one which I believe Nietzsche realized in his euphoric experience of the 'eternal return of the same'. The transformative potential of this profoundly captivating thought has obsessed, preoccupied and enraptured me from the 'tremendous moment' of its first encounter, leading me again and again to a strange kind of knowledge, one which is glimpsed at the very moment that the reflective powers are eclipsed. It is one of the abiding claims of this book that the notion of ecstasy which Nietzsche introduces in his early writings on tragedy, and subsequently amplifies in his later 'physiology of art', is the necessary condition for thinking eternal return. Indeed, it is my contention that Nietzsche's ecstatic philosophy shares a far greater intimacy with the aesthetic project inaugurated by Kant and developed by Schopenhauer, continuing in the twentieth century in the creative explorations of Deleuze and Bataille, than with the existentialist, phenomenological and deconstructive philosophies often characterized as its natural descendants. Despite the role which aesthetics has come to occupy as a specialism within philosophy, it is evident from its inception as a 'science of sensitive knowing' that it has always occupied a broader ambit than the philosophy of art. In so far as aesthetics constitutes an exploration of affectivity – of pleasure, of desire, of life – it maps a philosophical trajectory which circumvents cognitive judgements of being and perhaps circumvents being as such. Since ecstasy is the means by which *the form of identity is exceeded* it is hardly fortuitous that accounts of rapturous experience – be they aesthetic, erotic or mystical in orientation – should in turn yield vectors for rethinking Nietzsche's 'highest formula of affirmation'.

Nietzsche's thought of eternal return impacts as the foreshock of a sense in the process of being born. The sign of its arrival is ecstasy, as if the body were communicating a new knowledge to the self that it supports. To encounter this notion is to be intoxicated by ideas tuned to a different frequency, to catch the wave of another movement of thought. The philosophical writings which communicate this rush of delight are themselves born *of* ecstasy, attesting to the power of rapture to perpetuate the forces it provokes. For Nietzsche, this transposition of affect into thought stimulates that attraction for everything problematic, mysterious and uncertain that flares up again and again in the philosopher: this 'art of transfiguration *is* philosophy' (*GS* Preface, 3).

That Nietzsche should have proliferated so many versions of this 'doctrine', as if bemused by his own insights, may tell us something about the power of repetition as a transformative force. There is no essential truth of eternal recurrence, reproduced across numerous versions, only so many new pathways into the unknown. The enigmatic proposal that life returns eternally, elliptically presented in *The Gay Science* and *Thus Spoke Zarathustra* and explored at greater length in a series of contemporaneous notes, presents philosophy with a sign it cannot decipher. In the published work, the intimations of the thought of eternal return of the same frequently entail questions of *desire* and affirmation: 'Do you want this again and innumerable times more?; 'How well disposed would you have to become to yourself and to life to *long* for nothing *more* than this ultimate eternal confirmation and seal?'; 'All "it was" is a fragment, a riddle, a dreadful chance – until the creative will says to it: "But I willed it thus!"'; 'Oh how should I not lust for eternity and the wedding ring of rings – the Ring of Recurrence!'; 'Amor fati: let that be my love henceforth!' Eternal return is above all else a thought of the supreme affirmation of life but what it actually means to affirm life is highly questionable, a phrase too easily uttered and then abandoned unthought. If Nietzsche's announcement of the death of God is the decisive shattering of the anthropocentric ideal, one wonders what the affirmation of life, the eternal return of life, renders possible. If longing for this ultimate confirmation and seal is not commensurate with a psychological state – not a human desire in any obviously voluntarist sense – what effect can eternal return have for life? What is its value for life?

It is argued in this book that an *aesthetic* philosophy can suggest a way of understanding how thought can be *of* me but not mine. Nietzsche sees rapture as central to the reception and production of art – for which issues of sense and sensitivity are cardinal. It is through his reflections on ecstasy that Nietzsche shows that *adventures in philosophy involve experiments in physiology*. What it is possible to think depends on material conditions, a question of what a body can do. It is claimed that for Nietzsche ecstasy is a physiological condition for recreating nature – for transfiguring thought. In connection with this it is suggested that to think the thought of eternal return we have to create the categories that would render it tangible – which may also mean discarding many habits of thinking that have served us well. In the course of this enterprise I suggest some potential successors to Nietzsche's 'rapturous thinking' whose work strikes me as resourceful for the elaboration of a philosophy of ecstasy. These later thinkers include Bataille, Deleuze and Guattari, Irigaray, Klossowski and Bergson – philosophers who are not united by any obvious intellectual allegiance nor of whom could it be said that they constitute a 'tradition' as such. My aim is to show how certain works by the aforementioned develop an 'exploratory philosophy', one which pursues the 'matter' of thinking physiologically. In their different ways, each develop the 'art of transfiguration' as a philosophy of immanence, a series of exercises in 'living experimentally'.

Chapter 1 presents Nietzsche's philosophy as ecstatic inasmuch as it seeks liberation from sameness – *stasis*. *Stasis* has been tacitly equated with the Good (God) and this is why its *value* has gone unquestioned in the history of Western thinking. That ecstasy might be constitutive of the 'subject' is a thought advanced in certain contemporary hermeneutical philosophies such as phenomenology and existentialism which may seem to share an intimacy with Nietzsche's concerns. However, it could be said that even those twentieth-century schools of thought that have endeavoured to overcome metaphysics do not necessarily question the value of 'the same' at the level of the human (the horizon of finitude). In contrast to this, I show how in the work of Bataille and Deleuze the issue of physiology is foregrounded as a site for thinking beyond the human. Nietzsche poses the question of what *kind* of body is thinking here, one which is life-affirming or life-denying?

Chapter 2 considers Nietzsche's characterization of ecstasy in *The Birth of Tragedy* and related remarks in his mature philosophy which develop his understanding of recurrence and difference. It is proposed that the metaphysical priority accorded to the Dionysian conceals the more fundamental *libidinal* primacy of rapture. What it means to say that rapture exceeds the form of identity is elucidated here in an aesthetic rather than an epistemological register. This is achieved by indicating how, in terms of both Dionysian *and* Apollinian ecstasy, Nietzsche gestures towards a thought of sensitive or aesthetic *differentials*. The fact that both these dimensions of ecstasy 'fail to heed the single unit' is shown to be significant for thinking ecstasy positively rather than privatively and for understanding the interrelation of Apollinian and Dionysian non-oppositionally.

Chapter 3 situates Nietzsche's account of ecstasy within a lineage of thought stemming from Kant's account of disinterestedness as a criterion of aesthetic judgement. The chapter argues that disinterestedness is not an anti-sensuous state; on the contrary, here the *übermenschlich* may be accessed positively – sensed rather than 'known' – as a feeling of life. The claim that life expends itself 'without purpose' in art is addressed in terms of transcendental affectivity. It is argued that via Schopenhauer a latent anti-humanist strand of Kant's philosophy is deepened and intensified, prompting a new vocabulary of thinking which Nietzsche will later come to develop more fully in terms of 'the physiology of art'.

Chapter 4 explores the notion of rapture as an aesthetic state from the perspective of the 'creator' rather than the 'recipient' of art.

Drawing on Nietzsche's plans for a project entitled 'Towards the Physiology of Art', it sets out to explore what it means to say that the body is artistic and questions why rapture is given an indispensable role in artistic production. It then explores in what sense rapture is the precondition of all aesthetic activity by considering Kant's notion of genius. It is argued that ecstasy requires us to think of terms and relations as contemporaneous and that this exemplifies an extraordinarily rich philosophy of creative becoming, as pursued by Deleuze and Guattari.

Chapter 5 considers the emergence of ecstasy in thought as a site of immanent excess. This is explored in terms of 'exceptional states' of health and sickness which Nietzsche argues constitute the material conditions for both establishing and overcoming the 'form of the same'. Taking a cue from Nietzsche's reflections on the physiology of art, it is argued that the phenomenon of breakdown or collapse need not be understood privatively but may throw into relief an alternative mode of thought, a point then developed with reference to Schreber's *Memoirs*. From here, it is suggested that Nietzsche's attempt to overcome pessimism through its exacerbation illuminates the dynamic of convalescence.

Chapter 6 takes up the theme of identifying an exteriority or immanent excess at the core of a philosophy of the same and considers the extent to which a strategy of productive repetition succeeds in rendering a thought of difference. This is pursued through the sacred and erotic dimensions of rapture in mystical experience, the challenge being to think the notion of *union* without unity. Bataille and Irigaray, the two philosophers after Nietzsche who have been most searching and inventive in the pursuit of a sacred philosophy of ecstasy, have each identified mysticism as a site of primary affirmation and as a material condition for enabling an experience of intensity to break into thought. It is argued that in this endeavour they succeed in elaborating a philosophy of unknowing that bypasses the pitfalls of a speculative or dialectical discourse on the other.

Chapter 7 takes up the theme of identity in relation to notions of the self and asks what grants the limits of a human life. Exploring Nietzsche's thoughts on forgetting and the affective memory, I suggest that there is a libidinal time of the body which is concealed by the phenomenal time of the subject. The question of 'becoming what one is' is related to the experience of ecstasy as tragic oblivion and corporeal anamnesis. Insights from Hölderlin, Klossowski and Bergson are used to show how a philosophy of ecstasy is the condition for thinking the lived experience of eternal return. Here I seek to show that ecstasy opens thought to the excessive reaches of the inhuman.

Finally, in Chapter 8 I return to the question of eternal return as a transfiguring thought and consider its significance in light of these journeys into the horizon of the infinite.

After Nietzsche, the challenge for philosophy is to discover new ways of kindling an eruption of intensity in thinking. What breaks the circuit of reflexive knowing is a circling more vicious than anything yet dreamt – or perhaps only ever dreamt though never enacted. The thought of eternal return is the incursion of the inhuman into the bright sanity of philosophical practice, a compulsion to repeat sprung loose from the presupposition of prior identity. When thinking short-circuits, established connections are damaged but an alternative path is created through which an excessive current can flow. Ecstasy yields these new connections for thinking. For it is not in abandoning the desire to know that philosophy becomes ec-static: it is by increasing the charge.

Acknowledgements

I would like to thank colleagues and students at Bolton Institute for their support and interest in this project, Professor Joanna Hodge of Manchester Metropolitan University for her encouragement, Dr Gary Banham for his helpful editorial suggestions and John M. Smith for his assistance with the manuscript. Most of all I would like to thank Mark Price for his inspiration.

1
In the Horizon of the Infinite

In the Horizon of the Infinite – We have left the land and have gone to sea! We have demolished the bridges behind us, indeed, we have destroyed the very land behind us! Now, little ship, watch out! Beside you lies the ocean: it is true that it does not always roar and from time to time it lies spread out like silk and gold and reveries of goodness. But hours will come when you will realize that it is infinite and that there is nothing more terrible than infinity. Oh, the poor bird that had felt its freedom and now pushes against the walls of this cage! Woe, when you are assailed by homesickness for the land, as if there more *freedom* were to be found – and there is no 'land' any longer.

(*GS* 124)

The lure of the ocean is spellbinding for all who thirst to encounter the unknown. Its restless rise and fall communicates with an inner longing which laps at the edge of consciousness, insinuating its siren's song into all healthy terrestrial endeavour: 'Why go on clinging to this clod of earth, this way of life, why pay heed to what your neighbour says?' (*UM* III, 1). If the land promises security, community and a gentle haven from the need to think, the ocean offers a freedom so boundless that it exhilarates and terrifies to rival degrees. In the horizon of the infinite the dark and ambivalent relationship that exists between desire and destruction unfolds. The urge to escape boundedness is a desire so intense that it strives even to escape itself, the thrill of liberation and the anguish of abandon

1

describing the movement of a single wave. Such exploratory migrations are irrecoverable within any rationally grounded philosophy yet what becomes thinkable beyond its shores may stimulate a very different adventure in thinking. In the twilight of consciousness it is not the call of reason – much less of 'being' – that delicately torments our dreams.

From Descartes onwards, modern philosophy has sought to construct its intellectual edifices upon firm foundations, shielding itself from the surges of violent scepticism that might sweep it away. In a striking passage in the *Critique of Pure Reason* Kant likens the 'territory of pure understanding' to an 'island of truth' surrounded by 'a wide and stormy ocean, the native home of illusion' (*CPR* A235/B295). Where 'many a fog bank and many a swiftly melting iceberg give the deceptive appearance of farther shores', the 'adventurous seafarer' is 'incessantly' deluded with vain hopes which he is unable to satisfy yet can never fully relinquish (ibid.). Since the desire to migrate beyond the familiar is insatiable and prone to recur, Kant cautions against any contact with alterity which is not already safely anchored in the *form* of the same – the territory of possible experience. Indeed, given that the unknown (noumenon) is in principle inaccessible to experience, he suggests that it should function as 'a limiting concept' (*CPR* A255/B311), curbing the pretensions of sensibility and marking the coastline as the border of legitimate exploration. For the cartographer of reason, the possibility of navigating the vast expanses beyond the isle of 'the knowable' is a hazardous enterprise and one that can only be charted in relation to the land.

To 'leave the land' is to incur certain loss – the loss of certainty itself – for the price of a glory so captivating that it must engulf all who discover it. Such suicidal submission to the terrors of thought without foundation is decisively rejected by metaphysical and transcendental philosophy alike, the former by seeking to maintain, *inter alia*, a substance ontology of coherent subjects and objects, and the latter by thinking of the conditions of the real object of knowledge in terms of the conditioned – the 'I' of representation. Since that which eludes the *form* of being cannot be 'known', that is, it cannot be *re-cognized as the same*, philosophical consciousness can at best speculate about the unknown from the perspective of *terra firma*, commuting it to the status of an unknown *object* and thus maintaining the familiar relation of a subjective representation to what is objectively represented – as if the ocean were a mirror eternally reflecting the shore. The paradox of modern thought is that it strives to extend the boundaries of its contact with otherness by reinforcing the limits of its conditions in advance – like a sea wall protecting the subject from the threat of collapse. It is scarcely fortuitous that Freud should liken the project of shoring up the ego so that it can appropriate fresh portions of the unconscious to the work of land reclamation: 'Where id was, there ego shall be. It is a work of culture – not unlike the draining of the Zuider Zee' (*PFL* 2, 112).

It is for these reasons that Nietzsche characterizes the philosophical tradition as always having confused exploration with recognition, generously furnishing itself at the outset with the principles that it aspires to uncover. In a note from 1887 he writes:

> The *form* counts as something enduring and therefore more valuable; but the form has simply been invented by us; and however often 'the same form is achieved', it does not mean that it *is* the *same* form – *what appears is always something new* ... . (*WP* 521)

According to Nietzsche, concepts are generated by discarding individual differences between things, thereby furnishing a generic identity which 'simultaneously has to fit countless more or less similar cases – which strictly speaking are never the same and simply are dissimilar' (*TL* 1). Continual usage of the concept prompts the idea that in addition to individual particulars, an original 'form' exists which *governs and accounts* for the distribution of myriad differences. This reification of the principle of identity is epitomized by the concept 'God' which is abstracted from the 'flux of becoming' and then miraculously projected back upon it as its extrinsic explanatory principle. The conditions of production thus become confused with their products and we fall for our own subterfuge, believing in the validity of the 'truths' that we have forgotten are illusions (*TL* 1). Salvaged from the deep, these pearls of 'truth' shimmer with the lustre of eternity, steely and seemingly unengendered as if washed ashore from a world more perfect than our own.

No suggestion is made here that philosophy should 'renounce' concepts. On the contrary, Nietzsche argues that thinking 'must *assert* substance and sameness, because knowledge of something altogether fluctuating is impossible; it has to *conjure up* properties for being, in order itself to exist' (*KSA* 9/11[330]). What philosophy forgets, he suggests, is that the conditions of possibility for thinking are fundamentally 'illusory' – *a priori* fictions and finely honed metaphors which intelligent life skilfully fabricates in order to provide a narrative for itself. Since these illusions become progressively 'incorporated' into the human organism, 'conceptual thinking' will of necessity inhibit any genuine contact with alterity, for specific difference will always be mediated by representation within a concept of identity. In effect, philosophy establishes its so-called 'truths' by denying its primary inventiveness and (save to manufacture ever more baroque architectonics within which to 're-find' them) dissociates itself from its creative impetus.

To think, just for a moment, that the world might be organized otherwise is to submit to the vertigo of a world beyond identity, to awaken from dogmatic slumber to a different kind of dream.

> Only through forgetting this primitive world of metaphor, only through the petrification and paralysis of the mass of images that originally streamed forth from the primary faculty of human imagination in a fervent fluidity, only through the inassailable faith that *this* sun, *this* window, this table is a truth in itself, in short, only through forgetting that that he himself is an *artistically creating* subject, does the human subject live with any calm, security and consistency; if, just for a moment [*Augenblick*], he could get out of the prison walls of this faith, his 'self-consciousness' would slip away immediately. (*TL*1)

It is but a *moment* yet all of Nietzsche's philosophy unfolds in this dizzying instant of release. With Nietzsche, philosophy embarks on an exploratory enterprise which entails a departure from foundational thinking in all its forms. The voyage into the horizon of the infinite constitutes a journey away from the land – from the *ground as given*. Thought is no longer premised on transcendent forms nor channelled through the faculties and secured in the bedrock of the unitary subject. It is such *stasis*, such inertia of knowing, which precludes any connection with the strange, the unexperienced and the new.

Yet a disturbing problem now glimmers through the last mists of evaporating reality. However calcified these concepts might be, it is uncertain how philosophy could viably function in the absence of the coordinates of knowing. If there is no longer any 'land' in what sense is there still any 'sea'? Indeed, in default of the law of identity, in what sense are there any significant differences at all? In this regard, it is not without consequence that Nietzsche's 'In the Horizon of the Infinite' passage in *The Gay Science* should directly precede the famous 'The Madman' section in which the 'death of God' is announced:

> Where is God? [..] I shall tell you! *We have killed him* – you and I. All of us are his murderers. But how have we done this? How could we drink up the sea? Who gave us the sponge to wipe away the entire horizon? What were we doing when we unchained this earth from its sun? Where is it moving to now? Where are we moving? Away from all suns? Are we not plunging continually? Backwards, sideways, forward, in all directions? Is there still an up and a down? Are we not straying as if through an infinite nothing? (*GS* 125)

In the wake of God all is void and vacancy. Without foundation there is no point of orientation, direction, framework: no horizon of overarching truth, no sun to navigate by: 'We have abolished the true world: what world is left? The apparent one, perhaps? ... But no! *With the true world we have also abolished the apparent world!*' (*TI* 'How the "True" World Finally Became a Myth'). As absolute being haemorrhages into *infinite nothing* the chill horror of the *horizon of the infinite* impacts. If it is no longer possible to measure this transient, apparent world against the highwater mark of the true, then it is no longer possible to ground a coherent philosophy for, as Nietzsche so convincingly argues, knowledge and becoming exclude one another. The bloody sacrifice of God marks the disintegration of transcendent form and its reabsorption into the immanent productive process, the 'flux of becoming'. For Nietzsche, this is the moment at which the icy blast of nihilism impacts, provoking the terrifying realization that the *eternal values* invoked to render existence meaningful are merely exotic fantasies and that the world has no goals or ends as such (*WP* 12). Ironically, it is the 'truthfulness' cultivated by Christian morality that eventually turns against itself, discovering its teleology and brutally exposing needs for 'untruth' that can be no longer esteemed (*WP* 5). It is in questioning what grounds the ground that philosophy becomes *abyssal* – returns to the ocean upon which all order floats. Indeed, it is by virtue of striving to know (to err beyond the errors and illusions so effectively embedded in the species) that nihilism is encountered in its most *extreme* form: 'existence as it is, without meaning or aim, yet recurring inevitably without any finale of nothingness: "*the eternal recurrence*"' (*WP* 55). If one strives to know deeply enough *one returns to the depths* – the point at which knowledge becomes creative *once again*.

Nietzsche famously and provocatively asserts in *The Birth of Tragedy* that it is 'only as an aesthetic phenomenon that the existence of the world is *justified*' (*BT* 'Attempt..' 5). In this profound and extraordinary early work Nietzsche claims that it is as a consequence of the 'sublime metaphysical delusion' that thought can penetrate the deepest abysses of being that knowledge is conducted 'again and again to its limits at which point it must turn into *art – which is really the aim of this mechanism*' (*BT* 15). Rather than relinquishing the philosophical quest, it is through an augmentation of the desire to know that philosophy returns eternally to the conditions of its genesis. Hence for Nietzsche, artistic activity is no mere flight into an 'other' world of the imagination but a reconnection with the productive process that generates all idealities and forms – an active surrender to the ever changing waves of becoming. Everything rides upon how this plunge into the depths is to be thought if one is to avoid drifting as if through 'infinite nothing'. If, as Nietzsche readily concedes, thinking *must* assert substance and sameness, the challenge is to *evoke that which cannot endure*. The possibility of philosophy after the death of God must now be thought *from* the abyss.

Nietzsche acknowledges that it is 'some enigmatic desire' that compels an individual to 'think pessimism through to the bottom', to really gaze 'into the most world-denying of all possible modes of thought' – for in the process (and without intention) one may glimpse the opposite ideal, 'the ideal of the most exuberant, most living and most world-affirming man' who, beyond mere resignation, *wants* 'to have it again *as it was and is* to all eternity' (*BGE* 56). This craving fails to register on any intelligibly human scale. One has to thirst for one's ruin, be consumed by the rapture of the deep,

if one is to perceive – and wholly by chance – the devastating profundity of Nietzsche's thought. Perhaps by that very act one will
come to long *again* for one's ruin as if caught up in the maelstrom
of the *circulus vitiosus deus* (ibid.). For such explorers, the absence of
God, wholly affirmed, opens thinking to a horizon of transcendence
beyond the eternally transcendent One.

> [W]e philosophers and 'free spirits' feel, on hearing the news
> that the 'old God is dead', as if illuminated by a new dawn; our
> heart overflows with gratitude, astonishment, presentiment,
> expectation. Finally, it seems to us as if the horizon were free
> again, although perhaps not so bright; finally, our ships may set
> sail again, sail out towards every danger; every hazardous enter-
> prise of the knower is permitted again; the sea, *our* sea, lies
> open again; perhaps there has never yet been such an 'open
> sea'. (*GS* 343)

Significantly, Nietzsche does not announce a new beginning or
starting point for thinking but a *return*. The enterprise of the knower
begins (finally) again yet such a re-beginning is not grounded
within a pre-established horizon. The catastrophe of God's death
marks the collapse of the origin and *telos* according to which the
trajectory of thinking might be mapped and implicitly rediscovered.
If it is still intelligible to speak of relations between 'subjects' and
'objects' this can only proceed in default of the principle of identity
which has always served as a mooring rope, yoking knower to
known. With his voyage into the horizon of the infinite, Nietzsche
conducts philosophy into the dark, uncharted waters of repetition
without foundation.

If philosophy is to *become creative again* this 'again' is not to be
taken to imply a 'state' to be emulated and re-presented. If there is
no 'ground' – no 'same' or 'identical', then repetition cannot be a
return *to* the same. *We have destroyed the very land behind us.* Indeed,
no originality of occurrence is possible if sameness is thought conceptually, that is, as a retrieval of a forsaken identity within a closed
metaphysical economy of essences. On the contrary, Nietzsche
implies that what is at stake is a return *of* the same – the again and
again of an 'incessant' and 'enigmatic' *desire*. It would seem that it is
only by virtue of *intensifying* metaphysics – by willing nihilism to its

limit – that the possibility of a very different way of thinking might appear. One is reminded of Nietzsche's 'demon' who claims that the thought of *the eternal return of the same* has a tremendous transformative power: 'If this thought gained possession of you, it would change you as you are or perhaps crush you. The question in each and every thing, "Do you desire this once more and innumerable times more?" would lie upon your actions as the greatest weight' (*GS* 341). But what could it mean to become so 'well disposed' to oneself and to life *to crave nothing more fervently* than the ultimate, eternal 'confirmation and seal' of eternal return?

Such desire finds few advocates in the identifiably human realm but it is touched in those ecstatic moments that are shared with the demonic ('You are a god and never did I hear anything more divine!'). Amid the delirium of erotic love, of sublime entrancement, of visionary and hallucinatory bedazzlement, there is a joy that wills itself so intensely that *it wants itself more and again*. There are many readings of Nietzsche which champion a facile ethic of 'self-creation' ('Live as if every moment were worth reliving') but such a focus misses the vital sense of eternal return as an ecstatic thought. It is the thought itself which is aggressive – which changes the 'one' who thinks it. The tremendous moment is the point of an uncanny transition but one which must engulf its thinker in order to occur. From this point – which is the limit point of a human life – the horizon becomes free again. Once thought, one is eternally undone and nothing will ever be the same – rather, will only be the same – *again*.

The horizon is free but perhaps not so bright. The ecstatic revelation of the thought of eternal return is not a 'truth' that would anchor a new way of thinking, not a meaningful thought in any obvious sense. Indeed, after the death of God, it is dubious whether it is a thought that is available for *comprehension* at all. As Nietzsche so astutely observes, metaphysical philosophy depends upon its own logic of eternal return of the same, inasmuch as the reiteration of the identical across time and space is constitutive for conceptual reasoning as such. The question is how to exacerbate this logic, how to ride its wave such that it might be driven to use its own energy against itself. On the assumption that the 'reality' of the world of phenomena was first created by us and lies in 'continual recurrence of identical, familiar, related things in their logicized character' Nietzsche suggests that 'the antithesis of this phenomenal world is not "the true world" but the formless unformulable world of the chaos of sensations – *another kind* of phenomenal world, a kind "unknowable" for us' (*WP* 569). This is not the Kantian realm of things in themselves for as Nietzsche points out, 'thingness' is merely a metaphorical device and we have no way of knowing whether 'things' as such exist. His question is 'whether there could not be many other ways of creating such an apparent world' (ibid.). Such a world is strictly speaking 'unknowable' because it lacks the forms and formulations of logical identity but it may be sensed and encountered. Configured in this way, the unknown is no longer conditioned by the known – privatively determined as an unknown 'object' in default of representation. Exploration now emerges as a rather different endeavour – one which *returns* to the 'realm of appearances' once again.

This return is a transformative repetition, an inquiry into the matter of thinking anew. In suggesting that the processes through which the world of 'things' is constructed as such are not themselves explicable in terms of 'things', Nietzsche is doing rather more than making a transcendental point about the necessary conditions of experience. While the belief that things retain an identity is enshrined in the form of the concept which determines the possibility of repeatable experiences, the material flows which condition any given experience are the fluctuating, non-repeatable ground for the difference between instantiations of the concept. The concept can only explain the form that a *possible* actualization will take but it can never account for the existence of any real actualization.

> Has a force ever been noticed? No, only effects translated into a completely foreign language. However, we are so used to regularity in succession that we *never wonder at its oddity*. (*WP* 620)

Nietzsche's question is what makes a difference prior to representation – what generates a vital effect. This leads to his development of the notion of differentiation as a positive principle of production – the *material* difference of 'dynamic quanta in a relation of tension to all other dynamic quanta' (*WP* 635). Such a locution might be taken to imply an oppositional and inverse relation to the conceptual difference that organizes philosophical discourse, but perhaps this is not to say much since materialist discourse must also be rendered intelligible in this completely foreign language. The key point is that there is no reason to suppose that what makes no difference at the level of recognition makes no difference at all. For Nietzsche, this tensional dynamics is 'not a being, not a becoming, but a *pathos* – the most elemental fact from which a becoming and an effecting first emerge' (*WP* 635). It is in terms of a sense of power that intensive forces first differentiate themselves. In other words, the 'aesthetic' is the real condition of experience and it is from this material plenum that the conceptual is to be thought. Accordingly, the task for the philosopher after the death of God is to diagnose which forces are operative in a given phenomenon.

> Behind the highest value judgements that have hitherto guided the history of thought, misunderstandings of living constitution lie concealed – be it of individuals, ranks or whole races. All those bold insanities of metaphysics, especially answers to the question about the *value* of existence, may always be regarded first of all as symptoms of particular bodies; and if such world affirmations or world negations were to be scientifically measured lock, stock and barrel, without yielding a grain of significance, they are all the more valuable for historians and scientists as hints, as symptoms of the body, of its developments or failures, its plenitude, power, self-mastery in history, or its inhibitions, fatigues, impoverishments, its premonitions of the end, its will to the end. (*GS* Preface, 2)

Perhaps it is this recourse to the physiological that has been most misunderstood in Nietzsche's philosophy. Nietzsche's professed 'naturalism' has frequently been treated as a reductive materialism, an uncritical or positivist valorization of brute animality over and above the cultivated reaches of 'spirit'. Such a judgement tacitly assumes the polarity between the natural and the spiritual; indeed the assumption of the validity of bilateral disjunctions is made from a position which remains unilaterally idealist. Nietzsche's notion of differential forces resists the thought of an ideal limit marking the difference between transcendence and immanence. This is not simply a methodological point, for it already bears within it an evaluation of *physis* as a primary self-differentiating element. In other words, there is no suggestion that difference implies mutual discontinuity between terms. In a note from 1881 Nietzsche defines his task as 'the dehumanization of nature and then the naturalization of man, after he has reclaimed the pure concept of "nature"' – a thought which suggests the immanence of the human to nature with the latter as a primary term (*KSA* 9/525/11[211]).

When Nietzsche comes to embellish this remark in *The Gay Science* he refers to the task of 'de-deifying' nature (*GS* 109). His basic thought is that the values which have been 'incorporated' over the course of several centuries of Western history will not be extinguished by the mere 'event' of God's murder. Thus, even though the guarantor of truth, purpose, unity and design has met a bloody demise, humanist values continue to retain their cultural currency. It is not the case that there is anything intrinsically life-affirming or life-negating about the human. For Nietzsche 'the human' is an adjective rather than anything else. His point is simply that the cultivation of the human animal has been an exercise in harnessing potent energies and redirecting them against the self ('morality as anti-nature'). Consequently, his exploration of a post-human or *übermenschlich* physiology is integral to his attempt to 'transvalue' the 'form of the same'. In *The Gay Science* Nietzsche says that we should guard against all aesthetic anthropomorphisms which tempt us into positing the world as a living being modelled on the concept of the 'organic'. For Nietzsche the 'organic' is something 'unspeakably derivative, recent, rare and accidental' whilst the arch-anthropocentric tendency is to regard the 'crust of the earth' and its latest 'development', consciousness, as something 'essential, universal and eternal' (*GS* 109, 11) The modern scientific by-product of the belief in God is faith in the universe as an organism. Such a scientific view cannot fail to reduce superabundant nature to the servile mechanism of the 'organized' and the functional. Deeply contemptuous of this, Nietzsche emphatically rejects the suggestion that the universe 'obeys laws', that it has a drive for 'preservation' or any other kind of drive and that the ascription of moral judgements such as 'heartlessness' and 'unreason' are ever valid (*GS* 109). Unlike a living being this world does not grow or expand but it is 'in all eternity chaos' lacking every kind of order that might be attributed to it and expressing only *necessity*.

At first glance, Nietzsche's de-deification of nature appears purely negative, a simple withdrawal of all familiar predicates. In fact, this is only the necessary first stage of the reclamation of nature from its metaphysical accretions. The crucial point is to show how values are already *implicated* in matter. The imperative is to reassess from an atheistic and anti-humanistic perspective the series of determinations consonant with an anthropocentric determination of life (organization, integrity, self-preservation) as vectors of *value for life*. It would be precipitate to assume that 'slave morality' is entirely life-negating – a subtlety which Nietzsche's ambivalence towards the ascetic ideal seems to reflect. If it is fair to say that the human animal has largely been tutored to think its nature reactively – in terms of wants and needs and in terms of preservation from perceived dangers – the question might be how different evaluations of life are to be lived and embodied. In other words, how might an active or life-affirming physiology be nurtured and created?

In the Preface to *The Gay Science* Nietzsche draws an explicit link between affectivity and philosophical production. We are told that the philosopher gives birth to his thoughts out of his pain and endows them with heart, blood and fire: 'Life – that means for us, constantly transforming all that we are into light and flame – including everything that wounds us – we simply *can* do no other' (*GS* Preface, 3). For Nietzsche, it is only great pain, 'the long, slow pain that takes its time – on which we are burned, as it were with green wood' that compels the philosopher to descend to his ultimate depths and to put aside everything 'that is mild, that is medium – things in which formerly we may have found our humanity' (ibid.). From such depths of torment one emerges 'as a different person' with an ever renewed taste for all that is perplexing. Arising phoenix-like from the ashes, the thinker is literally 'on fire' for thought: his delight sparks up 'again and again [*immer wieder*] like a bright glow over all the distress of what is problematic' (ibid.). Having been charred to a husk he returns as the fire that rekindles his own thought, he has become the thought *of* fire. If the 'art of transfiguration *is* philosophy' it would seem that it is by redirecting the affects, making even the most painful experiences *productive* that 'we know a new happiness ...' (ibid.).

The importance of this 'art' ought not to be underestimated. Nietzsche suggests that it is only through the transformation of 'nature' that a transformation of thought is possible. There is a sense in which philosophy must become ecstatic if it is to succeed in thinking beyond the values which perpetuate the logic of the same. A philosophy which practises this art fails to commensurate with work or even with discourse, both of which forestall the tendency towards collapse. Rather, as a taste for all that is problematic, philosophy is a passion. The legacy of Nietzsche's philosophy will concern this appeal to affectivity. It is this that is to be understood if philosophy is to be renewed.

After Nietzsche

Having blazed an intense and glorious trail throughout the history of art, religion and philosophy, spanning classical accounts of 'divine inspiration' to Romantic and modernist notions of genius and transcendence, Eastern and Western spirituality from Christian martyrology to mystic and shamanic practices, the phenomenon of 'ecstasy' has resurfaced in the twentieth century as a dominant feature of a range of continental philosophies.[1] The conviction that a non-foundational philosophy must be *fundamentally* ecstatic is undoubtedly paradoxical but it is scarcely fortuitous that after Nietzsche this prospect should have claimed the imagination of so many thinkers. The concept of an ecstatic or self-transcending existence was most explicitly formulated by existentialist thinking to define the inner constitution of a 'groundless' subjectivity and to mark it apart from the 'objective reality' of classical epistemology. As Alphonso Lingis writes:

> Existential philosophy defined the new concepts of ecstasy or of transcendence to fix a distinct kind of being that is by casting itself out of its own given place and time, without dissipating, because at each moment it projects itself – or, more exactly, a variant of itself – into another place and time. Such a being is not ideality, defined as intuitable or reconstitutable anywhere and at any moment. Ex-istence, understood etymologically, is not so much a state or a stance as a movement, which is by conceiving a divergence from itself or a potentiality of itself and casting itself into that divergence with all that it is.[2]

As Lingis indicates, to 'exist' (or 'ex-ist' from Latin *ex-sistere*) means to 'stand out' but in its existentialist usage it signifies the dynamic notion of 'transport'. For existentialism, human existence is always already 'ecstatic' inasmuch as *ecstasis* (the Greek cognate of 'existence') defines the human animal as the being whose distinctiveness is constituted in and through its very evasion of 'essence'. In its transcendence of the determinate existence that would consolidate its identity 'in itself', the existentialist subject is always eluding the possibility of foundation. As Sartre says, the for-itself is always bound up in its 'worldly' projects yet is never wholly defined by them (the for-itself determines its being as *a lack*). In a similar manner, in its infamous 'return to the things themselves', phenomenological philosophy marks a thought of transcendence which is intraworldly, endorsing the Kantian insight that it is *paralogistic* to suppose that the subject can be determined or grasped as if it were a being somehow separable from its own functioning. Despite the considerable differences between the exemplars of these perspectives, the ecstatic imperative, if we may call it thus, is to think beyond the opposition between the 'apparent' and the 'true', not to restore certainty this side of the beyond. It is notable that in this endeavour, a number of influential thinkers have identified the ecstatic with the move beyond metaphysics and with the broader, ongoing attempt to rethink the transcendental.

To the extent that the phenomenological movement concerns itself with what Nietzsche so aptly calls 'the nearest things', it could be said to have taken inspiration from his attempt to re-evaluate 'appearance' after the death of God. It is also to be remarked that this process has often been identified with a rethinking of art and the nature of the artwork and that existentialism and deconstruction have been greatly informed by reflection on the literary. However, while there are family resemblances between Nietzsche's thought and the hermeneutical philosophies of a range of twentieth-century thinkers, there is no reason to suppose that all retreats from the philosophy of identity should be themselves identical. It could be said that while phenomenology and deconstruction have sought to think the immanence of Being to beings and to expose the confusion of the transcendent with the transcendental, it has not been the chief goal of these movements to explore a thinking 'beyond the same' at the level of value.[3] Arguably, it is Deleuze and Bataille who have been most alert to the 'materialist' implications of Nietzsche's attempt at a 'revaluation of all values' and in this respect could be said to contribute to a philosophy of physiology and desire which develops the resources for thinking how life affirmation might be embodied.

According to Deleuze, one of Nietzsche's central concerns is the radicalization of Kantian critical thinking. Deleuze suggests that Kant's genius was to conceive of an immanent critique but that he lacked a method which permitted reason to be judged from the inside. Kantian philosophy discovers conditions which still remain external to the conditioned: 'Transcendental principles are principles of conditioning and not of internal genesis' (*NP* 91). While Kantian critique brings itself to bear on dogmatic claims to knowledge and truth, it fails to criticize knowledge and truth as *values* (for example, the value of the *a priori* is never called into question). In *Nietzsche and Philosophy* Deleuze argues that Nietzsche's thinking impacts upon contemporary philosophical sensibility in terms of a fulfilment of the critical enterprise:

> [W]ith Nietzsche, we must begin from the fact that the philosophy of values as envisaged and established by him is the true realisation of critique and the only way in which a total critique may be realised, the only way to 'philosophise with a hammer'. (*NP* 1)

Deleuze suggests that for Nietzsche the fundamental values which support and frame transcendental philosophy have to be challenged. Evaluation presupposes values on the basis of which phenomena are judged, while values similarly presuppose evaluations – 'perspectives' of certain kinds of life. As Nietzsche puts its, the 'value of these values must be called into question' and for that there is needed a knowledge of the condition and circumstances in which they grew and changed (*GM* Preface, 6). Echoing this sentiment, Deleuze writes that the problem of critique is that of 'the value of values, of the evaluation from which their value arises, thus the problem of their *creation*' (ibid.).

Understood as material effects or symptoms of a living constitution, values are regarded by Nietzsche as orientations of *life* rather than simply determinations of being and this is as applicable to non-foundational philosophies as it is to the 'bold insanities of metaphysics'. Nietzsche suggests that 'when we speak of values we do so under the inspiration and from the perspective of life: life itself evaluates through us *when* we establish values' (*TI* 'Morality as Anti-Nature, 5). Something is sensed, is 'known' sensitively: 'the *will to power* is the primitive form of affect, [..] all other affects are only arrangements of it' (*WP* 688). Since evaluations are ways of being, 'conditions of life' for those who evaluate, they serve as principles for the values that these 'evaluators' use. For Deleuze, the crucial point is that '*high* and *low*, *noble* and *base*, are not values but represent the differential element from which the value of values themselves derives' (*NP* 2). 'High' and 'low' do not represent fixed points on a scale of evaluations but mark what type and degree of confrontation or relation of domination is operative between 'forces' – what conditions of life are determinative in any given state. No state is interpreted independently of the forces which instantiate it, consequently no phenomenon 'in itself' is incontrovertibly noble or base (not even the much maligned Platonism). What is no longer tenable is the concept of a *value in itself*; even 'truth' must be understood as the *product* of the differential element or interrelation of forces. Deleuze's aim in thus aligning Nietzschean genealogy with critique is to articulate a thought of difference which is not already constituted by identity. Hence Nietzsche's great insight: to reject the 'perspective illusion' of unity that the ego promotes and take instead the *body* as 'starting point' for critique (*WP* 492).

Following Nietzsche's cue, Deleuze relates a philosophy of difference to the physiological. Every force is related to other forces which either obey or command: 'What defines a body is this relation between dominant and dominated forces. Every relationship of forces constitutes a body[...] as soon as they enter into a relationship' (*NP* 40). Consequently, the 'being' of force is plural and is the prior condition of conceptual determination. This is not a 'given' sensory manifold because it is only the contingent relations between actual forces that constitute the 'being of the sensible'. Deleuze proposes that 'in a body the superior or dominant forces are known as *active* and the inferior or dominated forces are known as *reactive*' (*NP* 40). Active and reactive are the qualities which express the relation of force with force. Whereas an active force affirms its difference from another force, a reactive force merely 'denies all that it is not and makes this negation its own essence and the principle of its existence' (*NP* 9). The difference between a body conditioned by 'the form of the same' and an exuberant or transformative body starts to emerge at this point.

Nietzsche claims that the noble mode of evaluation 'acts and grows spontaneously', engaging its opposite only to affirm itself triumphally (*GM* I, 10). However, because active forces are non-teleological, unpredictable and excessive, they escape apprehension by consciousness (whereas reactive forces can be understood in relation to superior forces). Modern thought attends almost exclusively to the reactive aspect of forces, overlooking the 'essential priority of the spontaneous, aggressive, encroaching, form-giving forces' that give 'new interpretations and directions' (*GM* II, 12). A prime example of this is evolutionary theory which foregrounds concepts such as 'adaptation' and survival. Against this logic, Nietzsche insists that 'life is not the adaption of inner circumstances to outer ones, but will to power, which, working from within, incorporates and subdues more and more of that which is "outside"' (*WP* 681). Contrary to the Darwinists who construe life as fundamentally reactive – a tactics of environmental adaptation for survival – Nietzsche suggests that life is ineluctably superabundant, fervently creative and combative:

> The will to power can manifest itself only *against resistances*; it therefore seeks out that which resists it, – this is the original tendency of the protoplasm when it sends out pseudopodia and feels about. Appropriation and incorporation are above all a wanting-to-overwhelm, a forming and shaping and reorganizing until finally that which has been overwhelmed has merged completely into the power of the attacker and has increased it. (*WP* 656)

The insatiable drive to appropriate manifests itself in the riotous inundation and assimilation of whatever is alien, recalcitrant or weaker than itself. This is the most basic tendency of life as will to power, which even in its elementary animal forms 'seeks to incorporate into itself as much as possible, not just to *compensate* for loss – it is *acquisitive*' (*KSA* 9/490–1/11[134]). The restorative impulse is superseded by a thirst for expansion and conquest but it is an exorbitant desire, too great to be attributed to any perceived 'goal'. In fact, Nietzsche asserts that one 'cannot ascribe the most basic and primeval activities of protoplasm to a will to self-preservation, for it takes into itself absurdly more than would be required to preserve it; and above all, it does not thereby "preserve itself," it falls apart' (*WP* 651).

In this passage and in related notes Nietzsche explicitly denies that hunger or the drive to self-preservation are 'first causes' and emphasizes the point that such excessive engorgement is by no means a matter of 'restoring a loss' (*WP* 652). It is here that Bataille's thinking is at its closest to Nietzsche's. A hymn to the splendour of sacred expenditure, Bataille's philosophical writings succeed in giving voice to the *need for utter loss*, a thought as remote from the notion of desire as lack as it is from the logic of reciprocal exchange. In defining eroticism as 'assenting to life up to the point of death', Bataille declares that this site of excitations is 'in the first place an exuberance of life' – a way of dissolving the boundaries which inhibit a possible continuance of being beyond the confines of the self (*E* 11). Life as 'active incorporation' is sacrificial – fatally indifferent to its own self-preservation. If the challenge for an exploratory philosophy is to evoke that which cannot endure, the consummation of transcendental critique may now be said to entail the cultivation of *unproductive* or sacred values. Such an approach would depart from a thought of practical or 'worldly projects' and would resituate the ecstatic in terms of intensive states. Bataille speaks of seeking to grasp that which takes flight as soon as it is seen – a task he relates to the aesthetic. It is the futile and exultant efforts of the artist to create pathways for the 'endless reattainment of that which flees' which attests to the joy of the ungraspable (*VE* 241). Art has the force to attain the 'sacred instant' by its own resources, perhaps because it engages the affective states that reactive forces inhibit and negate. For Bataille, the 'sacred is only a privileged moment of communal unity, a moment of the convulsive communication of what is ordinarily stifled' (*VE* 242).

What is felt in these explosions of joy is the entry of active or 'life-affirming' values into thought. Accordingly, Deleuze's suggestion that the will to power produces values as the internal, differential and genetic element of forces is to be grasped in a physiological context as the growth of new capacities: 'The will to power *interprets* (it is a question of interpretation when an organ is constructed): it defines limits, determines degrees, variations of power' (*WP* 643). Since values are produced in accordance with the capacity for a life form to interpret itself (for example, as active or reactive) they simultaneously express an immanent evaluation of their mode of expenditure (growth) – an argument which relocates the *agency* of critique at the level of the physiological.

Nietzsche suggests that 'the task of *incorporating* knowledge and making it instinctive' is a task that human thought has only begun to glimpse (*GS* 11). The suggestion that humankind has hitherto only incorporated 'errors' is not necessarily to be taken negatively. The will to survive is not trivial but it only attains sovereignty when tested against the lure of self-ruin. As an exorbitant index of sacred desire, 'incorporation [*Einverleibung*]' connotes an openness to the 'horizon of the infinite' predicated on the thought of dissolvant boundaries. In other words, the receptivity to the unknown that is implied by this process of 'becoming-body' is not mediated by a pre-existent interiority: the body which incorporates is itself *created by incorporation*. Whatever is taken in 'from the outside' *forms* the 'inside' as such. In this way, what the body consumes or incorporates becomes the same as itself, a 'oneness' exorbitantly generated from diversity.

Since the 'logical' concept of the self-identical 'same' integral to the philosophy of identity is derived from the process of 'making the same', it is treated as an entity that has *finished* becoming: 'All thinking, judging, perceiving as *comparison* has presupposed a *"positing* as same", earlier still a *"making* the same". The making the same is like the incorporation of appropriated material into the amoeba' (*WP* 501). Nietzsche suggests that the *strength* of knowledge does not depend on its degree of truth but on its age, on the degree to which it has been incorporated, on its character as a condition of life (*GS* 110). These conditions, inherently corporeal, present the question as to whether a life form is able to expend itself – sacrificing its own 'ground' – or whether it seeks to preserve itself, inhibited by its thirst for secure terrain. Nietzsche says that the thinker is that being in whom the impulse for truth and those life-preserving errors clash for their first fight, after the impulse for truth has proved to be also a life-preserving power (*GS* 110). The question and the 'experiment' concern the extent to which truth can bear incorporation (ibid.).

Consequently, for the incorporating body the 'same' in no sense constitutes a substantive state, rather *materializes as immanent to the fluid, metamorphic movement of becoming.* This entails in turn that recurrence is no longer posited as a transcendent principle which modifies a given set of entities but is itself to be thought of as internal to becoming-the-same. Such a physiology is ecstatic in that it overcomes what it has become. In this respect it is possible to see how will to power functions as a principle of Nietzsche's own philosophy of eternal return – as the differential element where all forces will be played out. In Deleuzian terms it might be said that the will to power is a *derivative transcendental*, derivative because it is the plane generated by forces, yet transcendental because it is where forces synthesize. Diversity thus emerges as something that is *produced* by incorporation as irreducible indeterminate difference. The differential element expresses that which is shared in a multiplicity, a sameness which materializes in the process of incorporation.

These reflections on physiology will significantly shape the possibilities for philosophy after Nietzsche. The question to pose to any cultural phenomenon (including contemporary philosophies of ecstasy) is never merely ontological but is inherently perspectival: 'Is it hunger or plenitude (*Überfluss*) that has here become creative?' (*GS* 370). Following Nietzsche, it could be asked whether philosophies which express disdain for the natural or animal, which privilege values of utility, industry and responsibility, and which reify notions of the limits of 'our' history and conceptual heritage, flow from evaluations which are life-affirming or life-negating. Even a phenomenology of the body risks impoverishing 'life' if it resists those pulsions which lead beyond 'our world'. Perhaps Nietzsche is right to insist that 'it is only from the conception "I" that there follows, derivatively, the concept "being"' (*TI* 'Reason in Philosophy', 5). Thought in terms of life rather than being, the 'world' for Nietzsche is not the nexus of human meanings and involvements but is *will to power*.

> This world: a monster of energy, without beginning, without end [...] set in a definite space as a definite force, and not a space that might be 'empty' here or there, but rather as force throughout, as a play of forces and waves of forces, at the same time one and

many, accumulating here and at the same time diminishing there; a sea of forces flowing and raging together, eternally changing, eternally flooding back, with tremendous years of recurrence, with an ebb and flood of its forms [...] *This world is the will to power – and nothing besides!* And you yourselves are also this will to power – and nothing besides! (*WP* 1067)

In the wake of the death of God, the will to power emerges as a new syntax of thought, one in which difference of force is thought immanently in terms of the value economies it creates. In this turbulent ocean of becoming, forms ebb and flow beyond the rescuing shore of a world 'for us' and an economic vocabulary of tides, intensities, peaks and troughs supplants the semiotics of 'structure, sign and play'. Philosophies which fail to experience the death of God as the death of theological values will never succeed in taking the will to negation to the limit – will never experience the ecstasy of abandon – because the limit is always thought as that which co-exists with what has yet to cross it (*TP* 432). Ecstasy is no more in excess *of* stasis than the sea is in excess *of* the land. The ocean has no margins.

For Bataille, the death of God is not an ontological problem but an orientational one, a voyage into the *unknown* which 'is distinct from Nothingness by nothing which discourse can enunciate' (*IE* 114). The frequent references to be found in Bataille's work to a 'nostalgia' for continuity no more signify a 'return' to an Edenic nature prior to the Fall than Nietzsche's glorification of tragic dissolution signals a wistful yearning for the primitive. Those who would seek to dismiss sexual taboos and advocate a return 'to the good old days of animalism' fill Bataille with a genuine sense of dread. On his account, man differs from the animal in that he is able 'to experience certain sensations that wound and melt him to the core' (*ME* 140) but like Nietzsche with his fascination for slave morality, Bataille regards human nature as an ingenious aberration of matter and resists valorizing the pure spontaneity of the natural order – itself an abstraction. Enthralled by the tensions and torsions of affectivity that describe the arcs of discontinuity, Bataille pursues a base materialism which is the obstinate negation of all idealism and – at this level – of all philosophy (*VE* 45). Yet in his protracted meditations on the poignant, indeed violent impulses, alternatively of revulsion and attraction, to which sensibility and intelligence are 'inseparably attached' he resists proposing an ontological disjunction that demarcates self and other along epistemological lines (*ME* 138–9). It is only in the intolerable surpassing of itself that being is given to the human animal.

Since we have known only slavish values, have known only a negating will to power, Nietzsche does not strive to change values but seeks a change in the element from which the value of values is derived, that is, the will to power. According to Deleuze, reactive forces become active by affirming their own negation and in this spirit Nietzsche advocates an active destruction of the values that stasis represents – God, Eidos, Identity, the One – thereby conducting force to the limit of what it can do – at which point it becomes transformative. This is why he pursues an active destruction of nihilism rather than a nihilistic deconstruction. If the finite animal is the beast of finality – of goals, projects and ends – ecstasy impacts as a self-annihilating power that dispossesses and transfigures.

Let it be recalled that it is only when nihilism is intensified, when the desire to know becomes the impetus for the exacerbation of itself that a return to unknowing is realized. The enigmatic desire for the eternal return of the same, encountered ecstatically at the point of collapse, is a thought which *takes itself as its own object*, wills to have it again as it was and is to all eternity, eternally flooding back. To the inertial repetition of the same, Nietzsche counterposes a darkly inhuman philosophy of excitation. Thought in terms of the libidinal rather than the liminal, ecstasy describes *a feeling of life*, not the definition of self-exceeding presence. Perhaps this will mean that the philosopher must stammer in an alien tongue, translating the inner 'echoes of the world symphony' into the form of concepts (*PTAG*, 3). For all this, the problem which philosophy faces after Nietzsche is not one of language but one of *life*. How 'well disposed' would one have to become to oneself and to life to *crave nothing more fervently* than the ultimate, eternal 'confirmation and seal' of eternal return? To consecrate one's life to this thought one must have experienced a 'tremendous moment', have experienced a joy so extreme that one can only ever want it again. Nietzsche's philosophy is the anatomy of this longing, a series of notes towards a philosophy of ecstasy.

We aeronauts of the spirit! – All these bold birds which fly out into the distance, the farthest distance – it is certain! At some point or other they will be unable to go any further and will perch on a mast or a barren rock and will be even thankful for this pitiful lodging! But who could dare conclude from this, that there was *not* an immense, clear expanse before them, that they had flown as far as one *could* fly! All our great teachers and forerunners have finally reached a halt, and it is not with the noblest or most graceful of gestures that weariness comes to a halt: you and I will fare the same! But of what concern is that to you and me! *Other birds will fly further!* This insight and trust of ours flies with them and with this wager of theirs, up and away; it ascends above our heads and beyond powerlessness into the heights and from there looks out into the distance, sees flocks of birds far stronger than us ahead, which strive where we have striven, and where everything is still sea, sea, sea! – And where would we go then? Would we want to go *beyond* the sea? Where does this mighty craving draw us, this craving which is worth more to us than any pleasure? Why go just in this direction, where hitherto all the suns of humanity have *gone down*? Perhaps it will be said of us some day that we too, *heading westward, hoped to reach an India* – but that our fate was to be wrecked against infinity?Or, my brothers? Or? (*D* 575)

2
The Tempo of Becoming

> Oh, sea! Oh, evening! You are wicked mentors! You instruct
> human beings to *cease* being human!
>
> (*Daybreak* 423)

There are certain philosophical ideas that can be accessed only
through self-abandon. For Nietzsche, the insight of Heraclitus into the
'eternal wavebeat and rhythm of things' is the product of a raw and
restive meditation that has come to ebb and flow with this dark,
inhuman pulse (*PTAG* 5). It is one thing to declare: 'it is the fault of
your myopia, not of the nature of things, if you believe you see firm
land somewhere in the ocean of becoming and passing away': quite
another, as Heraclitus attests, to actually 'see nothing other than
becoming' (*PTAG* 5). According to Nietzsche, the herd beast *homo
sapiens* is spared the terror of the infinitely swallowing horizon because
it is simply incapable of imagining that reality might outstrip its capacity to perceive it: 'we are not sufficiently *refined* to see the ostensible
absolute flux of occurrence' (*KSA* 9/11[293]). It is thanks to our 'coarse
organs' that we drive impressions together, asserting the existence of
forms 'because we cannot perceive the most minute, absolute motion'
(ibid.). In fact Nietzsche suggests that 'in a world of *becoming*, 'reality'
is always only a *simplification* for practical ends, or a *deception* through
the coarseness of organs, or a difference in the *tempo* of becoming' (*WP*
580). The imposition of form upon flux has an indispensable survival
value for 'the clever beast' that has 'invented knowing', enabling it to
re-find and re-cognize its constructions in the mirror of its established
truths (*TL* 1). Its 'will to truth is a *making*-stable, a *making*-true and

24

durable' such that there is a reflux between its perceived reality and the reality of its perception (*WP* 552). 'Organs' become 'coarse' through their reduction of difference to sameness: the '*positing* as the same' presupposes a prior '*making* the same' (*WP* 501). Nietzsche goes so far as to suggest that subsuming a sense impression into a pre-existing series is analogous to the body's assimilation of inorganic matter (*WP* 511). It is thus that the organs 'organize' the body, 'metabolize' what is multiple and fluid, much like the amoeba assimilates nutrients from its environment. In so far as these 'illusions which we have forgotten are illusions' are necessary for human knowing, they become materially *incorporated,* that is, they come to constitute the *a priori* conditions of any possible experience. Yet Nietzsche contends that it is only when the 'tempo of growth' has slowed down that one senses anything as logically self-identical, the illusion of *stasis* being the consequence of such deceleration: 'an equilibrium *appears* to have been reached, making possible the false idea that *here a goal has been reached* – and that development has a goal' (*WP* 521).

As modern philosophers and cognitive scientists have suggested, the visual field is stabilized according to a discrete number of foci which gradually demarcate and limit what it is possible to view. Similarly, the auditory field is anticipated and somatically encoded according to the cultural norms that limit the tonal scale.[1] Nietzsche's reflections on the pace and pulse of physiological processes appear to reinforce the view that relatively robust systems, such as the human animal, succeed in preserving their form or identity through encrypting a certain perceptual rhythm, which is then commuted to a transcendental condition or 'natural law' for its *being.* However, while it might seem as if Nietzsche merely resituates Kantian arguments within a more explicitly materialist register, it is questionable whether the conditions under which 'representations' can relate to 'objects' are themselves invariant. If becoming lacks a subject distinct from itself, the body 'as such' is not to be regarded as a given. If the body is as much a constellation of the rhythm of things as the items in its perceptual horizon, then its status as a *form of the same* is as illusory as the things it surveys. To view the body in terms of becoming is to take seriously Nietzsche's suggestion that 'the isolation of the individual ought not to deceive us: something flows on *underneath* individuals' (*WP* 686). In the flow of becoming, material processes constantly combine to produce physiologies which, although 'distinct', are simultaneously continuous with forces which exceed them. In fact, the body is never regarded by Nietzsche as a self-sufficient entity but a multiplicity of forces which from a particular perspective share a common holding pattern (*WP* 641). If it is the case that 'at every moment' there are countless factors influencing us such as air and electricity which we seldom sense, there may well be forces that continually influence us although we never feel them (*WP* 676). Only a small fraction of bodily motions and changes actually impinge on consciousness despite the tendency to take the latter as the sole arbiter of significant activity. Coherent knowledge of 'our world' is only possible because we have forgotten that we fell from the sky as stardust and rain, that we exchanged our gases with plants and our fluids with ditches – that we flowed out through the capillaries of the earth into the vast, anonymous tidal swell.

If the body is not given, it is debatable whether the 'tempo of becoming' is given either. At first glance, Nietzsche's assorted remarks on tempo *seem* to constitute an empirical claim about relative rates of change, with decrease in tempo accounting for the illusion of fixity. However, it is noticeable that he frequently inflects this account with a genealogical diagnosis regarding value for life. For example, in *On the Genealogy of Morals*, he says of both science and the ascetic ideal: 'a *certain impoverishment of life* is a presupposition of both of them – the affects grown cool, the tempo slowed down' (*GM* III, 25). Similarly, in *Ecce Homo*, 'the tempo of the metabolism' is said to stand in a precise relation to the mobility or lameness of the spirit such that while 'the rapid metabolism' draws 'again and again' [*immer wieder*] on 'great, even monstrous quantities of strength', the sluggish metabolism generates the retarded idealist world view of eternal verities (*EH*, 'Why I am so Clever', 2). More significantly, perhaps, he often speaks positively of slow and gentle tempos of becoming, commending an '*andante* of development' as the necessary 'tempo of a passionate and slow spirit' (*GS* 10). He even writes that the impulse to construct form – to *idealize* – may be construed as a *creative compulsion* (*TI* 'Expeditions...' 8). It would seem precipitate then, to read Nietzsche's remarks on tempo as exemplary of a general metrics of becoming, calibrating respective flows of difference. In any case, this would be tantamount to instituting a 'form of the same' at the level of process. If tempo is a measure it is a non-determinate one, something more akin to an *aesthetic* registering of life, its *sense* of difference.

> To *communicate* a state, an inner tension of pathos through signs, including the tempo of these signs – that is the sense [*Sinn*] of every style; and considering that the multiplicity of inner states is in my case extraordinary, there exists in my case the possibility of many styles – altogether the most multifarious art of style that any man has ever had at his disposal. Every style is *good* which actually communicates an inner state, which makes no mistake as to the tempo of signs, as to the *gestures* – all rules of phrasing are art of gesture. (*EH* 'Why I Write Such Excellent Books', 4)

The tempo of 'inner states' is not something that can be quantified but it can be lived and felt. Perhaps tempo is less a question of speed than of speeding – a feeling of vital tension or differentiation, rather than conceptual determination of extension or velocity. For Nietzsche, it is the suppression of this feeling (the 'cooling of affect') that is the precondition of knowledge as recognition. This assimilation of difference to sameness is a slowing of tempo but interpreted from an immanent measure of value for life, not from a scale that is pre-given. As such, different tempos of becoming have no privileged ontological status as different degrees of being but must themselves be submitted to the genealogical question: is it hunger or superabundance that has here become creative?

We have noted that, for Nietzsche, the tensional dynamics of the will to power is to be understood affectively in terms of the *pathos* from which values for life emerge. Considered genealogically, any phenomenon, happening or physiology reflects a state of forces or 'perspectives' that are to be read 'symptomatically' as products of their environment. Rather than perpetuating the humanist tendency of regarding consciousness as a mediator in the relationship between conditions of life and value, Nietzsche proposes that forces be viewed as immanent perspectives on life, its internal differentiations. It is in this sense that will to power is Nietzsche's term for the production of values. In effect, this means that there is a reflexive relation between physiologies and their environments, such that values spawned of depleted life in turn deplete the 'systems' that they inhabit, just as poor conditions of cultivation yield a defective crop. Understood thus, the normative, functional physiology of the human animal is an achieved and reinforced product of its own utile, rational values: 'You put your will and your values upon the river of becoming [....] Now the river bears your boat along' (*TSZ* II, 'Of Self-Overcoming'). Like viruses, values become self-replicating when they become embodied, 'incorporated' – a point that Nietzsche constantly emphasizes. Indeed, the slave revolt in morality begins when *ressentiment* becomes creative and gives birth to values (*GM* I,10). As Nietzsche argues so insistently in 'On Truth and Lies in a Non-Moral Sense', the rational human being can only live with any security, repose and consistency by forgetting that the laws which impress him so much are ones which he brings to things. While never challenging the utility of this state of affairs, Nietzsche questions its value for life. Values of self-preservation *tend* to be constituted by physiologies which are 'life-denying' inasmuch as they seek merely to maintain themselves and their objects (hence 'truth' is a kind of error without which a certain kind of living being would perish). To the extent that the man of science requires shelter from 'frightful powers which constantly break in upon him' his world of logical identity is regarded by Nietzsche as the product of reactivity, a disavowal of the colourful and irregular configurations of myth, art and dream (*TL* 2). Indeed, it is only by forgetting that he is an aesthetically creating subject that he arrives at his *moral* 'feeling of truth' and places his behaviour under the rule of binding abstractions (*TL* 1). Such a life form fears a change of rhythm, the possibility that life might be lived otherwise. The 'immense construction and planking of concepts to which the needy man clings' is counterposed by Nietzsche to the superabundance of a luxuriant and audacious species of life which delights in the thought that *as in a dream* 'anything is possible at each moment' (*TL* 2).

> The waking life of a mythically excited people, like the ancient Greeks, takes it for granted that, as in myths, miracles are constantly happening and in fact it more closely resembles a dream than the waking life of the scientifically disillusioned thinker. (*TL* 2)

Inasmuch as it repels the thought that there could be many *other* ways of creating the apparent world, the waking life of the 'rational man' is literally one of *disaffection*.

To live life according to stranger, less predictable rhythms is strictly speaking only possible if different values are incorporated for *just as 'the body' is a product of an idea, its ideas are products of its body*. What it is possible to *think* given the kind of physiology that is actually cultivated is less a question of what a body *is* than what it can do or *become*. Perhaps one of the chief reasons why Nietzsche remained so fascinated by the tragic culture of the ancient Greeks is that for him they embodied in their art an estimation of life quite alien to the scientific ethos of Enlightenment Europe. In interpreting the Greek predilection for the 'pessimistic' art form of tragedy it is physiological preconditions that he sees as decisive. Posing to Greek tragedy 'the big question mark concerning the value of existence', Nietzsche asks whether such 'pessimism' springs from 'decline, decay, a state of failure, wearisome and weakened instincts' or is prompted by 'well-being, by overflowing health, by the *fullness* of existence' (*BT*, 'Attempt…', 1). Arguably, it is easier to be persuaded by the 'reactive' interpretation of tragedy which views this art form as an expression of dissatisfaction with life, a spectacle of the horrors of existence, performed to relieve and purge dangerous emotions. This is because such a rational, moral conception of tragedy is essentially governed by humanist values of self-preservation – the Socratic (and Aristotelian) virtues which according to Nietzsche have helped to shape and nurture the physiological type of modern European man. This human being is a triumph of moral husbandry, a beast that has been bred to be '*calculable, regular, necessary*' – whose entire nervous and intellectual system has been hypnotized by 'fixed ideas' and now beats to the rhythm of the industrial calendar (*GM* II, 1, 3). It is perhaps more difficult to connect with Nietzsche's diagnosis of life-affirming values because such a perspective fails to commensurate with this model of human life and yet everything he has to say about eternal return can only be accessed from this perspective. If we have been tamed to take our being as the measure for things – and for good reason – how is it possible for the human animal to transcend the value judgements of its 'coarse organs', to embody different rhythms of life, to 'see nothing other than becoming'?

Dreams and intoxications

Nietzsche says of Heraclitus that only 'aesthetic man' is able to gaze at the world of perpetual 'becoming and passing away' without any 'moral ascription' (*PTAG* 7). The 'ever self-renewing drive' to artistic 'play' calls 'new worlds into life' but such an ebb and flood of forms is 'invisible to the common human eye' (*PTAG* 7). Not quite insensate perhaps but barely capable of deviating from its repertoire of project and plan ('being-for-self'), the herd beast has become progressively immune to the magic and majesty of great art – at best able only to perceive the 'play of the signifier'. Yet for Nietzsche, those kinds of art that communicate a world-altering power supply a vital conduit to the ever-renewing streams of becoming that the civilizing process breeds out. Works of art which *'excite the state that creates art'* (*WP* 821) reconfigure the being that they hold captive, retuning its senses to hitherto unknown frequencies and treacherously discrediting the crucial signs of an avowedly human past. This is a power 'which it is senseless to resist, indeed, which renders irrational and incomprehensible every way of life previously lived' (*UM* IV, 7).

> Set outside ourselves, we swim in an enigmatic, fiery element, no longer knowing ourselves nor recognizing the most familiar of things; we no longer possess any standard of measurement, everything lawlike and rigid begins to shift, everything gleams in new colours, speaks to us in new signs and characters. (Ibid.)

At the core of the bedrock of things burning matter ebbs and flows. The 'aesthetic man', a voyager in the deep recesses of inhuman vitality, translates all that he is into light and flame. Configured thus, art might seem to constitute a supreme transcendence of the 'world', a flight into the beyond disturbingly akin to the metaphysical idealism it purports to resist. Yet it is important to note that Nietzsche expresses a stinging antipathy for 'romantic pessimism', detecting in its otherworldly aspirations the scent of renunciation, failure and defeat (*HH* II, Preface 7). For Nietzsche, *tragic* pessimism is not the fruit of poverty but of plenitude, less a question of attempting to escape 'this life' than of helping 'this life' to escape the structures that imprison it. Accordingly, he regards Greek art as a *return to the body* but an *inhuman* one, as if life now shook itself free from its parasite self. From the moment that Nietzsche begins to write about the mythically inspired Greeks he rejects the language of concept and logic in favour of a vocabulary of libidinal drives and trans-individual affects – 'artistic energies' that 'burst forth from nature itself *without the mediation of the human artist*' (*BT* 2).

In an early text entitled 'The Dionysian Worldview', Nietzsche writes that 'one reaches the blissful feeling of existence in *dream* and in *rapture*' (*KSA* 1, 553). These superlative physiological states contour Nietzsche's entire treatment of Greek art, indeed the supreme joy of which he speaks again and again in these reflections has no obvious correlate in the social world of practical human involvements. The 'Apollinian' drive to dream and the 'Dionysian' drive to intoxication are vital compulsions which fail to heed 'the single unit' – forces of becoming which register their effects beyond the discrete boundaries that seem to demarcate individual being, enchanting the body with excitations which it can neither control nor fully recognize as its own. In the name of Apollinian powers of image-making and Dionysian energies of destruction, Nietzsche maps out an economics of artistic production and enjoyment of such burning libidinal intensity that it might seem at first glance to offer more to the history of desire than to classical aesthetic scholarship. Yet for Nietzsche, aesthetics is not obviously a region of philosophy delimited from other supposedly non-sensuous areas of thought, just as art is not obviously in and of itself life-affirming. Indeed, seen through the prism of 'value for life', there is a sense in which all philosophical questions are reformatted aesthetically, that is to say, *sensitively*, as material evaluations springing from paucity or plenitude. This means that any cultural product – artistic or otherwise – is estimated in terms of the mode of existence that it presupposes. In his retrospect on *The Birth of Tragedy*, Nietzsche comments that the aim of this 'audacious book' was '*to look at science in the perspective of the artist, but at art in the perspective of life* (*BT* 'Attempt', 2). Such an orientation leaves open the possibility that science might prove itself to be the progeny of superabundance and, by the same token, that art might show itself to be the botched and decadent offspring of declining vitality. In no sense then, is art privileged over *Wissenschaft* because of any essential quality or ontological primacy. Nietzsche's interest in art, and with tragic art in particular, is with its *transformative* potential for life – its role as 'the great stimulant of life, rapture with life, a will to life' (*WP* 851).

It is fundamental to the thought of will to power that *physis* is self-transcending, that life is 'that *which must overcome itself again and again*' (*TSZ* II 'Of Self-Overcoming'). Understood energetically as forces of becoming, life has no identity in and of itself – other than being that which perpetually differs from itself. Because life is that which wills to be 'more' than itself, a living thing must above all, '*expend* its energy' (*BGE* 13). Perhaps one of the chief reasons why ecstasy plays such a crucial role in Nietzsche's thinking is that it exemplifies most vividly this *feeling* of the superabundance of life. These new sensual continents are created, not discovered, born of rhythmic excitations that do not pre-exist their being sensed. For the human animal, the eruption of 'new worlds' into being is glimpsed all too fleetingly in exhilarating experiences which defeat explanation in familiar terms – hence the devastating allure of erotic adventures, mystical revelations, and, of course, dreams and intoxication.

It is notable that in *The Birth of Tragedy*, Nietzsche reserves the term *Rausch* – ecstasy, rapture, intoxication – for his discussion of Dionysian affects, distinguishing the latter from Apollinian intensities at the level of both physiology and art. His persistent allusion to the Dionysian in his later philosophy, particularly in the context of life-affirmation, might seem to license the view that the Apollinian occupies a subordinate position or marks a 'reactive' pole in his thinking, unrelated both to his ecstatic researches, and, consequently, to eternal return. However, in his general characterization of the transfigurative power of art and in numerous notes from the 1880s, Nietzsche underscores the thought that *Rausch* is the 'physiological precondition' for 'any sort of aesthetic activity' and that Apollinian and Dionysian are 'both conceived as kinds of rapture' (*TI* 'Expeditions...', 8 & 10). Even the most cursory reading of *The Birth of Tragedy* confirms that Apollinian art is life-transfiguring and that its 'rapturous vision' reflects and elicits extraordinarily intense pleasures (*BT* 4). Why Nietzsche should initially differentiate Apollinian and Dionysian in terms of dream and intoxication may tell us more about the *libidinal primacy of rapture* than the metaphysical primacy of the Dionysian, the latter being notoriously overdetermined by Nietzsche's adaptation and adoption of Kantian and

Schopenhauerian formulations. In fact, it is only through reading *The Birth of Tragedy* in terms of Apollinian and Dionysian ecstasy that it is possible to discern beneath its 'offensively Hegelian' dialectics another dynamics – one which reveals a burgeoning thought of libidinal difference refractory to the oppositional logic of 'the same'.

In an intriguing note from 1888, Nietzsche writes as follows:

> In Dionysian rapture there is sexuality and voluptuousness: they are not lacking in the Apollinian. There *must* also be a difference in tempo in the two conditions. ... The *extreme calm in certain sensations of rapture* (more strictly: the deceleration of the feelings of time and space) likes to be reflected in a vision of the calmest gestures and types of soul. The classical style essentially portrays this calm, simplification, abbreviation, concentration – the *highest feeling of power* is concentrated in the classical type. Slow to react; a great awareness; no feeling of struggle. (*WP* 799)

In this extraordinary note, Nietzsche characterizes Apollinian and Dionysian rapture in terms of a difference in tempo, with the tantalizing suggestion that the greatest *feeling* of power lies with the Apollinian. Since the Dionysian is so explicitly presented as the dominant power in *The Birth of Tragedy*, especially in its incarnation as the spirit of music from which tragedy is 'born', it seems initially difficult to imagine how the modest and decorous Apollinian could be thought of as the more intense force. Indeed, one of the complexities of *The Birth of Tragedy* is the alignment of the Apollinian with the Schopenhauerian 'principle of individuation', an association which seems to invite a conceptual parallel with the reactive 'rational man' who, like the Apollinian Greek, could be said to seek 'freedom from the wilder pulsions' (*BT* 1). Moreover, we are told that the Apollinian Greek trusts in the principle of individuation as soberly as a sailor navigates a stormy sea that 'unbounded in all directions, raises and drops mountainous waves' (*BT* 1). Yet instead of presenting this image of the human as life-negating, Nietzsche characterizes it from the outset as the embodiment of Apollinian glory – of the joy, beauty and 'wisdom of "semblance" [*Schein*]' (ibid.). Interpreted metaphysically, this conception of the human seems exemplary of self-preservative values yet, interpreted libidinally in terms of Apollinian rapture a rather different picture begins to emerge.

In characterizing the Apollinian and Dionysian as 'artistic energies that burst forth from nature itself *without the mediation of a human artist'*, Nietzsche complicates the classical conception of art as *mimesis* by failing to rigorously distinguish art from nature. Such a gesture inhibits any precipitate determination of art as agent governed, a point Nietzsche underscores by signalling the absence of the human artist from any mediating role in the emergent process. Nevertheless, he insists that it is the role of the representative artist to *imitate* the Apollinian pulsions in the production of poetry, visual art, sculpture and drama, just as the Dionysian artist must imitate the natural artistic energies, despite the fact that Dionysian art – lyric poetry, music and dance – is non-imagistic. While it might seem as if this gesture reinscribes a traditional model of the imitative role of art, it becomes progressively clear when examining the Apollinian and the Dionysian that the activity of the artist is not to be equated with a simple copying.

Indeed, from the outset the Apollinian is presented less as a representational force than a visionary power. First defined as the creative impulse operative in and through dreams, Apollinian energy is hailed as the formative force of the 'the beautiful shimmering of the dream world [*der schöne Schein der Traumwelten*]'. The forms and figures of the dream world are such that we take immediate delight in their *showing* or *Schein*. Bedazzled by their resplendence, the beholder is conducted beyond the 'everyday world' and a different quality of knowing comes into its own: 'We delight in the immediate understanding of figure; all forms speak to us; there is nothing inessential or unnecessary' (*BT* 1). To the extent that the Apollinian compels the dreamer to take delight in images *as* images it is an entrancing power, yet Nietzsche is careful to mark the fact that Apollinian pleasure in sensible form must respect a delicate limit: 'It is essential to include in the image of Apollo that delicate line which the dream image ought not exceed lest it have a pathological effect, in which case semblance [*Schein*] would deceive us as if it were crude reality' (*BT* 1). In fact, Nietzsche suggests that even when this 'dream reality' has the most intense vitality, the sensation glimmers through that it is still 'mere semblance [*Schein*]'. The intense pleasure taken in the beautiful shining of the dream world is thus wholly sensuous. Forms and figures appeal immediately to sensibility irrespective of their theme – which may be troubled or lugubri-

ous. Indeed, it is sensitivity to limit or measure that prohibits the
dreamer from mistaking semblance for actuality. This said, absorption in the image is unusual. Inasmuch as the dreamer 'lives and
suffers' with the dream he or she is *rapt* in the image. One does
not become fused with what one sees but nor does it flicker before
one like a mere 'shadow play'. Moreover, Nietzsche contends that
many, himself included, will recall how amid the dangers and
terrors of dreams they have sometimes been able to courageously
spur themselves on with the thought 'It is a dream! I shall dream
on!' (*BT* 1). The dreamer is entranced by the dream, as if attuning
to a different rhythm of life. It is in this sense that Apollinian
rapture pleases for its own sake. As in Kant's account of the
beautiful, this pleasure concerns delight in form rather than faith
in its existence. It revels in that which is bounded – abbreviated,
simplified.

In contending that the dreamer delights in *Schein*, Nietzsche
could be construed as merely privileging fantasy over reality, especially since he goes so far as to contrast the 'higher truth' and the
'perfection' of these states with the 'incompletely intelligible everyday world' (*BT* 1). He even considers the possibility that the waking
world is but an imitation of the realm of the dream and not vice
versa (*KSA* 7, 323/9[133]). Indeed, there is something peculiar about
the mimetic relation at issue here. As John Sallis points out, the
Apollinian would seem to constitute an 'inversion of the usual sedi-
mented Platonic ordering of image and original', since it is the
image and 'not the original which it images' that is superior.[2] This
strange inversion notwithstanding, Sallis remarks that it would seem
that the image is 'an image *of* an original: one dreams always *of*
something' (ibid.) – the implication being that the world of waking
reality remains the implicit 'standard' or measure against which
Apollinian rapture is defined.

That dreams are essentially the detritus of the day is something of
a commonplace. It is notable that Merleau-Ponty endorses precisely
this view in his consideration of dreaming.

> Bereft of the waking state, dreams would be no more than instan-
> taneous modulations and would not even exist for us. During the
> dream itself we do not leave the world: the space of the dream is
> entrenched from the space of clear thinking, but it utilizes all its

articulations; the world obsesses us even during sleep and it is about the world that we dream. (*PhP* 339, *PP* 293)

For Merleau-Ponty, it is the waking self that has authority over the dreaming state, for the latter can give no account of itself that would be useful 'for us'. But perhaps this definition of 'reality' is only 'a *simplification* for practical ends', the prejudice of a normative physiology which takes its variation in the tempo of becoming as definitive of all other corporeal modulations. That dreams might constitute an alternative stream of coherence, having their own cumulative reference and logic, is an impermissible proposition for a kind of life that screens out all intense and unpredictable sensations, particularly those sensations that would threaten to undermine consciousness as the ultimately decisive material flow. If one always dreams *of* something, could it not be said that what one dreams of is *the dream*?

Nietzsche's deployment of *Schein* as self-showing semblance in *The Birth of Tragedy* seems important here. It is to be recalled that for Kant the wild and stormy ocean is the native source of *Schein* – that which tempts the bold explorer to attribute predicates to things-in-themselves beyond the 'land of truth' (the lawful domain circumscribing possible experience). Within this isle, that which constitutes the necessary and *a priori* relations of things as phenomena are the transcendental principles of experience in general, but for Nietzsche the conditions of experience are themselves actual not possible (that is, particular and contingent rather than universal and necessary). Nietzsche does not assume that the normative physiology of the human animal is the exemplary self-identity that is momentarily exceeded in rapture. The body 'as such' is not given. To this extent, he is influenced by Schopenhauer's tendency to view the Kantian *a priori* as evidence of the 'subjective' nature of the forms of intuition and understanding rather than as the condition of objectivity and indeed, in the opening section of *The Birth of Tragedy* he obliquely alludes to the Schopenhauerian view that the world must be recognized, 'from one aspect at least, as related to a dream, indeed as capable of being placed in the same class with a dream' (*WWR*, II, 4). While Nietzsche has little interest in upholding the metaphysical distinction between phenomenal illusion and noumenal reality – which his notion of the higher truth of *Schein* clearly disturbs – he remains persuaded by Schopenhauer's proposal that dreaming has a reality or continuity in itself. Perhaps the 'higher truth' of shining semblance which 'perfects' incomplete reality need not be read metaphysically as a claim about the way things really are, but aesthetically, as one of the many other ways of creating the apparent world. Characterized thus, the distinction between 'this world' and the realm of the dream does not hinge on the opposition between appearance and reality: 'For 'appearance' [*Schein*] here means reality *once more*, only selected, strengthened, corrected…' (*TI* 'Reason in Philosophy', 6). Whereas Merleau-Ponty commutes dreaming to the form of the same – the phenomenological reality of 'our world', Nietzsche's insights stem from the lived perspective of dream. There is a 'joyous necessity' to this dream world, one that is exemplified in the dreamer who is able to 'continue the causality of one and the same dream over three or more successive nights' (*BT* 1). The way in which dreams may return, recapitulating and diversifying their unworldly preoccupations, attests to the power of unconscious physiological flows to create reality *once again* but no longer in the image *of* a daylit originary world.

In so far as dreams are already proto-artistic forces, free from any merely mimetic relation to 'our world', the artistic imitation of dream energy in epic poetry, visual art and sculpture is by definition difficult to reinscribe in the classical model of art, despite Nietzsche's allusions to this theory (*BT* 2). Implicitly invoking Schopenhauerian metaphysics once more, he goes on to suggest an equiprimordiality between dream and art in that both could be construed as the '*Schein des Scheins*', although art could equally be viewed as the semblance of semblance to the second power (*BT* 4). However, to think of dreaming as the semblance of semblance *once again*, that is, as an imaging power *unanchored in the world of identity* is to go some way towards explaining why the embodied reality of the Apollinian Greek differs from that of 'rational man'. We are told that 'Apollinian rapture alerts above all the eye [literally 'holds it aroused'], so that it obtains the power of vision. The painter, the sculptor, the epic poet are visionaries *par excellence*' (*TI* 'Expeditions…', 10). Perhaps here the artist is able to see what is 'invisible to the common human eye' – the emergence of new worlds into life. For in Apollinian rapture sight is made powerful, is intensified. The pleasure in *Schein* is the affective yield of a vision which perceives what cannot be seen – the appearance *of* appearance but now thought as a visionary power which seizes the visible *as it appears*. Consequently, the Apollinian compulsion to idealize – to prolong the dream by perpetuating yet further dreams of dreams – is a superlative concentration *of its own force*, its primary self-overcoming or self-differentiation. This explains why it is both a life-affirming power and a potent formative force. Whereas the reactive rational man constructs his concepts by negating unique, sensitive experience (*TL* 1), Apollinian form is achieved through supreme concentration of its energy. This clarifies Nietzsche's assertion that idealization is not a matter of deducting the petty and the secondary but involves 'an immense *forcing out* of the principal features' (*TI* 'Expeditions...', 8). In short, it is not a different possibility of a given perceptual power that is here invoked but a *difference created within the power of perception*. The 'organs' refine themselves.

Nietzsche says that nature's art drives are 'directly satisfied' in the image world of dreams 'the completeness of which bears no relation to the intellectual depth or artistic culture of a single being' (*BT* 2). There is no impetus here to think of dreams as partial fragments of 'everyday reality' or to think of Apollinian ecstasy as a deviation from the 'unit' of identity. Indeed, there is an internal succession to Apollinian re-imaging that is both differential and continuous. In proliferating simulacra, rather than likenesses or copies 'of the world', the Apollinian repeats itself as self-differentiating, creating effects of resemblance by means of difference. For certain conceptually driven thinkers, such simulacra are 'copies of copies', inscribed within 'ambivalent', 'undecidable' mimetic 'play'[3] but from the perspective of ecstatic philosophy it is possible to see how Apollinian rapture is a tempo of becoming that is self-perpetuating, a power that actualizes its internal virtuality. Since nothing proceeds by re-cognition *anything is possible at any moment*. As such Apollinian energies are not defined in relation to a given concept (for example, the 'form of the same' of a normative physiology) nor are they defined dialectically or negatively in terms of limitation by what they are not. This may help to account for the fact that the Apollinian is described both as a specific tempo of intoxication and as part of a dynamic interplay with the Dionysian. As we shall shortly see, when thought libidinally, this wider dynamic also eludes the form of dialectic.

If Apollinian rapture names a differential power of concentration and contraction, the Dionysian designates a force of dissolution and dilation. Initially introduced in *The Birth of Tragedy* as a potent compound of destruction and delight, the Dionysian announces both the terror and 'blissful ecstasy' [*wonnevolle Verzückung*] that wells up from nature at the collapse of the principle of individuation (*BT* 1). Whether under the influence of narcotic draughts or with the intoxicating power of nature's blossoming bounty, Dionysian excitations are aroused, exacerbated and transformed. *Rausch* designates this vital upsurge, the effervescent and explosive power of life. As with the image world of dreams, intoxicated reality 'likewise does not heed the single unit' (*BT* 1). It is immediately clear that, like the Apollinian, Dionysian rapture is a self-differentiating power, a force 'in the intensification of which, the subjective vanishes into complete oblivion' (*BT* 1). As Nietzsche comments in 'The Greek Music Drama': 'The all-powerful, suddenly emerging effects of Spring here also intensify the life forces to such excess, that ecstatic states, visions and belief in one's own enchantment everywhere come to the fore' (*KSA* 1/521–2). Similarly, in a note from 1869 Nietzsche writes: 'in those orgiastic festivals of Dionysus such a degree of being-outside-of-oneself – of *ecstasis*, held sway that people acted and felt like transformed and enchanted beings' (*KSA* 7/10/1[1]). In the overwhelming and entrancing *ecstasis* of Dionysian rapture, life differentiates itself transversally. Unlike Apollinian rapture, which concentrates and proliferates forms of itself, Dionysian rapture is trans-formative, both in the sense that it is a destructive, metamorphic power and in the sense that it seems to migrate between forms. Nietzsche suggests that Dionysian ecstasy impacts as 'a mystic feeling of oneness', a reconciliation with nature, but this sense of oneness is strangely non-unifying (*BT* 1). Dionysian ecstasy names a nomadic ubiquity, a *sense* of 'sameness' forged through constant differentiation between individuals: 'the essential thing remains the ease of metamorphosis, the inability *not* to react' (*TI* 'Expeditions...', 10). Like the hysteric, the Dionysian takes on any role at the slightest suggestion (ibid.). This is stressed all the more emphatically in a contemporaneous note in which Nietzsche tellingly extends the notion of *ecstasis* to cover *all* forms of art.

All art demands a 'being-outside-of-oneself', an *ecstasis*; it is from here that the step to drama takes place by which we, in our *ecsta-*

sis, do *not* return to ourselves [*wir* nicht *in uns zurückkehren*] but reside in an other being; therewith we behave as if enchanted. Hence the deep astonishment when watching drama: the ground shakes, the belief in the indissolubility of the individual likewise.

Also, in lyric poetry, we are astonished to feel our ownmost feelings again, to have them thrown back to us from other individuals. (*KSA* 7/ 54–5/ 2[25])

This passage may invite the conclusion that *ecstasis* signifies movement *from* one identity *to* another (not unlike the endless play of the signifier or 'polyvalent identities'). Since the formulation 'being-outside-of-oneself' implies a self that is exceeded it would seem that Dionysian ecstasy must at some level be addressed in relation to a 'form of the same', despite the fact that this limit between self and non-self is transgressed. As John Sallis remarks: 'Thus, in ecstasy transgression cannot but disrupt the limit. And yet, transgression is possible only in relation to the limit; that is, one can be *outside oneself* only if the self within continued somehow to be delimited' (*C* 55). Dionysian ecstasy both exceeds the limit by which the self would be identified and it exceeds its own exceeding for 'to disrupt the limit definitive of the opposition would be to disrupt the very limit by which the transgression, the being outside, would be defined (ibid.). Sallis concludes from this that 'there can be transgressive disruption of the limit only if the limit is also redrawn, reinstated, as the very limit to be transgressed' (ibid.). Yet it seems that what must be acknowledged is that this need not entail a return to the *same* self ('we, in our *ecstasis*, do *not* return to ourselves'). Ecstatic passage requires the thought of a becoming-other which is not transcendent to its terms. For Nietzsche tragedy is an art form born immanently from the participants, from the dangerous, contagious energy flowing through the rapturous throng. It is the nature of 'the Dionysian man' to constantly overcome his own becoming: 'He enters into every skin, into every affect: he transforms himself constantly' (*TI* 'Expeditions...', 10). In no sense, then, is change measured relative to the being that we are (or fail to be). Becoming-other is not the endless Sartrean process of becoming what one is not. In fact, to understand ecstasy in terms of the exceeding of limits of self ensures that the self which is exceeded continues to function as a 'form of the same' governing the movement of difference. However, for

Nietzsche, the antithesis between inner and outer is a completely inappropriate opposition for all that lives (*UM* II, 4). What *The Birth of Tragedy* succeeds in doing is thinking physiology in terms of self-differentiating processes within which 'identities' are produced – but *felt* not cognized. *Both* Apollinian and Dionysian are already 'outside-of-self' but the self is a relational network rather than a limit, the effect of different tempos of becoming.

> If we give up the effective *subject*, we also give up the *object* which is effected. Duration, identity with itself, being inhere neither in that which is called subject nor in that which is called object: they are complexes of events, apparently durable with regard to other complexes – e.g. through the difference in tempo of the event (rest – motion, firm – loose: all opposites that do not exist in themselves and that actually express only *differences in degree* that from a certain perspective appear to be opposites...). (*WP* 552)

If Apollinian and Dionysian *Rausch* are different in tempo rather than in kind, it may be possible to understand each as different degrees of the self-differentiating power of *physis*, thereby circumventing the dialectic entirely. However, it still remains to be seen how these energies differ from one another. Given that the Dionysian lacks imaging powers it cannot be thought in terms of simulacra: 'The plastic artist, like the epic poet immediately related to him is absorbed [*versunken*] in the pure intuition of images. The Dionysian musician is without any images, utter primordial pain and its primordial reverberation [*Urwiederklang*]' (*BT* 5). Indeed, Dionysian ecstasy articulates a 'bliss born of pain', excruciating pleasures become audible in devilishly enchanting tones. Nietzsche's remarks about this primordial re-echoing are of crucial importance. He claims that in Dionysian ecstasy, something never before experienced struggles for utterance. To express 'oneness as genius of the race, indeed of nature', a 'new world of symbols' is required, an 'entire symbolism of the body' [*die ganze leibliche Symbolik*] (*BT* 2). This symbolism is 'not merely the symbolism of the mouth, face and words but the entire, rhythmically moving dance gestures of all members' which incite the growth of other symbolic powers – of rhythm, dynamics and harmony (*BT* 2). In fact, in the Dionysian state 'the entire affective system is alerted and intensified' so that it discharges all its powers 'at the same time [*zugleich*]' (*TI* 'Expeditions...', 10). This is exemplified in Dionysian music where 'the shuddering power of the tone [*die erschütternde Gewalt des Tones*]', the singular flow of melody and the 'incomparable world of harmony' constitute the collective, intensive vibrations of *pre-personal* affectivity. Here Nietzsche seems to be alluding to what he describes in a note as the '*tonal sub-ground*' from which the 'reverberation [*Wiederklang*] of sensations of pleasure and pain' originate (*KSA* 7, 362/12[1]). In a Schopenhauerian idiom (although departing from its spirit) Nietzsche claims that the only clue that we have to 'all becoming and willing' is this 'tonal sub-ground' that accompanies all representations as a 'figured bass' and to which 'our whole corporeality' is related (ibid.). So-called 'gestural' language is rooted in this sub-ground, the multiplicity of languages appearing as a 'strophic text of this primordial melody of pleasure and displeasure language' (ibid.). The power to represent is thus generated *from* the pre-conceptual rhythms of *pathos*. In *Beyond Good and Evil*, Nietzsche relates the 'tempo of metabolism' to different qualities of linguistic style, underscoring the point that the physiological rhythms of a people are communicated in the cadences of their language. Similarly, in *The Birth of Tragedy* he contends that the image world of the poem is generated from this pre-personal melody: 'The melody gives birth to the poetry out of itself and does so ever again anew [*immer wieder von Neuem*]; *the strophic form of the folksong* says to us nothing other than this' (*BT* 6). Perhaps even more interesting still, Nietzsche asserts that the Dionysian melody which in conjunction with the Apollinian 'gives birth' to poetry, leaves residual traces in the folk song 'just as the orgiastic movements of a people eternalize themselves in its music' (*BT* 6).[4] The lineaments of sacred joy are carved in this rhythmic cascade – not as immortal motifs (eternity) but as self-perpetuating material energies (eternalizing processes). Apollinian imaging powers are recurrently reborn from the tempo of this erotic intensity. And it is *of* this that the Apollinian dreams.

We are now in a position to see why the Apollinian is also a dimension of *Rausch*. It is distilled from the metamorphic forces that reverberate in the Dionysian but this effect is only achieved because the difference between Apollinian and Dionysian *ecstasy* is already thought *within* the Dionysian. Nietzsche's remarks on the 'spirit of music' from this period are often difficult to disentangle from the Schopenhauerian theory of will with which they are interlaced, but Nietzsche remains constant on one point: images cannot generate music. However, music has the 'wonderous power' to put us in an enchanted state because it excites the affective realm *as such*. Melody, which is 'primary and universal', does not serve to illustrate dramatic dialogue. Rather, poetry is produced by the rapid variation and mad haste of the continuously generating melody. The *strophic*, 'turning' form of the song marks the perpetual falling back of the melody into itself. Thus it embodies the generative power – so alien to epic poetry – which 'ever again anew' gives birth to images.

The modifier 'ever again anew [*immer wieder von Neuem*]' that accompanies the Dionysian element in Nietzsche's text, articulates a power of perpetual overcoming, the trajectory of which may not be determined in advance. While stately rhythm observes the laws of form and measure and as rules of composition may be *taught,* the mad haste of the continuously generating melody animates 'the entire symbolism of the body', suggestively communicating its pulsions to a language which strains to give it shape. The vital rhythms of the dancing, frenzied, orgiastic body which 'reverberate' at the core of the body of nature now resound in poetic images, repeating Dionysian insights at another level. The Dionysian impulse to repeat 'ever again anew' serves to reactivate the Apollinian drive to eternalize, like a wave that in its enigmatic pulsion and recurrent rise describes the impetus to compose once again the oceanic flux. In this way the Dionysian impulsion to dissipate coupled with the Apollinian urge to distend attain a double becoming that rises and falls in time to the beat of a thoroughly sexual longing.

If rapture is the precondition for all art, the Apollinian is the *intensification* of this primordial affective excitement. It is in this respect that it constitutes the supreme feeling of power. Indeed, the transformative power of repetition is expressed here as immanent differentiation of life. As Nietzsche shows in his account of the interrelation of Apollinian and Dionysian in lyric poetry, dark insights into the suffering 'will' are embraced so intensely that they are taken to the limit at which they become something else – supreme joy.

First of all, as a Dionysian artist he has become completely one with the primordial unity, its pain and its contradiction, and he produces the copy of this primordial unity as music, assuming that music has been correctly termed a repetition and a second casting of the world. Now however, under the Apollinian dream-influence, this music becomes visible to him again as in a *symbolic dream-image*. That imageless and conceptless reflection [*bild-und begrifflose Wiederschein*] of primordial pain in music, with its redemption in semblance [*Schein*], now engenders a second mirroring as an individual symbol or example. The artist has already given up his own subjectivity in the Dionysian process. The image which now shows him his unity with the heart of the world is a dream-scene which represents the primordial contradiction and primordial pain together with the primordial joy of semblance [*Urlust des Scheins*]. Thus, the 'I' of the lyrist sounds out from the abyss of being; its 'subjectivity' in the sense of modern aestheticians is an illusion. (*BT* 5)

Nietzsche's account of the lyric poet shows that the groundless is not undifferentiated but is reverberating intensity *without identity* – imageless and conceptless *Wiederschein*. If the 'ground' is difference (perpetual differentiation) then repetition cannot be *of* the same but only of the different – the renewal of the different. Non-identical repetition is the vibrating movement that constitutes differences but it is not 'instants' that are repeated: it is the whole. It is this differential material plenum that Deleuze might designate the real transcendental field. Apollinian and Dionysian only affirm themselves by differing from themselves prior to their unilateral differentiation as a duality, with the entire affective system of the Dionysian as the primary term. The imageless and conceptless *Wiederschein* is a re-shining power – one that intensifies and repeats the Apollinian drive to *Schein*. If the 'bliss born of pain' in Dionysian ecstasy is the Apollinian symbolization of Dionysian intensities it now becomes evident why 'the wisdom in semblance' of the Apollinian is a *sensitive* knowing, a non-conceptual recognition of physiological consanguinity with these darker forces. The Apollinian Greek 'was compelled to feel' that 'his entire existence with all its beauty and measure, rested on a concealed substratum of suffering and of knowledge, disclosed to him once again by the Dionysian' (*BT* 4). The Apollinian gives way to the Dionysian once again but it is to be noted that this 'once again' is inscribed at the outset of the dynamic interplay between the two forces. It is a primordial repetition – a primordial reverberation, we might say.

To see becoming

Nietzsche says that 'we have to understand Greek tragedy as the Dionysian chorus which ever again anew [*immer von neuem wieder*] discharges itself in an Apollinian world of images' (*BT* 8). As in the folk song, intense Dionysian rapture is released 'ever again anew' into an Apollinian vision of resplendence. The Apollinian furthers what the Dionysian repeats, intensifying the wild pulsions of the body, concentrating them, idealizing them. If Apollinian vision represents a difference within the power of perception we can now say that it thereby represents a difference within the Dionysian – it comes to illuminate the only clue we have to all becoming and willing. In Apollinian ecstasy, the eye acquires a power of vision that enables it to see semblance as *Schein*, and, at its apex, to reflect in tragedy the Dionysian forces that cannot show themselves. Tragedy is made 'visible and intelligible from the inside' (*BT* 24).

The tragic myth is to be thought of as a symbolization of Dionysian wisdom through Apollinian artifices, which 'leads the world of appearance to its limits where it denies itself and seeks to flee back again into the womb of the true and only reality' – the 'rapturous ocean's billowing swell' – to cite a line of Wagner (*BT* 22). This is the nature of the uncanny delight in tragedy: one ceases to identify with the suffering hero but comes to identify with the 'ground' or primal one of tragedy: one becomes ecstatic. Nietzsche says that in tragedy there is a thirst to see which is so intense that it longs to be blind and desire to hear that at the same time bears within it a longing to get beyond all hearing:

> [I]n both states we have to recognize a Dionysian phenomenon that ever again anew [*immer wieder von Neuem*] reveals to us the playful construction and destruction of the individual world as the outflow of a primordial pleasure; in a similar manner, the worldbuilding force is compared by Heraclitus the dark to a child at play who places stones here and there, builds sandcastles and smashes them again. (*BT* 24)

In the crashing torrents of the Dionysian sea of forces, the Apollinian emerges as a vortical power – a whirlpool of apparent stability in a turbulent and ever-changing swell. Its uncanny calm, its slower tempo, gives it a semblance of difference from the surging waves but it is of the ocean and cannot exist without it. Such is to say that the Apollinian differs from the Dionysian without the Dionysian differing from it. Both Apollinian and Dionysian are differentiating powers without unity but there is a difference in tempo between them. The Apollinian is a power of individuation that differentiates the dissipative Dionysian energies and distinguishes itself from them without negation. Nietzsche counterposes the 'eternalizing' power of both Apollinian and Dionysian in terms of the 'becoming-eternal' of the phenomenon and the 'eternal becoming' of the Dionysian 'will' and it is this subtlety that marks the resistance of their sacred continuity to ideal abstractions (*BT* 16). It is Dionysian insights that the Apollinian comes to eternalize. The Dionysian provokes the Apollinian power to the point at which it becomes something else – the illumination of the depths. Perhaps this is why the dreamer is compelled to dream on, despite the terrifying nature of the dream. There is necessity to this rush which is compulsively beautiful.

3
A Feeling of Life

> I want to learn more and more to see as beautiful what is
> necessary in things; then I shall be one of those who makes
> things beautiful. *Amor fati:* let that be my love henceforth!
>
> (*The Gay Science* 276)

There is a contented way of living that is not only commonplace
but strangely encouraged and even envied. Its hallmarks are moder-
ation, utility, a faith in means–ends reasoning and damage limitation – the value of which all goes unchallenged for it appeals to the
familiar and the habitual without questioning the nature of its
appeal. Nietzsche claims that all human arrangements are actually
designed to distract thought to the point at which one ceases to
have any 'sensation of life' (*UM* III, 4). Few of the contented many
suspect the proximity of savage and unbearable passions which,
once touched, consign their convenient pleasures and tolerable
pastimes to permanent exile. The prospect that supreme joy might
be catastrophic is safely alien to a species that has perfected the art
of bovine satisfaction. But to have experienced a joy so profound
that one can only want what one will always want *again* is an
affliction which far outweighs the discomforts of disturbed equilibrium. Is this why the artist, the lunatic and the lover live with an
urgency quite disproportionate to any perceived necessity and
more intensely than strictly they can bear? Shattered by a life that
is too much, they struggle to minimize, to master, to contain – in
the process, magnifying and augmenting the catastrophe that
seethes beneath the surface. The horror of burning up from within

is superseded only by the horror of indifference to ruin, which in turn is outstripped only by the horror of finally failing to burst into flames.

No good will come of these monstrous passions and yet they claim us with a ferocity that makes us ache for more. Could it be that the cruellest pleasures are always the ones which are so disarmingly pure? Nietzsche suggests that the craving for beauty among the ancient Greeks may have concealed a more perverse desire, the craving for the ugly, the frightful, the evil. Initially, the Apollinian is presented as a veiling power, one which seeks to conceal the horrors of the Dionysian abyss. Yet even at the level of the dream, the Apollinian has the power to take pleasure in the gruesome and grotesque as if able to find beauty even here. While the Dionysian may seem to occupy a superior position in Nietzsche's philosophy, Apollinian rapture may ultimately prove to be the more complex libidinal charge.

The compulsive lure of the useless

The thirst for the beautiful is something which many thinkers have sought to explain, its brazen inutility aggressing against the reasoned order of civilization. In *Civilization and its Discontents* Freud writes that: 'The enjoyment of beauty has a peculiar, mildly intoxicating quality. Beauty has no obvious use; nor is there any clear cultural necessity for it. Yet civilization could not do without it' (*PFL* 12, 270—1). With reassuring predictability Freud argues that beauty derives from the domain of sexual feeling and that 'the love of beauty seems a perfect example of an impulse inhibited in its aim' (*PFL* 12, 271). Freud's analysis proposes that beauty is aim-inhibited desire, that decency is the bandage of the incurably depraved. Our delight in the beautiful is forged in a crucible of erotic longing, our ideals the evaporating smoke of infelicitous passion. Yet whatever the significance or cogency of this might be, its 'truth' is never grasped by its simple acknowledgement. There is something unteachable here which is fully commensurate with its sublimated dynamic. Beauty – so ambivalently delicate and brutal – is an ideal which mysteriously thrives upon its own withholding. If the desire for the beautiful always conceals something that we cannot acknowledge, it is not because we 'repress' the truth, but simply that we cannot *know* it.

Yukio Mishima cites the following passage from Dostoyevsky's *The Brothers Karamazov* as an epigraph to *Confessions of a Mask*.

'... Beauty is a terrible and awful thing! It is terrible because it never has and never can be fathomed, for God sets us nothing but riddles. Within beauty both shores meet and all contradictions exist side by side. I'm not a cultivated man, brother, but I've thought a lot about this. Truly there are mysteries without end! Too many riddles weigh man down on earth. We guess them as we can, and come out of the water dry. Beauty! I cannot bear the thought that a man of noble heart and lofty mind sets out with the ideal of the Madonna and ends with the ideal of Sodom. What's still more awful is that the man with the ideal of Sodom in his soul does not renounce the ideal of the Madonna, and in the bottom of his heart he may still be on fire, sincerely on fire, with longing for the beautiful ideal, just as in the days of his youthful innocence. Yes, man's heart is too wide, too wide indeed. I'd have it narrower. The devil only knows what to make of it! But what the intellect regards as shameful often appears splendidly beautiful to the heart. Is there beauty in Sodom? Believe me, most men find their beauty in Sodom. Did you know this secret? The dreadful thing is that beauty is not only terrifying but also mysterious. God and the Devil are fighting there, and their battlefield is the heart of man. But a man's heart wants to speak only of its own ache. Listen, now I'll tell you what it says...'[1]

There is something about the urgent, painful ardour of these words – spoken from the heart to the heart – that attests to the futility of knowing our desires. This pathological lunge towards our splendidly beautiful collapse is something that we can 'identify' yet its observation fails to tell us anything from which we can ever learn. But then, perhaps pleasure in beauty is badly construed as a feeling which 'we' have. Perhaps it is a feeling which somehow 'has' us.

According to Nietzsche, the beautiful is that which 'pleases, arouses joy, as *Schein*' (*KSA* 1, 573). It is the scintillating show, the subtle sparkling that lends a luminosity to the world far exceeding that which is merely perceived. Apollinian art enables the viewer to see the world anew, as if animated by a visionary power. It is as if a second nature blossomed forth from nature, captivating the enraptured spectator by the sheer radiance of its sensible form. This subtle holding power is perfectly measured, free from rule yet necessary. In beauty, the world is revealed in its higher truth, in its perfection.

In characterizing the beautiful thus, Nietzsche appears to draw on the account of pleasure in the beautiful advanced by Kant in the *Critique of Judgement* and embellished by Schopenhauer in *The World as Will and Representation*. To suggest a contiguity between the ideas advanced in these texts and Nietzsche's account of Apollinian rapture may seem initially surprising, given Nietzsche's retrospective regret regarding *The Birth of Tragedy* that he had struggled to express strange and new evaluations by means of Kantian and Schopenhaurian formulas (*BT* 'Attempt...,' 6). Indeed, in *Daybreak* he objects that the thinking of Kant and Schopenhauer lacks the 'passionate history of a soul', that Kant's philosophy is the 'biography of a *head*', whereas Schopenhauer's is 'the description and mirroring of a *character*' (*D* 481). Kant in particular is taken to task for failing to exploit the possibility that even the most solitary and quietest of lives can burn 'with the passion of thinking' (ibid.). Yet, these caveats notwithstanding, it is notable that in *The Birth of Tragedy* and related writings of the period Nietzsche explicitly endorses the Kantian notion of 'disinterested' aesthetic judgement, making it central to his explanation of lyric poetry. Furthermore, in *On the Genealogy of Morals* he does not so much reject this specific formulation as the ascetic value economy within which it is inscribed (*GM* III, 6). As we shall see, a 'transvalued' conception of disinterestedness is integral to Nietzsche's own thinking of Apollinian and Dionysian rapture and the different tempos of affectivity which unite them.[2]

That delight in beauty is useless, gratuitous and literally good for nothing is a conviction that Kant establishes at the heart of his account of aesthetic pleasure, despite competing attempts to align beauty with the moral good and despite the more far-reaching goal of consummating the Critical System through the transcendental critique of reflective judgement. In the *Critique of Judgement* Kant insists that beauty exists only for beings that are both fatally imbricated in the swamp of embodiment yet endowed with a capacity for Ideas of reason which transcends 'mere' nature. Yet if beauty is a humanizing power it must sustain the rift in order to bridge it: here 'both shores meet and all contradictions exist side by side'. In the opening sections of the *Critique of Judgement*, Kant takes care to distinguish 'liking for beauty' from the grubby needs of appetite, the lofty aspirations of morality and the brute teleology of 'interest'. Indeed, for an aesthetic judgement to be pure it is imperative that it be free of any interest that would *account* for our favouring the object of our delight. In suggesting that our liking appeals to sense without making sense in its terms, Kant inaugurates the thought of aesthetics as gratuitous (sacred) pleasure.

> This pleasure is [...] not practical in any way, neither like the pleasure arising from the pathological basis, agreeableness, nor like the pleasure arising from the intellectual basis, the conceived good. Yet it does have a causality in it, namely, to *preserve* [*erhalten*] the state of presentation itself and [to hold] the cognitive powers preoccupied, without any further intention. We *linger* [*weilen*] in our contemplation of the beautiful, because this contemplation strengthens [*stärkt*] and reproduces itself. (*KU* 138, *CJ* #12, 68)

Pleasure in beauty is a self-sustaining and regenerating force – irresistibly strong if elusive at the level of meaning. Interestingly this passage may help to contextualize Nietzsche's memorable description of the dreamer continuing the *causality* of one and the same dream over successive nights, an experience which we have already identified with the self-differentiating power of Apollinian rapture. Kant's notion of an 'inner causality' which preserves the state of a presentation itself without further design, characterizes the 'subjective purposiveness' of aesthetic pleasure in the beautiful. In much the same way as sheer joy in the *Schein* of the lingering dream is independent of waking reality, delight taken in the form of the beautiful does not depend on the existence of an object as such. This must be so for Kant because pure aesthetic reflective judgement is 'disinterested'. Since Kant defines 'interest' as a liking that we connect with the presentation of an object's existence (which always refers to our power of desire) pure contemplative delight bears on that which I make out of the representation in myself (*KU* 117, *CJ* #2, 46). It is worth making the point that desire, for Kant, concerns the egoic, empirical interests of the subject whereas pure disinterested contemplation is transcendental in nature and hence 'free' of reality. Accordingly, the purposivity that is germane to Kant's account here is of a particular kind, namely that which is encountered in 'reflective judgement'. In the *Critique of Judgement* Kant argues that judgement in general is 'the ability to think the particular as contained under the universal' and that this is determinative when the universal (the rule, principle, law) is given whereas it is *reflective* 'if only the particular is given' and judgement has to 'find the universal' for it (*KU* 87, *CJ Second Introduction* #IV, 18-19). Kant insists that the transcendental principle given by reflective judgement 'can only be given to itself' for if it were to take it from somewhere else it would then be determinative (*KU* 88, *CJ Second Introduction* #IV, 19). Understood as an ability to *reflect*, in terms of a certain principle, on a given presentation so as to make a concept possible, reflective judgement enables beauty to be estimated on the ground of conformity to an end without an end or 'purposivity without purpose'.

The suggestion that we linger in our contemplation of the beautiful because this contemplation strengthens and reproduces itself is clarified by Kant's requirement that aesthetic pleasure be located in terms of how a subject 'feels himself' affected by a presentation, an event which he in turn refers to that subject's 'feeling of life' under the name of the feeling of pleasure or displeasure (*KU* 115, *CJ* #1, 44). It is particularly significant that Kant should propose that representations be referred to this *Lebensgefühl* because this implies that aesthetic judgement always entails an *evaluation of life* – a consideration of its pains and pleasures. Pleasure is aligned with a sense of life enhancement ('the furtherance of life') whereas displeasure signifies a sense of its inhibition or restriction. Much of the first half of *Critique of Judgement* is devoted to exploring these feelings of life in terms of pleasure elicited by beauty and displeasure provoked by the sublime. The notion of 'disinterestedness' is central to both of these enterprises, for Kant seeks to distinguish aesthetic judgements from all other kinds of judgements on the basis of the *formal* nature of these feelings. Accordingly, Kant claims that the feeling of life grounds 'a very special power of discriminating and judging' that compares 'the given presentation in the subject with the entire presentational power, of which the mind [*Gemüt*] becomes conscious in feeling its own state' (*KU* 116, *CJ* #1, 44). In making this reference, Kant ensures that mere sensory receptivity to presentations, including the appeal that material aspects of an object might have for our senses, are not confused with transcendental feeling in which pleasure and judgement are a-subjectively united. In other words, 'disinterested' pleasure (or pain) is not a merely private state of sensation (which relies on the real existence of the object) but a 'pure' subjective feeling of mental life.

Rudolf Makkreel notes that in the *Anthropology from a Pragmatic Point of View* (1798) Kant coins the term 'interior sense' to describe 'an intermediate, responsive mode of consciousness which involves a sensitivity of feeling to the state of the subject' (*IIK* 94; *AP* 446). Interior sense is distinguished from both 'inner sense' which is a 'passive' power of empirical perception (for example, the apprehension of the flow of time) and from the 'activity' of the understanding. The claim is that certain sensations can be both sensed and felt – that is, they are sensations which at the same time arouse an attentiveness to the state of the subject. Such responsiveness expresses either affirmation or rejection of the state of the representation as such. Makkreel argues that 'it is clear that the feeling of enhanced vitality of the subject involved in aesthetic pleasure belongs to this interior sense' (ibid.). Makkreel also notes that Kant introduces a notion of 'vital sense' in the *Anthropology* (*AP* 446) which involves the 'more generally encompassing sensations that pervade the entire system of the body' and he suggests that 'whereas inner sense synthesizes the discrete givens of the five outer senses, the interior sense may be said to respond to the content of vital sense' which although physiological is not localized in any specific organ (*IIK* 95). These notions of interior and vital sense suggest a way of understanding the evaluations of the human animal in physiological terms which, on the one hand, seem to unite the 'subject' as a whole, while on the other, seem to dissipate its normative requirements of perception and cognition.

We have seen that the pleasure taken in Apollinian rapture is a concentrated self-intensifying power, one which takes itself as its own object and is not to be referred back to empirical sensations emanating from 'our' waking world. Intriguingly, Kant's text emphasizes that the liking for the beautiful carries with it directly 'a feeling of life's being furthered [*ein Gefühl der Beförderung des Lebens*]' (*KU* 165, *CJ* #23, 98) – that is, boosted, increased, *transported* beyond itself. Such a feeling is regarded by Nietzsche as the more intense feeling of power – the slowing, strengthening force of Apollinian rapture. Delight in the beautiful holds its 'subject' with a sense of utter neccessity yet mysteriously so because it bears no relation to the 'self' as an intentional agent. To say that such a judgement is 'free' from interest means that I cannot choose whether to have a liking for beauty, it chooses me, *it compels me*. In a curious sense aesthetic judgement is *of me* (is grounded in sensations of pleasure and pain) without being obviously peculiar to me ('interested'). Kant's suggestion is that the universal communicability of the judgement (and hence its intersubjective validity) rests upon this essential indeterminacy. Our feeling of life is enhanced and intensified by the sensation of the 'enlivening' yet indeterminate play of the two powers required for cognition in general – imagination and understanding (*KU* 133–4, *CJ* #9, 63). Yet Kant's argument for the universality of this feeling seems equally to make the case for its anonymity. The judgement excludes *me* at the moment that I think it. Kant's remarks about a feeling of life are so astounding because they appeal to the *horizon of the infinitive* – to *indeterminate* vital pulsations which 'flow beneath' transcendental subjectivity, feelings which transport us.

For this reason, Kant's reference to 'preserving' the feeling of life in judgements of beauty must be distinguished from the will to 'self-preservation' which Nietzsche identifies as generally indicative of a reactive will to power. The life which is boosted and furthered is not inherently or exclusively 'human' in any obvious sense. Furthermore, Makkreel points out that Kant's account of preserving the state of a representation in judgements of beauty constitutes a divergence from the account of synthesizing representations offered in the *Critique of Pure Reason*. There, in the Transcendental Deduction, Kant suggests that there are three subjective sources of knowledge, each with its respective transcendental synthesis. In the first synthesis, multifarious impressions of sense are apprehended as one manifold; in the second, past representations are reproduced in a present manifold; and in the third, past and present representations are recognized as connected. In short, Kant argues that the imagination synthesizes representations as discrete, momentary items in the successive flow of time. What is distinctive about the *Critique of Aesthetic Judgement* is Kant's consideration of the *state* of a representation which persists for an indeterminate period of time, *reproducing itself* without any acts of imaginative synthesis:

> Thus we can distinguish the synthesis of reproduction of the first *Critique* from the aesthetic self-reproduction of the third *Critique*. In the former, the imagination recalls a representational content that has disappeared in the succeeding moment; in the latter a formal response to a representation persists over a period of time. (*IIK* 93)

When enraptured by beauty, the intuition of the flow of time is stalled and intensified. This lingering calls to mind Nietzsche's assertion that Apollinian rapture reflects a heightened sensation of calmness and differs in tempo from the Dionysian in terms of the retardation of the feelings of time and space (*WP* 799). This distended pleasure concentrates spatial and temporal sense: it reconfigures the limits of the 'coarse organs', enabling us to experience the world in a strangely impersonal yet pleasurable way. As Nietzsche puts it, '"becoming more beautiful" is a consequence of *enhanced* strength'; it is the 'expression of a *victorious* will, of increased coordination, of a harmonizing of all the strong desires, of an infallibly perpendicular emphasis [*Schwergewicht*]' (*WP* 800). It is as if a new centre of gravity is found for the body, refocusing its conditioning powers. We might say that the power of interior sense is felt as a pleasurable release from the limits of inner sense but that what it discloses is a strangely non-human feeling – a calm yet exultant *triumph* of an asubjective physiology over the cognitively conditioned body. Beauty undoes us and we thirst to prosecute our own collapse.

If it is legitimate to align pleasure in the beautiful with Apollinian rapture, it seems that Kant's analysis of the sublime maps out the libidinal terrain of those excitations Nietzsche associates with the Dionysian. The theory of the sublime is presented as an annex to the 'Analytic of the Beautiful', and as of lesser importance, owing to its inability to indicate anything purposive in nature itself. This said, one of the striking features of Kant's account is the extraordinary enthusiasm he brings to the task of explaining why what is terrifying for sensibility is 'at the same time' horribly attractive. The sublime is the aesthetic state stimulated by the experience of nature as formless ('unbounded') hence contrapurposive for our power of judgement. Here the transcendental subject is forced to confront that which it is unable to recognize or render harmonious, an experience which involves a more ambiguous 'feeling of life'. Unlike experience of beauty where nature freely accords with form, carrying with it a seductive sense of the furtherance of itself, the feeling of the sublime is a pleasure 'which only arises indirectly, being produced by a feeling of momentary inhibition of the vital forces [*das Gefühl einer augenblicklichen Hemmung der Lebenskräfte*] followed immediately by an outpouring of them that is all the stronger (*KU* 165, *CJ* #23, 98). In so far as the mind is not just attracted to the object prompting the judgement 'but is alternately also ever again [*immer wieder*] repelled' the liking for the sublime deserves the special name of 'negative pleasure' (ibid.).

Pleasure and pain in the experience of the sublime appear to participate in an energetic dynamic of perpetual overcoming formally analogous to that observed in Nietzsche's account of the recursive libidinal reverberation of the Dionysian. The 'pure primordial pain and contradiction' that re-echoes in the lyric poet and which 'ever again anew' discharges its pressure into Apollinian images is an explosive impulse that Nietzsche locates at the heart of his account of tragedy. We have already seen how for Nietzsche, Apollinian pleasure and its self-intensification appear to be primordially generated from *within* the Dionysian as the primary term. The thought that begins to glimmer through Kant's text is a disturbing one – although perhaps splendidly beautiful to the heart. Maybe beauty only emerges as a supremely *pure* and *idealizing* power when re-energized by the Sodom of 'our' destitution and despair. Love of beauty would constitute an affirmation of the pain of existence, indeed would consummate self-abandon as *supreme* joy, albeit cruelly compelling. That Kant argues to different conclusions is in its own way telling. It is significant that for Kant it is the chaos of nature in its 'wildest, most ruleless disarray and devastation' that arouses ideas of the sublime, and more importantly, that he should resist the thought that the human might be shattered by its encounter. For Kant, sublimity cannot indicate anything threatening or indeed purposive in 'raw nature' itself (*KU* 167, *CJ* #23, 100). Indeed, he denies that bold, overhanging rocks, thunderclouds piling up in the sky, lightning, volcanoes, hurricanes and the heaving boundless ocean are to be called sublime (*KU* 185, *CJ* #28, 120). On the contrary, we are able to make 'use' of our intuitions of raw nature so that we can feel a purposiveness in ourselves 'entirely independent' of nature (*KU* 167, *CJ* #23, 100). In the case of the mathematical sublime we intuit the transcendent order of reason ('a superiority over nature itself in its immensity') whereas in the dynamical sublime we discover that we are able to judge ourselves independent of nature as subjects of 'moral feeling' (*KU* 185, 194, *CJ* #28, 120, #29, 128). Kant is adamant that these overwhelming experiences reinforce a sense of our humanity, but the substance of his analysis may teach us something rather different.

A striking feature of Kant's argument is that subjective purposiveness is felt through an experience of the sustained *conflict* of the presentational powers of the faculties; indeed 'negative pleasure' is stimulated by a discord between imagination and reason that is not dialectically resolved. Kant writes that in presenting the infinite in nature the mind feels *moved*: 'This movement (above all in its inception) can be compared with a vibration [*Erschütterung*], i.e. with a rapidly alternating repulsion from, and attraction to, one and the same object' (*KU* 181, *CJ* #27, 115). In the case of the mathematical sublime this oscillation describes the attempt by the imagination to apprehend in an intuition that which is excessive for it – 'an abyss, as it were, in which it is afraid to lose itself' (ibid.). This excess is nature's magnitude, the 'absolutely vast' – such as the starry sky – the singular intuition of which defeats our animal powers. Yet this is not excessive for reason's idea of the supersensible, rather, it conforms to reason's law to give rise to such strivings by the imagination, thereby disclosing 'a different, non-sensible measure that has this infinity itself under it as a unit' (*KU* 185, *CJ* #28, 120). Similarly, when confronted with nature's might we triumph over our physical impotence and are driven to present the ideas of practical reason. This recognition of our supersensible vocation stimulates a feeling of pleasure but it is to be noted that this pleasure is consequent upon the displeasure experienced in the defeat of imagination's powers of synthesis. From here it is but a short step to Nietzsche's thinking of the secret of tragic joy: it is as if 'bliss born of pain' resounds from the 'abyss of being' (*BT* 4;5).

While Kant appears to be committed to the view that pain precedes pleasure in the experience of the sublime, perhaps even to speak of succession here is misplaced in so far as he insists that we hear his account of the reverberating rhythm of pleasure and pain atemporally. While the role of the imagination in the *Critique of Pure Reason* is to synthesize the progressive sequence of representations in time, in his discussion of the sublime Kant relates the imagination's activity to reason and to a 'regression' which nullifies the condition of time *once again*.

> Measurement of a space (as apprehension) is at the same time a description of it and so an objective movement in the imagination and a progression. On the other hand, the comprehension of multiplicity in a unity, not of thought, but of intuition, and therefore the comprehension in *one* moment [*Augenblick*] of what is apprehended successively, is a regression which again annuls [*aufhebt*] the time condition in the progression of the imagination and makes *coexistence* [***Zugleichsein***] intuitable. Hence, (since temporal succession is a condition of inner sense and of an intuition) it is a subjective movement of the imagination *by which* it does violence to inner sense and this violence must be the more significant the greater the quantum which the imagination comprehends in one intuition. (*KU* 182, *CJ* #27, 116)

We shall have cause to return to this fascinating passage somewhat further on in our explorations but here it suffices to note that the cancelling of the *a priori* form of intuition (time as the form of inner sense) reveals a new power of the imagination, one which violates the schemas that phenomenalize time. For our current purposes, it should be recognized that – as in the case of the beautiful – disinterested reflective judgement in the sublime discloses a pre-representational, pre-individual domain of aesthetic 'feeling' or physiological intensity. Makkreel suggests that in the sublime, the displeasure of our vital sense gives way to the pleasure of our interior sense as it forces us into ourselves and discloses a moral-rational power to improve our life rather than simply to preserve it (*IIK* 97). The 'violence' done to inner sense in the sublime is *transformative*: it changes inner sense into an interior sense through which we instantaneously feel the vitality of the '*whole determination* of the mind' (*KU* 182, *CJ* #27, 116). While for Kant, sublime pleasure is explicable in terms of human transcendence, our superiority over mere nature, it is noticeable that it is the defeat of animality which is experienced as pleasurable. The reference to 'coexistence' becoming intuitable could be taken, at least provisionally, to imply that pleasure and pain are mutually reinforcing sensations in the feeling of the sublime and are to be thought together. The pleasure that reason draws from the displeasure felt by the imagination is described by Nick Land as 'an anti-pathological eroticism, in which the body lusts after the agonized convulsions that stem from its own negation'.[3] In a complementary vein, Jim Urpeth notes the 'abattoirial odour' that pervades the negative pleasures of the Analytic of the Sublime and the darker themes of violence and sacrifice which mark out the particularly exquisite libidinal-affective economy of Kant's delight in the humiliation of imagination.[4] Indeed, rather than regarding the crushing of animality as pleasurable because of the revelation of our supersensible vocation, it might be construed as the euphoric opening of animality to the infinite and abyssal through the collapse of time. Kant says that the feeling of the sublime repels our sensibility yet attracts us 'at the same time', because it is a force which reason exerts over sensibility only for the sake of expanding it according to the requirements of its own domain (the practical) and 'letting it look outward toward the infinite' which for sensibility is an 'abyss' (*KU* 190, *CJ* #29, 124). Could it be said that the pleasure of the sublime is discovered at the heart of the abyss of time, indeed is rediscovered again and again when delight becomes a function of a primordial negative pleasure? This gives some context to the claim that attraction and repulsion are experienced 'at the same time' and that pain is also primary (an asymmetry that Nietzsche inscribes in the Apollinian–Dionysian relation). The pleasure of the triumph of reason cannot be separated from the sacrificial violation of the imagination but perhaps this is to triumph in joy at the furtherance of life which is no longer *mine* – that which must overcome itself once more.

Such would be to find beauty in Sodom, the *more intense feeling of life* which is conditioned by the momentary inhibition of the vital forces. As Gary Banham shows, the dynamical sublime tends to lead us back towards the ideal of beauty in so far as the respect we feel for ourselves and for nature concerns the ends of reason, the insight being that this disqualifies it as a pure judgement.[5] If we overlay

Nietzsche's philosophy of ecstasy on the Kantian text we might now say that beauty is only ever aim-inhibited, only glimpsed as an ideal when the reproductive powers of cognition are eclipsed. This means that the pure form of non-sensuous delight can no more be renounced than the ferocity of the desire fuelling its 'illusion' [*Schein*] can be acknowledged. In the horizon of the infinite, the most intense joys are generated *from* the boundlessness of nature in its ruleless disarray. At times the ocean spreads out like 'silk and gold and reveries of goodness' – prompting dreams of the moral good, perhaps – but these playful shadows are conditioned by devastation – the raging ocean of inhuman desire.

The passion of ferocious denial

As is often remarked, Schopenhauer was more alert to the idealist implications of Kantian thinking than to his transcendental arguments. Rather than viewing causality as objectively (*a priori*) valid, Schopenhauer held that causality exists 'only in the understanding' (*WWV*, I, 50, *WWR*, I, #5, 15), that the epistemological vocabulary which supports metaphysical reasoning is strictly speaking a fabrication, and that empirical experience is genuinely analogous to dreaming, having 'a continuity [*Zusammenhang*] in itself' (*WWV*, I, 55, *WWR*, I, #5, 18). For Schopenhauer, the powers of the intellect are among the most superficial elements of life, indeed, space, time and causality (the 'principle of sufficient reason') are merely human representations which render existence coherent if ineluctably mundane. Since representational knowledge is by definition limited only to phenomena, Schopenhauer concedes that we cannot have representational knowledge of the thing-in-itself – the blind, impersonal strivings of nature or 'will'. However, he argues that the thing-in-itself can be 'known' *non-representationally* via the body. Indeed, he contends that since we are not merely knowing subjects but also belong to those entities we require to know, it follows that we ourselves *'are the thing-in-itself'*.

> ... a way *from within* stands open to us, so to speak, a subterranean passage, a secret connection, which, as if by treachery, transfers us all at once into the fortress which could not be taken by attack from without. (*WWV*, II, 257, *WWR*, II, #18,195)

In regarding the human body as part of a pre-empirical materiality refractory to the projects and plans of the ego, Schopenhauer gestures towards a thought of chaotic or lawless nature prior to the empirical nature of constituted experience. This said, his commitment to the notion of *will* as 'ultimate reality' seems to mark his philosophy apart from transcendental thinking, especially if we take the latter to be a form of explanation which makes no appeal to the 'true' constitution of subjects and objects. Indeed, in claiming that we 'know' the thing-in-itself more intimately than the phenomenal through bodily feeling, which in turn becomes the key to 'the knowledge of the innermost being of the whole of nature', Schopenhauer's metaphysical convictions could not be more explicit (*WWV*, I, 176, *WWR*, I #21, 109). He even goes so far as to claim that the force that 'sprouts and vegetates in the plant, indeed the force through which the crystal shoots, the force that turns the magnet to the North Pole [...] which acts so powerfully in all matter, pulling the stone to the earth and the earth to the sun' is the same according to 'inner nature', namely *will* (*WWV*, I, 176–7, *WWR*, I #21, 110). Will involves no representation of any object yet is continuously characterized as an unconscious impulse impelling movement, transformation, conflict and tension. For the human being will is experienced in terms of a savage will-to-live, cunningly disguised by nature as sexual love, 'the strongest and most active of all motives' (*WWV*, II, 691, *WWR*, II, #44, 533). Schopenhauer is unrelenting in his depiction of how thoroughly wretched and deleterious its influence can be: 'it appears on the whole as a hostile demon, endeavouring to pervert [*verkehren*], to confuse, and to overthrow everything' (*WWV*, II, 692, *WWR*, II, #44, 534). Since for Schopenhauer will is a material, impersonal energy, to 'know' it (as a human being bound by the principle of sufficient reason) is merely to 'feel' its splintering effects. Yet Schopenhauer insists that when willing is disengaged from the teleological structure of desire through aesthetic experience a *different feeling of life* is rendered possible. It is in part due to the metaphysical legacy that he inherits that he persists with the language of representation to present this account. However, to the extent that he concerns himself with the conditions under which representations relate to objects unaccompanied by the 'I think', his philosophy points the way towards a transcendental philosophy beyond the boundaries of self-consciousness.

In what is tantamount to the claim that one must abdicate from the human condition in order to attain knowledge of fundamental reality, Schopenhauer singles out asceticism and aesthetic activity as privileged corporeal conduits to the 'truth' of pre-individual desire. Dissatisfaction and perpetual misery are inevitable, given the impossibility of achieving genuine well-being in 'this world' of pointless striving, but disciplined attempts at suppressing the will through sensory deprivation of all kinds (e.g. starvation, lack of sleep, solitude) may yield an experience of 'reality' which is uncompromised by egoic investments and goal-orientated urges. A temporary silencing of the imperious individual will is also possible via aesthetic contemplation of beauty and sublimity and in enjoyment of the supreme art of music. To stipulate, as Schopenhauer does, that aesthetic contemplation be *will-less* is clearly problematic given his account of reality as will, leading one to deduce that it is object-orientated willing that is to be suppressed, not willing as such. In fact, this is the only way in which it is possible to make sense of the claim that music gives us pleasure (since unlike the other arts which are copies of Platonic Ideas, music is an immediate objectification of the will). Thought in this way, the accent of Schopenhauer's aesthetics appears to fall on unconscious and impersonal affectivity, a feeling of life that is achieved when we are suddenly 'raised out of the endless stream of willing' and knowledge is snatched from 'servitude to the will' (*WWV*, I 289, *WWR*, I, #38, 196). While the Platonic legacy of Schopenhauer's thinking is not to be denied (for it is *eros* which impels the thinker) it seems that in Schopenhauer a transition from human (goal-orientated) desire to inhuman (non-teleological) willing is negotiated in terms of a philosophy of ecstasy which *returns* to the body. As we shall see, it is from *this* body that a new possibility of thinking emerges.

When enraptured in an encounter with beauty or the sublime, the subject undergoes a sudden and exceptional transformation. Knowledge is 'torn free' from the service of the will and its familiar relations to the world. All ties with the phenomenal constructs of space, time and causality fall away and one becomes '*pure* will-less, painless, timeless *subject of knowledge*' (*WWV*, I 265, *WWR*, I, #34, 179). In such a moment we are mentally transported from 'the ordinary way of considering things' and '*lose* ourselves entirely' in the ostensible 'object' of our gaze (*WWV*, I, 265, *WWR* I, #34, 178):

Further, we do not let abstract thought, the concepts of reason, occupy our consciousness, but, instead of all this, surrender the whole power of our mind [*Geist*] to intuition [*Anschauung*], sink so completely therein and let our whole consciousness be filled through the calm contemplation of the natural object actually present, whether it be a landscape, a tree, a rock, a building or anything else.' (Ibid.)

Consciousness in this enraptured state is empowered by intuition rather than reason but its 'disinterestedness' is also de-individuating. We 'forget our individuality, our will, and continue to exist only as pure subject, as clear mirror of the object, so that it is as though the object alone existed without anyone to perceive it' (ibid.). Such an account calls to mind the well-known thought of Merleau-Ponty that 'the seer is caught up in what he sees', that it is in a strange sense, the landscape that sees (*V&I*, 139). Yet Schopenhauer's thinking of aesthetic disinterestedness empties the category of the subject of all intentionality. Indeed, the surrender of the will springs from a desire to liquidate being-for-self. The pleasure this evokes is a negative one in that the subject is liberated from the chains of desire that anchor it to the frustrating pursuit of self-gratification. However, by the same token, the 'object' of knowledge changes from the familiar perceptible features of the apparent landscape to the immediate objectivity of the will in the form of the eternal *Idea*. Pleasure in the contemplation of beauty is said to spring from these two inseparable constituent parts, sometimes more from the one than from the other (*WWV*, I, 288, *WWR*, I, #38, 195–6). This entails the further consequence that aesthetic enjoyment is not wholly life-denying because the source of aesthetic enjoyment will lie sometimes in the apprehension of the known Idea, sometimes in the 'bliss and peace of mind' of pure knowledge free from all willing, and thus from all the pain of individuality (*WWV*, I, 310, *WWR*, I, #42, 212). There are grounds for regarding the pleasure of knowledge as superior to the pleasure of release from will in that the former pleasure is more apparent when the object contemplated is a high grade of objectification of the will (a human being, for example). All this notwithstanding, the values driving Schopenhauer's account of rapture betray a view of the will as inherently evil and his privileging of aesthetic experience as a 'denial of the will-to-live' constitutes a triumph of representation over the ugly, pointless striving of mere nature. Yet in spite of this, Schopenhauer, not unlike Kant, tells us something about the source of the pleasure driving his own account of desire.

Schopenhauer suggests that the blissful release from the world attained in contemplation of beauty requires minimal effort: the abundance of natural beauty invites contemplation and even presses itself upon us (*WWV*, I 290, *WWR*, I, #38, 197). Indeed, something is regarded as very beautiful if it *compels* this contemplation (and Schopenhauer implies that there are grades of bliss depending on the grade of objectification of the will). By contrast, in the case of the sublime, the pure state of knowing is gained first of all by a 'conscious and violent tearing away' from the world (*WWV*, I 296, *WWR*, I, #39, 202). As in Kant, exaltation is consequent upon this initial experience of pain, and in similar fashion Schopenhauer proposes that the trauma of self-annihilation gives way to an inner sense of superiority over nature. However, there is a significant difference. Schopenhauer explicitly rejects Kant's explanation of the 'inner nature of this impression' in moral terms. If in contemplating the vastness of the universe we feel drawn to reflect on the millennia past and to come, or if we see in the starry heavens 'innumerable worlds' before our eyes, we 'feel ourselves reduced to nothing, feel ourselves as individuals, as living bodies, as transient appearances of will, like drops in the ocean, disappearing and melting away into nothing' (*WWV*, I, 301, *WWR*, I, #39, 205). At the same time, there arises 'the immediate consciousness' that the immensity of this and all possible universes exists only in our representation and that our dependence on the world is annulled by its dependence on us. Yet Schopenhauer goes on to remark our *continuity with nature* in order to reinforce his point:

> All this, however, does not come into reflection at once, but shows itself only as a felt consciousness, that in some sense or other (which philosophy alone makes clear) we are one with the world, and are therefore not oppressed but exalted by its immensity. (Ibid.)

The obscure sense which it is the role of philosophy to make clear – a philosophy of ecstasy, we might conjecture – is an 'elevation beyond our own individuality', something that can only be felt and not accessed at the order of reflection. As in Kantian thinking, absorption in the sublime presupposes a reflection of the subject on its own state which is strangely anegoic. Yet for Schopenauer, the notion of aesthetic disinterestedness as a feeling of oneness with the world constitutes an allergic reaction to the moralizing role of the Ideas of reason and succeeds in excavating and deepening the anti-humanism latent in Kant. This pleasure is negative at the level of the value accorded the will to life but the negative pleasure of dis-interestedness indicates a sacred delight in material continuity with nature for which retreat from egoic action (or existentialist project) is wholly positive. Ultimately it is in terms of music that this thrill finds its most affirmative expression and perhaps here too Schopenhauer finds his beauty in Sodom.

As is well known, Schopenhauer singles music out for special con-sideration in his philosophical system because, unlike the other arts, it is a direct objectification of the will. Since music is not a copy of phenomena but a copy of the will itself, Schopenhauer claims that we could 'just as well call the world embodied music as embodied will' (*WWV*, I, 377, *WWR*, I, #52, 263).[6] However, if this is the case it seems difficult to explain how it is possible that music could delight us since the will is savage, evil and the source of all misery to which the human animal is heir. Commuting the will to the sphere of representation cannot solve the problem because music is as immediate an objectification and copy of the whole will as the world itself. If it could be argued that aesthetic representation differs in that it delivers its spectator or recipient from the pain of willing (and Schopenhauer does advance this claim) his account of the pleasures of music seems to point in the opposite direction. Indeed, in delineating the scales of the will's objectification in terms of the song of the earth, Schopenhauer warms to his theme. Firstly, the 'ground-bass' is recognized in the inorganic mass of the planet, which is the material support inseparable from the grades of the will's manifestation, just as a certain degree of pitch is inseparable from a tone as such (*WWV*, I, 371, *WWR*, I, #52, 258). The whole gradation of the Ideas in which the will objectifies itself stretches between the bass and the melody, the latter revealing the secret history of the intellectually enlightened will. Every effort, agitation, and striving of the will is sounded here (*WWV*, I, 373, *WWR*, I, #52,

259). Furthermore, the nature of melody is a constant digression and deviation from the keynote in a thousand ways, 'yet there always follows an endless turning back [*endliches Zurückkehren*] to the keynote' just as the will strives, is satisfied and strives ever again anew (*WWV*, I, 374, *WWR*, I, #52, 260). In disclosing the 'deepest secrets of human willing and feeling' melody constitutes a transvalued feeling of life (ibid.). The 'innermost nature of the world', encountered physiologically as the torment of sexual agitation, is disclosed in music as supremely delightful. Rapid melodies without great deviations are merely cheerful whereas slow melodies that strike painful discords and wind back to the keynote only through many bars are sad 'on the analogy of delayed and impeded satisfaction' (ibid.). Yet far superior to rapid music which speaks only of ordinary happiness which is easy of attainment is the *allegro maestoso* which with its great phases, long passages and wide deviations expresses 'a greater, nobler striving towards a distant goal, and its final attainment' (*WWV*, I, 375, *WWR*, I, #52, 261).

> The *adagio* speaks of the suffering of a great and noble effort that scorns all petty happiness. But how wonderful is the effect of a *minor* and *major*! How astonishing that the change of half a tone, the entrance of a minor third instead of a major, at once and inevitably impresses on us an anxious and awkward feeling, from which we are again delivered just as instantaneously [*augenblicklich*] by the major! The *adagio* in the minor key reaches the expression of the keenest pain, and becomes the most shuddering [*erschütterndesten*] lament. (ibid.)

Given this revelling in the exotic joys of protracted, reverberating suffering it is difficult to see how music could be the 'panacea to all our sorrows' (*WWV*, I, 376, *WWR*, I, #52, 262). Is it not rather the exacerbation of them? And again, is not the slower tempo the more exquisite and excruciating pleasure? If music and nature are two different expressions of the same thing, it would seem that music has a different universalizing power. Whereas concepts contain only the forms abstracted from perception, music gives 'the innermost kernel preceding all form', the heart of things (*WWV*, I, 378, *WWR*, I, #52, 263). Most importantly, if music is to express the inner stirrings of the will it must proceed from the immediate knowledge of the inner nature of the world and this must be unknown to the faculty of reason otherwise it would merely imitate the phenomena of perception. The 'truth' that music speaks is universal yet not individuated, distinct yet not determinate. For the man who gives himself up entirely to the impression of a symphony 'it is as if he saw all the possible events [*Vorgänge*] of life and the world passing by within himself' – a transpersonal feeling of life (*WWV*, I, 374, *WWR*, I, #52, 260). Finally, Schopenhauer asserts that if the world as representation is only the visibility of this will, then art is the elucidation of this visibility, the *camera obscura* that shows the objects more purely. Schopenhauer concludes that the pleasure of everything beautiful enables one to forget the cares of life but that the cure should sting more keenly than the affliction is the enigma that knowledge cannot resolve. We guess at it as we can and come out of the water dry. Schopenhauer never renounces the ideal of beauty but perhaps this is because it is fuelled by the Sodom it so serenely intensifies.

Between Kant and Schopenhauer

According to Nietzsche, Kant commuted the ecstasies of aesthetic delight to the categories of knowledge with all the ignorance in erotica of a country parson; Schopenhauer, by contrast, saw art as 'lupulin and camphor' for the tortures of the vile urgency of sexual longing (*GM*, III, 6). The humanist values underwriting the Kantian project and the anti-humanist yet life-denying values of Schopenhauer's thinking are both signally rejected by Nietzsche in his philosophy of ecstasy. Nevertheless, the concept of disinterestedness, so central to each thinker's work, is retained by Nietzsche in a transvalued form. With sardonic glee, he suggests that the demand for art and beauty is an indirect demand for the ecstasies of sexuality, an 'unconscious reminder' of 'aphrodisiac bliss' (*WP* 805). Despite their respective allegiances to the ascetic ideal (or perhaps because of its rare libidinal intensity) there are moments in the writing of Kant and Schopenhauer when a feeling of ecstasy tremors, shakes and finally explodes into thinking with all the force of sexual trauma. Art heightens the 'feeling of life' by prompting the unconscious physiological drives to augment and repeat themselves at the level of signs and judgements. Indeed, it is the combined effect of Kant and Schopenhauer's philosophy which results in the astonishing synthesis that Nietzsche calls 'tragedy'.

We have already noted how Nietzsche's distinction between Apollinian and Dionysian energies shares profound affinities with Kant's understanding of the beautiful and the sublime. The 'feeling of life' engaged in these glorious encounters conducts the human animal beyond the boundaries imposed by the 'coarse organs' to intense inner landscapes of the unknown. Nietzsche's notion that a 'tonal subground' (the 'reverberation of sensations of pleasure and pain') accompanies all our representations as a 'figured bass', clearly inherited from Schopenhauer, describes the immense range of libidinal adventures that a transpersonal physiology implies.[7] In a fragmentary essay, 'Music and Words', he emphasizes that feelings may symbolize music but they are too saturated with representations – with worldly concerns – to inspire its production (*KSA* 7/364/12[1]). By contrast, our emotions are stimulated by music because it appeals to an intermediate realm of affects. As we know, music excites the affective realm in general: these states intensify themselves and do not conduct us back to the objects of 'our world'. In 'The Dionysian Worldview' Nietzsche attributes to Schopenhauer the view that feeling is 'a complex of unconscious representations and states of the will' (*KSA* 1, 572) – a thought which resonates with the notion that these strivings of the will are externalized (quantatively differentiated) as pleasure or displeasure in innumerable representations.[8] Nietzsche's invocation of rhythm, dynamics and harmony, located within the physiological 'experience' of Dionysian rapture, is inspired by this notion of 'will' as a richly nuanced continuum. It could be argued that this is simply to reconfigure ecstasy within the Kantian confines of possible experience but it is not clear that the transcendental distinction between the phenomenal and the noumenal survives this move intact. While Nietzsche uses Kantian formulations with the seeming intention of distancing himself from Schopenhauer's metaphysics of music, this does not connote the outcome of a simple choice of positions. In fact, it is the thought of ecstasy which is the vital hinge in the relation which Nietzsche forges between the transcendental critique of Kant and the anti-humanist energetics of Schopenhauer. Schopenhauer succeeds in expanding and elaborating a thought of rapture latent in Kantian aesthetics, recasting it in more overtly physiological terms.

Persuaded by the Critical turn in philosophy inaugurated by Kant, Nietzsche rejects Schopenhauer's appeal to the possibility of knowing the thing-in-itself and the life-negating value economy it supports yet he seems to detect in Schopenhauer's aesthetics the possibility of another kind of 'knowing'. This sensitive, sensual intelligence conflicts with the role accorded to transcendental subjectivity in the Kantian project, but is latent in Kant's own thinking about the pleasures and pains subtending aesthetic judgement. In the space between Kant and Schopenhauer's thinking of rapture, Nietzsche develops a transcendental physiology, increasingly pursued as notes towards a philosophy of ecstasy.

Following Deleuze, it could be shown that a radicalization of critique devolves on a genealogy of values. Nietzsche submits both Kant and Schopenhauer's aesthetics to genealogical analyses which diagnose the kind of will operative in their respective notions of disinterestedness.[9] Here, it is imperative to remember that the body is not given, that it is a product of evaluations. This is why an appeal to affective states or rhythms as such has no meaning. Feelings of pleasure and pain are not simply effects of force but effects of evaluations, and this applies to economies of pleasure and pain as well as to their rhythms. For example, Nietzsche conjectures that one *could* regard pleasure in terms of *stasis* or a constant level of the feeling of power, but such a model would only have states of unpleasure by which to set its standards (*WP* 695). This would be to understand desire in terms of lack – a perspective in which Nietzsche claims the memory of stronger moments of pleasure would weigh on present feelings of pleasure in a depressing way. If, on the contrary, life is thought of in terms of a will to increase, then pleasure is felt as the will's drive to master what resists it, a thirst renewed 'ever and again [*immer wieder*]' (*WP* 696).

Nietzsche insists that pain is something different from pleasure, not its opposite. He speculates that if it is possible to consider pleasure as a '*greater feeling* of power [*ein **Plus-Gefühl von Macht***]', consequently a 'feeling of difference, presupposing a comparison' it may be possible to understand pleasure in terms of overcoming of hindrance (*WP* 699).

There are even cases in which a certain kind of pleasure is conditioned by a certain *rhythmic sequence* of smaller, unpleasurable stimuli: in this way a very rapid increase of the feeling of power, the feeling of pleasure, is achieved. This is the case, e.g. in tickling, also the sexual tickling in the act of coitus: in such a way we see displeasure active as an ingredient of pleasure. It seems a small hindrance [*Hemmung*] is overcome and immediately followed again by another small hindrance that is again overcome – this game of resistance and victory arouses most strongly that total feeling of surplus, superfluous power that constitutes the essence of pleasure. (*WP* 699)

In orgiastic excitement, pleasure reveals its potential for ceaseless augmentation, beyond any fixed structure of the organism and against any normative restraint. The waves of voluptuosity that animate the ecstatic body have an escalating tempo. The rhythmic sequence is the primordial reverberation of primordial pain, the condition of the Dionysian musician which in tragedy exacerbates and conditions Apollinian pleasure, producing perhaps a greater eroticism, the greatest feeling of power. Nietzsche suggests in this note that the really specific quality of pain is always the 'protracted shuddering [*die lange Erschütterung*]' or 'after-trembling [*Nachzittern*]' of a terrifying shock in the cerebral centre of the nervous system' (ibid.) – the violent vibrations that so innocently delight Kant and Schopenhauer. The tenor of Nietzsche's remarks tend to imply a theory of pain and pleasure that can be accommodated within a merely 'biological' theory of life but in the same note he emphasizes the point that a 'cumulative experience is summarised' in the judgement that something is 'harmful' and that 'there is no pain as such'. In other words, a certain judgement has been so effectively 'incorporated' that it has become instinctive. Further notes reinforce the idea that this dynamics of pleasure and pain has to be contextualized genealogically in terms of value for life. Pain and pleasure are not 'causes' but 'value judgements of second rank' presupposing a ruling value such as 'useful' or 'harmful' and here too 'one still has to ask in a hundred different ways "for what?"'(*WP* 701). On this point, Nietzsche adds: 'I despise this *pessimism of sensibility*: it is itself a sign of a deeply impoverished life.' This is why Nietzsche rejects the pessimistic evaluation of 'dissatisfaction', arguing instead that the latter 'acts rather as an agitation of the feeling of life [*Lebensgefühl*], as every rhythm of small, painful stimuli *strengthens it*, despite what pessimists may tell us' (*WP* 697).

Kant in the *Anthropology* remarks that satisfaction is the 'feeling of the furtherance [*Gefühl der Beförderung*] of life', pain that of its obstruction, but that life itself is a 'continuous play of the antagonism between the two' (*AP* 551). He declares that pain is always primary and holds the 'continual furtherance of life' in check, forestalling 'a rapid death from *delight*' (ibid.). As Nick Land puts it, citing this passage:

> Life is not consumed by death at its point of greatest depression, but at its peak, and inversely; it is only the brake provided by suffering that preserves the organism in its existence. It is pain that spares life for something other than an immediate and annihilating delight.[10]

In *Twilight of the Idols*, Nietzsche remarks that the psychology of the *orgy* 'as an overflowing feeling of life and power in which even pain itself acts as a stimulus' had provided him with the key to the '*tragic* feeling' (*TI* 'What I Owe to the Ancients', 5). This unleashing of desire in its savage immediacy is *felt* within the bodies of the tragic participants as the primordial pain of the body of nature itself – a pain which reverberates in the spirit of music. Yet, Nietzsche also speaks of an eternal joy of becoming which is attained in the erotic union of Apollo and Dionysus, where the striving of the spirit of music towards visual and mythical revelation reaches its most intense peak. The tragic hero is presented as the 'highest illustration' of the 'highest intensification' of music, within whose body the 'swelling flood of passions' becomes 'sensuously visible'. Moreover, the Apollinian spectator who delights in the drama is said to feel the actions of the hero to be justified, and is nevertheless still more elated when these actions annihilate their agent. One shudders at the sufferings which befall the hero, and yet anticipates in them a higher, much more overpowering joy (*BT* 22). In this manner the Apollinian in tragedy – rather than veiling the torments of existence – comes to relish the spectacle of pain and even feel a libertine's delight in its intensification. Indeed, the Apollinian wrests the human from its 'orgiastic self-annihilation' only to deliver it up to an image of more sublimated cruelty (*BT* 21). It is, he says, thanks to the Apollinian power of the drama that the almost shattered individual appears restored and

> where, breathless, we imagined ourselves coming to an end, in the convulsive paroxysm of all our feelings and little remained to tie us to this existence, we now hear and see only the hero fatally wounded, yet not dying, with his despairing cry: 'Longing! Longing! In death still longing! for very longing not dying!' (*BT* 21)

Could this perhaps be the secret violence of Apollinian rapture? It attenuates the moment, retards the feeling of space and time, stalls the orgasm of Dionysian frenzy, *refuses to let go*. This is not the conservative activity of the functional body, eternally sheltered against desires which would delight to death. It is a far more subtle yet highly charged knowledge, an eroticism which palpably 'knows' its bounds, presses tantalizingly up against its carefully retained limits.

The glorious insights of Kant and Schopenhauer into the erotic economy of aesthetic pleasure illuminate the 'feeling of life' that expends itself and is consecrated in tragedy. It becomes increasingly apparent that it is in terms of tragic pathos that Nietzsche approaches the question of life-affirmation at the core of eternal return – a feeling which emerges in the Dionysian throng as an affective rhythm. Here oneness is expressed as the genius of the species, indeed of nature. But this feeling of life is not something that is simply registered: it is enhanced, strengthened and overcome. Nietzsche declares that he wants to increasingly see as beautiful what is necessary in things for such would be to *make things beautiful*. But beauty is a terrible thing and its riddle is such that to solve it is to resuscitate its mystery. The appropriate response to the gratuitous upsurge of life is to squander in return. The body becomes artistic.

4
Men of Fire

> 'I tell you: one must have chaos in one, to give birth to a dancing star.'
>
> (*Thus Spoke Zarathustra,* 'Prologue', 5)

Artists, like dreamers, share a humbling illiteracy before their creations. They blaze across the star-splashed night in chaotic flights of inspiration only to drop like a stone into the blinking day, where poetry expires with the dawn. As Nietzsche writes in *Ecce Homo*:

> If one had the slightest residue of superstition left in one, one would scarcely be able to reject the idea that one is merely incarnation, merely mouthpiece, merely medium of overpowering forces. (*EH* 'Thus Spoke Zarathustra', 3)

A thought comes to us from beyond. It is not certain that we have the means for grasping it or the ability to account for it. Yet it excites something in us, awakens something in us that has the power to think. Without knowing how, one incarnates the thought that seems to arrive unbidden. Ideas impact which surpass the powers of recognition yet engender a sense of absolute necessity, as if truth were being remade in the heart of the unknowable:

> The concept of revelation, in the sense that something suddenly, with unspeakable certainty and subtlety, becomes *visible*, audible, something that shakes [*erschüttert*] and overturns one in the depths, simply describes the fact. One hears, one does not seek;

one takes, one does not ask who gives; like lightning a thought flashes up, with necessity, formed without hesitation – I have never had any choice. A rapture [*Entzückung*], whose monstrous [*ungeheure*] tension from time to time resolves itself in a flood of tears, while the pace now involuntarily rages forward, now becomes slow; a complete being-outside-of-self with the most distinct consciousness of countless subtle shudders and shivers down to one's toes; a depth of happiness in which the most painful and gloomy things appear – not as opposites, but as conditioned, provoked, as a *necessary* colour within such a super-abundance of light; an instinct for rhythmic relationships, spanning wide spaces of forms – length, the need for a *wide-spanned* rhythm is almost the measure for the force of inspiration, a kind of compensation for its pressure and tension. (Ibid.)

Ruthlessly, inexorably, lightning bursts of anonymous creativity take over a body, redirecting its powers and modifying its thresholds, convulsing the artist with unheard-of enchantments and the urge to enchant. In this ecstatic state, a different kind of consciousness is sparked into life – distinct yet completely outside of 'self'. Multiple shudders, shivers and tremulous rhythms are triggered by a *thought* yet this hypersensitivity also seems to condition its visibility, its amplitude. In this haunting, reverberating, corporeal intelligence it is difficult to say whether it is thought which enraptures the body or the body which enraptures thought.

On 14 August 1881, Nietzsche wrote to Peter Gast: 'Thoughts have arisen on my horizon, the likes of which I have never seen' (*SB* 6, 136, 112). Confessing that the intensity of his feelings make him shudder and laugh, that extreme paroxysms of 'tears of rejoicing' at his 'new vision' leave his eyes inflamed, he declares that truly he is one of 'those machines that can *explode*' (ibid.). This vision comes from inhuman heights – '6,000 feet beyond man and time' – yet Nietzsche says that something 'decisive in the depths' preceded this revelation, a sudden and ominous transformation of 'taste', above all in music (*EH* 'Thus Spoke Zarathustra', 1). The judgements of the body inspire and augment its skyward reflections, as if this vision from outside were also illuminating a landscape from within.

The thought of eternal return came to Nietzsche as a bolt of lightning in the inner darkness of the body, in the night of consciousness and its manifest signs. Yet what is it for a thought to *become visible, audible*? To see and hear in the depth of things requires a new thinking of the body, a different way of *enabling the body to think*, not a new theory about the body as an object of knowledge. Voyages in thought are always at some level 'experiments' with the body, attempts at navigating otherwise. Rimbaud famously cultivated the path of the *visionary* through a '*long, immense and calculated derailment of all the senses*'.[1] But the journey 'out there' is not a clairvoyant intimation of an alternative reality. It is an exploration in thought which creates the conditions for its own rediscovery, a philosophical undertaking of a deviant kind. If the body is the conduit to the unknown, this is not because it thinks itself (its idea of its function, its cohesion, its 'self') but because *life* thinks through it in innumerable ways. For Nietzsche, this thought of the outside takes place in rapture.

If the body thinks beyond itself when enraptured, we might wonder how this is achieved. How can the body realize its own transfiguration? In what sense is physiology artistic? We have seen that for Nietzsche, physiology is always at some level a matter of *aesthetics* in so far as values for life are approached in terms of the *pathos* of will to power. However, this does not in itself guarantee any primacy to art, which can be symptomatic of both life-enhancing and life-negating values. In the 1880s Nietzsche began to develop a series of reflections on the philosophy of art and *physis* under the prospective title 'Towards the Physiology of Art'. In a number of places in his published and unpublished work, Nietzsche refers to aesthetics as 'applied physiology' (*KSA* 6, 418) and suggests that art as *physis* is a 'return to the *hellenic* concept' (*KSA* 7, 510 / 19[290]). Although never systematically organized in a published work, many of Nietzsche's thoughts on the 'physiology of art' are elaborated upon in more extensive notes from this period, a large number of which appear in *The Will to Power*.[2] Familiar preoccupations from *The Birth of Tragedy* period resurface in these writings (which are dominated by the themes of 'rapture'[*Rausch*] and embodiment) but while the Apollinian and Dionysian still figure as 'fundamental types', the consideration of ecstasy is no longer confined to the sphere of Greek art. The association between rapture and plenitude (increase in force and the *feeling* of power) is strongly emphasized while the diagnosis of the 'impoverished body' in terms of 'abstractness', 'neutrality' and 'objectivity' – all hallmarks of conceptual thinking – becomes more pronounced. Tantalizing allusions to health and sickness, to pathology and 'tonic practice' are scattered throughout the notes (and we shall return to this theme in Chapter 5) yet the guiding thought uniting these fragments is the indispensability of rapture to artistic practice, the most succinct formulation of which is to be found in *Twilight of the Idols*.

> For there to be art, for there to be any kind of aesthetic activity and beholding, one physiological precondition is absolutely necessary: *rapture*. Rapture must first of all have intensified the sensitivity [*Erregbarkeit*] of the whole machine: before that there is no art. All kinds of rapture, however differently conditioned, have the power to do this: above all, the rapture of sexual arousal, the oldest and most original form of rapture. Likewise, rapture which comes in the wake of all great desires, all strong affects; the rapture of festivity, of contest, of bravura, of victory, of all extreme agitation; rapture of cruelty; rapture in destruction; rapture under certain meteorological influences, for example, the rapture of Spring; or under the influence of narcotics; finally, the rapture of the will, the rapture of an inundated, swollen will. – The essential thing about rapture is the feeling of intensified power and plenitude. (*TI* 'Expeditions...', 8)

At first glance, it seems obvious that if rapture is a prerequisite for artistic activity it must be logically prior to the activity (irrespective of how the stimulation has been achieved). This prompts the thought that rapture functions as an extra-genealogical term in Nietzsche's lexicon and as such is exempt from the evaluative economy of will to power. However, it is notable that Nietzsche's works are scattered with scathing remarks about the frenzied artworks of frustrated geniuses who seek to excite the emotions with their romantic and histrionic outpourings.[3] Indeed, the 'experience of *rapture*' proves misleading when those who are 'poor in life' acclaim the highest type of power: 'when the exhausted appeared with the gesture of the highest activity and energy, when degeneration conditioned an excess of spiritual or nervous discharge, they were *mistaken* for the rich' (*WP* 48). This begs the question of the value of rapture for life, its aesthetic value. If rapture is the physiological precondition of art, it makes a difference whether it animates a life-affirming or life-negating physiology: 'Is art the consequence of *dissatisfaction with reality*? Or, an expression of *gratitude for happiness enjoyed*?' (*WP* 845).

Closer scrutiny of 'The Physiology of Art' notes sheds some light on this important distinction. The body which is 'impoverished' is 'inartistic', it lacks the power to create beyond itself. As we have seen, ideas are material products of bodies but bodies are also products of the ideas that sustain them. The 'impoverished body' is nourished by an environment which reflects and reinforces its fundamental values: objectivity, neutrality, abstraction, 'mania for mirroring'. Having transposed its values on to the world it then becomes 'petrified' by its own reflections. Thanks to its psychological and perceptual prejudices that the world is 'given', it is assumed that it is the 'same' self which thinks, believes, imagines, remembers, that these are the 'same' objects apprehended, admired and addressed, that this is the 'same' world in which encounters between subjects and objects exist.[4] For life forms which swim in this sea, rapture as an aesthetic state is a symptom of nihilism, a desire to *escape* the very reality it has created and then denied.

Art which expresses gratitude for happiness enjoyed seems to spring from a physiology that differs from the impoverished body to the extent that it differs first and foremost from itself. Nietzsche writes that the essential thing about rapture is a feeling of plenitude and increased energy.

> In this condition one enriches everything out of one's own abundance: what one sees, what one desires, one sees swollen, pressing, strong, overladen with force. The person in this condition transforms things until they again reflect [*wiederspielgeln*] his power – until they are reflexes of his perfection. This *compulsion* to transform into the perfect is – art. (*TI* 'Expeditions...', 9)

The 'artistic body', if we might call it this, achieves its identity through a process of self-overcoming which cannot be assimilated to any exercise of the faculties or any strictly deliberative activity of the 'self'. This dynamic of transfiguration also complicates the temporal logic of primacy that would position rapture as a catalyst – a point which is elaborated upon in a series of related notes in which Nietzsche suggests that there is an ongoing reflux between the creator and his or her creations. We infuse 'a *transfiguration and fullness*' into things through an 'overflowing fullness and bodily vigour' which is in turn reactivated by things which display this transfiguration and fullness (*WP* 801).

> Art reminds us of states of animal vigour; it is on the one hand an excess and outpouring of blooming physicality into the world of images and desires; on the other, an excitation of the animal functions through images and desires of intensified life; a heightening of the feeling of life [*Lebensgefühl*], a stimulant to it. (*WP* 802)

Nietzsche makes it clear in these notes that only those physiologies which suffer from the 'pressure of abundance [*Nötigung des Reichtums*]' – the primary artistic state – are capable of receiving the aesthetic stimulus and returning it anew. The 'empty, the weary, the exhausted, the dried up (e.g. scholars)' are locked out of this process because they are unable 'to give' (*WP* 801). Instead, they feel constrained by the 'given'. To experience life as compelling rather than constraining is to feel bound by a different kind of necessity, one which forces thinking to surpass itself.

To blossom with fire

To see life swell and to swell with life in turn is an experience which seems to characterize some of the finest and some of the most tortured of artists. In a remarkable essay, Blanchot speaks of a divine inspiration which made of Hölderlin a vessel for new and unsurpassed poetic vision: 'one can speak of an excessive experience, a plenitude of light, too immediate an affirmation of the sacred' (*MPE* 115). We are told that in a letter to Bühlendorf, in December 1801, Hölderlin wrote: 'In the past, I exulted to discover a new truth, a greater conception of what surpasses and surrounds us; now, I just fear resembling the ancient Tantalus who received from the gods more blessings than he could stand' (ibid.). Again, in a letter to the same friend the following year, Hölderlin exclaims: 'As it is said of heroes, I can well say that Apollo has struck me' (ibid.). Unbearable bounty spills into consciousness, populating an austere and well-ordered world with more meanings than it can sustain. Scorched by a luminosity too brilliant and prodigious, Hölderlin consecrates his life to the 'onrushing word'. It is Apollinian rapture that speaks in the language of Hölderlin's poetry – the monstrous, overlit clarity which enriches everything out of its abundance.

> A serene life I see blossom around me in the shapes of creation, because not unfittingly I compare it to the solitary doves of the churchyard. But the laughter of men seems to grieve me, for I have a heart. Would I like to be a comet? I think so. For they possess the swiftness of birds; they blossom with fire and are like children in purity. ('In lovely blueness...')[5]

In this beautifully labyrinthine weave of associations, figures of superabundant life proliferate, as objects of all kinds are lent a blossoming power. For Hölderlin, 'art is the bloom, the perfection of nature' for nature only 'becomes divine' by its connection with art which harmonizes with nature as it differs.[6] A man may 'look up' to the heavenly and compare himself with the divinity which manifests itself as the poetic becoming of the world:

> Is God unknown? Is he manifest as the sky? This rather I believe. It is the measure of man. Full of acquirements, but poetically, man dwells on this earth. ('In lovely blueness...')

A vision of the heights is amplified, is measured by the blossoming of the world of which 'man' is a part. Poetically it becomes more.

> In lovely blueness with its metal roof the steeple blossoms. Around it the crying of swallows hovers, most moving blueness surrounds it. ('In lovely blueness...')

The imagery of 'In lovely blueness' calls to mind Van Gogh's rippling landscapes and bursting stars which violate the senses, swallowing the horizon that would situate the spectator at a certain remove from the immensity of the sky. Hölderlin's 'most moving blueness' – which blossoms alongside the world it frames – is matched by Van Gogh's flaming star streams, burning as much as glowing, with all the ferocity of a solar sacrifice. Indeed, in viewing Van Gogh's paintings one has the sensation of intense proximity, as if one could with eyes closed nevertheless feel the cold burn of stars on one's face. If the human is the 'measure' of this world it is an acentred, fluid perception that it reflects and embodies. Like Hölderlin's late poetry, Van Gogh's paintings tremor with the burgeoning power of intoxicated reality, a world within which human sensations become dissociated from their concordant, coherent physiology, operating at different tempos, different tensions and rhythms.

One of the few contemporaries of Van Gogh to enthuse about his work was Albert Aurier, who characterizes his genius thus:

> What particularizes his entire work is the excess, excess in strength, excess in nervousness, in violence of expression. In his categorial affirmation of the character of things, in his frequently headstrong simplification of forms, in his insolence in depicting the sun face to face, in the vehement ardour of his drawing and of his colour, and even in the slightest particularities of his technique, he reveals a powerful being [...] an ebullient brain which irresistibly pours its lava into all the ravines of art, a terrible and highstrung genius, often sublime, sometimes grotesque, almost always on the edge of the pathological.[7]

Van Gogh's remarkable ability to convey visually a heightened sensation of the tactile blossoms from a superabundant physicality. His work is *vibrant* – the progeny of an excessive 'feeling of life' which infuses transfiguration and fullness into things, making them bloom with his excruciating vigour. Blanchot writes that the great works of Van Gogh are 'overwhelming beyond all measure' but it is not 'our world' which speaks to us here (*MPE* 113). A call arises from this work 'acting upon us productively by pressing us to transform ourselves in the vicinity of what is still the inaccessible' (ibid.). His art excites the state that creates art – rapture.

In the context of an early essay in praise of Wagner, Nietzsche asserts that the power of the great artist resides in his 'demonic *transmissibility*' (*UM* IV, 222). Such an artist embodies an overflowing energy through which 'he' (the pronoun is not generic) is able to communicate with other natures, to both surrender to alien forces and to receive them in turn. Images of intensified life thus spark new intensities, drawing other lives into a new, intoxicating flow. Yet this power does not simply flow between beings, it flows between bodies, unmaking the 'being' of the body in the process. Sensations no longer converge on a common object, but work against and upon one another in deviant rhythms, replacing synchronized perception with synaesthetic couplings. Nietzsche says of the great art-work that all that is visible strives to become more intense and profound by becoming audible whereas all that is audible strives to emerge into the light and acquire corporeality (*UM* IV, 223). The beholder is thus impelled 'to translate visible movement back into soul and primordial life, and on the other hand to see the most deeply concealed inner weavings as appearance' and to clothe them with the shining glow or 'appearance-of-a-body [*Schein-Leib*]' (ibid.). It is as if nature were in the process of remaking itself, re-embodying itself through art.

This gives some context to an enigmatic fragment from 'The Physiology of Art' notes in which Nietzsche seems to give the power to create over to nature rather than to the artist.

> The work of art where it appears *without* an artist e.g. as body, as organization [...] To what extent the artist is only a preliminary stage. What does the 'subject' mean – ? The world as a work of art that gives birth to itself— (*KSA* 12, 118–19/2[114])

Yet one might now ask in what sense works of inspiration are works of art rather than works of nature. If ecstasy names an illicit receptivity to forces beyond what the subject can recognize as its own, in what sense does the artist 'act' and 'see'? If the artist is a vessel for transmission of energies it seems as if the 'aesthetic activity and beholding' that 'rapture' alerts are works of nature *once again*.

Recreating nature

To present the world as a work of art that gives birth to itself may appear to risk blurring the key terms in a distinction which – as Hölderlin notes – are harmoniously yet heterogeneously entwined. The mutually reinforcing relationship between art and nature is central to Kant's account of aesthetic reflective judgement which we considered in Chapter 3. For Kant, judgements of taste are grounded in our necessary ability to see nature by analogy with art; indeed, the concept of nature as *art* is a concept that arises originally from judgement 'as its own concept' (*KU* 17, *CJ* First Introduction, #2, 393). We do not know if nature is intentionally designed but we must judge it to be so if the empirical diversity of nature is to be seen as lending itself to judgement's search for systematic organization. To judge nature thus is to judge 'artistically' according to a principle that is universal but indeterminate (*KU* 26, *CJ* First Introduction, #5, 402). Accordingly, Kant argues both that nature is to be judged *as if* it were art (that is, *as if* intentionally ordered and hence consonant with the power of judgement to discern systematic unity) *and* that fine art is only to be judged as fine when it 'looks to us like nature' (indeed, judgements of taste relate directly to the feeling of pleasure stimulated by a sense of 'purposivity without purpose') (*KU* 241, *CJ* #45, 174). These stipulations – which always threaten to engulf the inquiry in a vicious circularity – come to the fore in Kant's account of *genius* for this is the point at which his analysis of the conditions of possibility for judgements of taste has to be reconciled with an account of the 'production' of works of fine art. Since a pure judgement of taste is 'disinterested' a work of art must *seem* to be as free of rule-governed design as a natural artefact if its form is to be judged 'beautiful', yet because it is a *work*, there is an additional criterion for judging fine art, namely attention to the concept of what the thing is 'meant to be' (*KU* 246, *CJ* #48, 179). In other words, we must *know* that the object of our delight springs from human intention but we must not be able to conceptually *determine* the intention if our 'feeling of life' is to be pleasurably excited. The peculiarity of this situation is that this must be equally true for its author.

Described as a 'natural endowment [*Naturgabe*]' and 'innate productive ability' that 'gives the rule to art', genius is presented by Kant as a talent for producing something for which no *determinate* rule can be given (*KU* 241, *CJ* #46, 174). Indeed, the foremost property of genius is originality, a special facility that exceeds mere technical skill. The latter is indispensable for the production of great art (distinguishing it from 'original nonsense') but since techniques can be learnt by following rules or imitating the talent of others, they are necessary rather than sufficient conditions. What the artwork comes to reflect is the excessive natural force that cast it into being – a force that cannot be communicated to another in precepts despite its exemplary status. Genius itself cannot describe or indicate scientifically how it brings about its products for it is 'as *nature* that it gives the rule' (*KU* 242, *CJ* #46, 175). Consequently, if an author owes a product to his genius, he himself 'does not know how he came by the ideas for it' (*KU* 243, *CJ* #46, 175). Works of genius, by consequence, have an unusual status because they embody a rule which could not have been predicted in advance. These products serve as *exemplars* for other potential geniuses but in a rather special sense. Since imitation is foreign to the nature of genius, the rule the great work comes to embody is not to be aped by the would-be genius. Rather, the work serves to arouse the 'feeling of his own originality' (*KU* 255, *CJ* #49, 187). Since the productions of genius *exceed* any combination of presentations generated by conceptual activity, re-ordering matter in surprising and unpredictable ways, the resulting art-work also occasions the very pre-conceptual play of the imagination in which judgements of taste are grounded. The ensuing pleasure, indicative of the universal yet indeterminate *a priori* principle of judgement, is thereby linked to the 'involuntary' feeling of 'freedom' from rule-governed activity that characterizes genius when it creates 'another nature out of the material that actual nature gives it' (*KU* 250, *CJ* #49, 182).

In his meditations on genius, Kant seems to resolve the difficulty encountered when it is claimed that art-works are 'naturally fashioned'. Inspired productions are not unrelated to cognitive activity for a considerable deal of 'academic' skill is required to manipulate the material through which ideas are to be conveyed. Moreover, Kant suggests that works of genius embody 'spirit', an animating principle which imparts to the mental powers a purposive momentum or play. This principle is the power to exhibit 'aesthetic ideas' – presentations of the imagination which stimulate 'much thought' but for which no determinate concept can be adequate. As such, the aesthetic idea is the counterpart to a rational idea which is a concept to which no intuition (presentation of the imagination) is adequate. These aesthetic ideas, which strive towards something that lies beyond the

limits of experience, are inner intuitions which exceed conceptu-
ality and give a completeness for which no example can be found
in nature. Accordingly, the aesthetic idea animates the mind by
opening up for it an 'immense [*unabsehliches*] realm of related
presentations' (*KU* 251–2, *CJ* #49, 183–4). The genius is able to
apprehend 'the rapidly passing play' of the imagination's power
and to communicate it without the constraint of rules (*KU* 254,
CJ #49, 186). This is because imagination in its productive capacity occasions freedom from the laws of association which attach
to its empirical use. Although it is under the law of the latter that
nature 'lends' us material, we can process this material into
'something *quite* different', that is, into something that 'surpasses
nature' (*KU* 250, *CJ* #49, 182).

Yet there is something quite curious about this process, indeed,
intoxicating. While it is central to Kant's account of aesthetic
judgement that the human subject must be capable of seeing the
world in a way which harmonizes with its faculties, that is, of
organizing nature through judgement which lends it form, his
account of the production of art implies that imagination does
more than merely supplement rational ideas. Aesthetic ideas
prompt the intuition of a nature *other than the one actually given to
us*. Indeed, aesthetic ideas reveal the capacity of the productive
imagination to stimulate thought by creating nature *once again*.
This activity which proceeds without concepts is a burgeoning
power which remakes thought, *materially realizes* ideas beyond the
limits of that which the faculties can recognize. It is in this sense
that physiology is 'artistic'. Yet if imagination has the power to
do this, this must include the thoughts which the body has about
itself, its mental powers, its transcendental unity, its 'self'. Taken
to the limit this means that imagination produces the self by
which it is supposedly governed. The body starts to twist itself
inside-out. What we can think, see, do, is no longer limited to
what we can 'know' – or else we can 'know' otherwise, a consciousness which is distinct but completely outside of self.

Explosive expenditure

In 'The Physiology of Art' notes, Nietzsche writes that the exalted
feeling of rapture enables one to survey tremendous distances and

divine much that is extremely fine and fleeting (*WP* 800). Indeed, the 'sensations of space and time are altered' and one seems to see in an extraordinarily expansive way (ibid.). In Kant's terms it could be said that an immense world of kindred presentations are intuitively apprehended, as if communicating the imagination's 'rapidly passing play'. What it is possible to see, to do and to feel when in this enchanted state seems to conduct the body beyond itself, folding it back upon its own conditioning powers. The excessive power of the genius prompts exploration into a different 'intuition' of space and time: the imagination learns to schematize 'productively', to generate 'illegitimate' relations. For example, in contrast to 'given' perceptual experience in which the world is seen according to ideal constructs of space and time, the rapturous experience of genius reveals a non-rationally mediated world of subject and object. If the perception of the 'impoverished body' functions by occluding that which fails to attain coherent form, just as certain kinds of figurative art fail to engage with the migrant sensations which flood the pre-conceptual field, genius (or artistic physiology) perhaps signifies the turning of sensation back on itself, intensifying synaesthetic rhythms and rendering new forces sensate. One might say that the faculty of sight becomes intensified, becomes *visionary*, as if able to see that of which the 'phenomena' are mere manifestations. Seeing *itself* is made visible – the production of the process of intuition is intuited – as if the body were now seeing itself from the inside.

We recall Nietzsche's remarks about the power of great art to stimulate the beholder through images of intensified life. Intoxicated by a spectacle such as tragedy, for example, he will sense that his visual faculty is no longer merely confined to surfaces but is 'capable of penetrating into the interior' (*BT* 22). It is as if he now sees before him, with the aid of music, the 'waves of the will, the conflict of motives, and the swelling stream of passions, sensuously visible' like 'a fullness of vital moving lines and figures' (ibid.). The delicate secrets of unconscious excitations seem almost tangible, as if the world were in the process of being born. This is not something strictly determinable but its reverberations can be felt – in the depths, as it were. Van Gogh's wild starscapes which swirl and pulsate with the delirial energy of nature straining to be *more* seem to embody this power. One might say that Van Gogh turns up the *volume* of the colour in his painting so that one can only see that which cannot be seen, making the invisible shine and amplifying the inaudible. As Albert Aurier says of Van Gogh:

> above all, he is a hyper-aesthete with obvious symptoms who perceives with abnormal and possibly even painful intensity the imperceptible and secret character of lines and forms, and even more of colours, of light, of the magic iridescence of shadows, of nuances which are invisible to healthy eyes. And that is why the realism of this neurotic [and] his sincerity and his truth are so different....[8]

Without any trace of irony, Schopenhauer designates the genius as one who is 'naturally abnormal', a precious deformity whose surplus powers are 'foreign to the will, i.e., to the authentic [*eigentlich*] I' (*WWV*, II, 492, *WWR*, II, #31, 377). If the genius is able to 'intuit otherwise' this is because inspiration discloses a de-individuated feeling of life which cuts across the ownmost possibilities of *Dasein*. According to Schopenhauer, genius is the capacity to 'hold oneself purely in intuition', to 'lose oneself in intuition', indeed, to completely relinquish one's 'personality' so that one might become a '*pure knowing subject*, the clear eye of the world' (*WWV*, I, 274, *WWR*, I, #36, 185–6). Because the power of anegoic knowledge is excessive in the genius, he is able to liberate his intellect from the service of the will and 'perceive a different world' to those individuals for whom being-in-the-world is goal-orientated (*WWV*, II, 491, *WWR*, II, #31, 376). Indeed, the genius emerges in his age 'like a comet in the paths of the planets, to whose well-ordered and visible arrangements its completely eccentric path is foreign' (*WWV*, II, 511, *WWR*, II, #31, 390). Whereas the common human being sees the world simply in terms of causal relations relevant to his or her projects, the genius sees the universal or 'life as such' in terms of the 'Ideas'. Schopenhauer's notion of 'Idea' – inspired by both Plato and Kant but idiosyncratically so – is wholly perceptive. In contrast to the 'dead receptacle' of the concept, the Idea is 'like a living organism, developing itself and endowed with generative force' which brings forth – via the genius – that which was not previously given to it (*WWV*, I 340, *WWR*, I, #49, 235). In fact, Schopenhauer claims that the genius is able to see not what nature has actually formed but what it endeavoured to form (*WWV*, I, 276, *WWR*, I, #36, 186). To this end, it is through genius that nature perfects itself as art – as if a medium for overwhelming forces. As in Kant's account of inspired creation, Schopenhauer insists that the genuinely inventive individual is not conscious of the aim and intention of the art-work, adding that the latter acts out of 'pure feeling and unconsciously, indeed, instinctively' (*WWV*, I 340–1, *WWR*, I, #49, 235). The task of the genius is to 'perfect' these illicit intuitions through the power of imagination – by virtue of which he is able to 'extend his horizon far beyond the reality [*Wirklichkeit*] of his personal experience', thus enabling 'almost all the possible images of life to pass by within himself' (*WWV*, I, 275, *WWR*, I, #36, 186). The 'feeling of life' that is heightened in the production and subsequent reception of art is swollen and exaggerated: both transpersonal and transphysiological. As Schopenhauer puts it, 'the artist lets us glance into the world through his eyes' (*WWV*, I, 287, *WWR*, I, #37, 195).

While the artist is able to enhance life through emphasizing the essential Ideas and thereby stimulate the rapturous state on the part of the spectator once again, Schopenhauer exclaims with characteristic *ennui* that 'life is *never* beautiful, only the images of life, namely those [shown] in the transfiguring mirror [*im verklärenden Spiegel*] of art or poetry' (*WWV*, II, 489, *WWR*, II, #30, 374). However, it is still possible for the non-genius to view the things of nature in a picturesque or poetic way. Schopenhauer comments that the sight of the moon and the stars delight us as objects of intuition rather than as objects of conceptualization because they are unknown to our willing – just as the sight of a strange town can delight us because it holds no associations for us; indeed, travelling is pleasant for precisely this reason (*WWV*, II, 484, *WWR*, II, #30, 370–1). In a similar vein, Kant insists that if we are to call the sight of the starry sky sublime, this must not be because we base our judgement on concepts of worlds inhabited by rational beings, conceiving of the 'bright dots' that fill 'the space above us' as being these worlds' suns (*KU* 196, *CJ* #29, 130). Rather, we must base our judgement regarding it merely on 'how we see it', as a vast vault encompassing everything. Moreover, we must be able to view the ocean as 'poets do', merely in terms of what 'manifests itself to the eye [*was der Augenschein zeigt*]' (ibid.). Strangely enough we must view the 'evidence' of nature through the eyes of the genius – through the *Schein* that they embody in their recreation of nature – if we are to avoid dreaming of other worlds. It seems that we must learn to look at the world monstrously, inhumanly, if it is through sublimity that our supersensible vocation is to be confirmed.

Van Gogh dreamt of travelling to reach a star, of voyaging into the horizon of the infinite. Perhaps one must become a star to see into the heights, to see as a star might see. In a letter from Arles to his brother Theo in mid-July 1888 he writes:

> In a painter's life death is not perhaps the hardest thing there is. For my own part, I declare I know nothing whatsoever about it, but to look at the stars always makes me dream *as simply* as I dream over the black dots of a map representing towns and villages. Why, I ask myself, should the shining dots of the sky not be as accessible as the black dots on the map of France? If we take the train to get to Tarascon or Rouen, we take death to reach a star. One thing undoubtedly true in this reasoning is this, that while we are *alive* we *cannot* get to a star, any more than when we are dead we cannot take the train. So it seems to me possible that cholera, gravel, phthisis and cancer are the celestial means of locomotion, just as steamboats, omnibuses and railways are the terrestrial means. To die quietly of old age would be to go there on foot.[9]

The star is the limit of human vision – the most distant point which the eye can touch. If star travel is only possible once the human condition has been vacated, the undoing of the body is the prerequisite for making contact. Nietzsche argues in *The Will to Power* notes that if we analysed our body spatially we would gain precisely the same image of it as we have of the stellar system and the distinction between the organic and the inorganic would cease to be noticeable (*WP* 676). His thought is that just as one no longer needs to explain the motions of the stars as effects produced by entities conscious of a purpose, one is equally justified in abandoning this belief in regard to bodily motions and changes. The human body, like the stellar body, has order without transcendent agency. It 'informs' itself. It organizes itself.

The delicate infolding reflux between the body and its world is acknowledged by Heidegger who argues that the pleasure derived from 'what is ordered' is a 'fundamental condition of embodying life' (*N*, I, 121). Rapture in Nietzsche's reflections, he suggests, signifies 'an embodying attunement, an embodied being that is contained in attunement, attunement woven into embodiment' (*N*, I, 105). Indeed, in exploring the life-enhancing power of rapture as an aesthetic state he emphasizes 'seeing more simply and strongly' as a major feature of the creative process (*N*, I, 117).There is a clear privileging of the Apollinian in Heidegger's account but not because it constitutes a heightening of sexuality or a more relentless libidinal insurgency. In fact, Heidegger is reluctant to explore those aspects of 'The Physiology of Art' notes which discuss sexuality, delirium or animality – the white-hot matter of the sacred. His inclination towards the Apollinian seems to reflect his desire to locate rapture within an intraworldly horizon in which forms can be grasped by a phenomenological consciousness: 'Form, as what allows that which we encounter to radiate in appearance, first brings the behaviour that it determines into the immediacy of a relation to beings' (*N* 119). While the relation of subject to object is presented as being wholly inappropriate to a thinking of rapturous *Stimmung*, Heidegger's notion of rapture as the glorious victory of form arguably still privileges a perceptual relation to the world that is centred by human authenticity: for example, beauty is an 'attuning' which 'thoroughly determines the state of man' (*N*, I, 123). That rapture might also be an 'explosive state' – as Nietzsche asserts (*WP* #811) – is dismissed by Heidegger as 'a chemical description, not a philosophical interpretation' and only relevant to creation 'as a life-process' (*N*, I, 115). Yet the starry night of the intense fluid body is a non-organic becoming, an intuition *of* nature that creates a second nature out of vibrant, migrant intensities. As Deleuze and Guattari express it: 'we are not in the world, we become with the world' (*WIP* 169). Perhaps *Stimmung* or 'mood' remains too overdetermined as an originary form of transcendence for there-being[10] to capture the monstrous force of rapture. Deleuze and Guattari employ the term *percept* to describe '*non-human landscapes of nature*' (ibid.). When they say that 'the landscape *sees*', their thinking is closer to that of Schopenhauer than Merleau-Ponty, despite the former's denial of the will-to-live. It is the human subject that must die if 'we' are to reach a star. Percepts are sensations which do not refer to perceived objects or perceiving subjects but to transversal becomings: we have passed into the landscape and are part of the compound of sensations exceeding individual lives. Although bound up with an unorthodox metaphysics of will, Schopenhauer's Ideas point the way for percepts in that they embody the excessive richness and plenitude of a transfigured world and are the conduit for non-human intuitions. Whether of the immense heights or the intimate depths, percepts lend to the vista of existence abnormal dimensions 'as if swollen by a life that no lived perception can attain' (*WIP* 171).

These inhuman perceptions unfold in the heart of the unknowable, where nature is intensified, made anew. Nietzsche says in 'The Physiology of Art' notes that artists exhibit 'the extreme sharpness of certain senses, so they understand a quite different sign language – and create one – the condition that seems to be a part of many nervous disorders' (*WP* 811). In the most extraordinary way, the genius lives the forces which generate forms. Indeed, ecstasy becomes a method of intensifying and exploring its own sensations, remaking the 'rules' for what it is possible for the body to think. Perhaps it could be said for artists such as Hölderlin and Van Gogh that another form of comprehension emerges, gained through a 'greater spiritualization and multiplication of their senses' (*WP* 820). Genius lends the world a completeness or perfection beyond the limits of experience, beyond any form that is given. It is here that nature thinks beyond itself, materially realizing a body that surpasses its 'given form'. If sublime experience marks the failure of human intuition, its collapse forces an aesthetic comprehension of *what cannot be seen, what must be seen*. In sublime experience we struggle to see what it is impossible for us to see and it is *this* that we see. We see becoming.

This process is one in which nothing can remain 'the same', rather, can only *return* as the same. As we have seen, for Nietzsche, the enraptured 'subject' transforms things until they 'reflect again his power – until they are reflexes of his perfection'. In this way the artist comes to embody the landscape of his inner life in his inspired exterior projections. In a rapturous state he exudes his blooming physicality into the world of images and desires: what he sees, he desires to see overladen, swelling with force. One gives to things, compels them to take, idealizes them by 'forcing out' their principal features (*TI* 'Expeditions...', 8). But the world then reflects these images of intensified life *once again*, restimulating the drive to create a second nature out of nature. The exterior becomes an intimate glowing landscape, it becomes-body, a *Schein-Leib*. We *incorporate* our environment, make it the 'same' as ourselves but this is already to make it different, to differentiate *life* once more.

If a thought *becomes visible*, audible, this is because the thinker becomes with the world, his body resonating with what it perceives, what it is made of, what it eternally renews. Nietzsche writes that enjoyment of semblance 'impels the *becoming* of genius, that is to say, of the world. Each engendered world has its pinnacle some-where: in each moment a world is born, a world of semblance [*Schein*] with its self-enjoyment in genius.' (*KSA* 7, 203/7[167]). The world created anew in every moment is prompted by the ever-self-renewing drive to artistic play, which as Heraclitus notes, is 'invisible to the common human eye' (*PTAG* 7). The recoming of becoming is celebrated in Nietzsche's account of tragic art as the most intense realization of the fecundity of life, the coupling of Apollinian *Schein* with Dionysian *Rausch*. We recall from Chapter 2 that 'oneness as genius of the race, of nature itself' is articulated through the incomparable symbolic excitations and harmonic exal-tations of the body in Dionysian rapture and their eternalization in Apollinian splendour (*BT* 2). The tragic age of the Greeks is identified by Nietzsche as a triumph of becoming over stasis, the incorporation of form into the reverberating Dionysian will – the tonal subground of pleasure and pain: 'The Greek world a blossom-ing of the will. Where did the elements of resolution come from? Out of the blossoming itself. The monstrous sense of beauty which had absorbed itself in the idea of truth, gradually set it free' (*KSA* 7, 73/3[45]). As Nietzsche notes, if the Greeks 'suffered' it was precisely from overfullness, from their craving for eternal transfiguration: 'Did those centuries when the Greek body bloomed and the Greek soul foamed over with life perhaps know endemic ecstasies?' (*BT* 'Attempt...', 4)

> When the Greek body and the Greek soul 'bloomed' and not in conditions of morbid exuberance and madness, there arose that mysterious symbol of the highest world affirmation and transfiguration of existence that has ever been attained on earth. Here a *measure* is given according to which everything that has

grown up since is found too short, too poor, too narrow. (*WP* 1051)

Eternal return is a thought embodied in the blossoming of life. As such, it cannot function as a measure *according to which* life unfolds. This blossoming life 'is' the measure, a thought of the unknown which reveals itself *as* unknown in ecstasy. The symbol of return arises as mysterious, a thought which cannot be conceptualized but can only be rapturously undergone. In the words of Hölderlin: 'Is there a measure on earth? There is none' ('In lovely blueness').

Yet the immense pleasure of tragic affirmation is conditioned by pain, a pain which the genius is fated to experience in seeking to reflect the world will in one consciousness. Significantly, this pathos is expressed as the condensation of time and the intimation of perpetual becoming.

> [S]inking in appearance is the highest pleasure: when the will is completely externalised. It achieves this in the genius. In each moment the will is simultaneously highest ecstasy and highest pain: to think of the ideality of dreams in the brain of the intoxicated – an infinite time and compressed in a second. Appearance as that which *becomes*. (*KSA* 7,199/7[157]).

Van Gogh knew these dreams that damage and delight: 'Sometimes moods of indescribable mental anguish, sometimes moments when the veil of time and the fatality of circumstances seemed to be torn apart for an instant.'[11] Life is renewed in every moment as the artist *becomes* with the world but art and nature are held in a double capture, creating themselves eternally once again. When the depths are projected into the heights, the nature one embodies is transfigured and it is difficult to say whether the starry sky above is not somehow already within.

Perhaps the artist develops a sense for being sensed, for being-looked at by the landscape which swallows up his horizon.

> Oh sky above me [...] are you watching me? Are you listening to my wondrous soul? When will you drink this drop of dew that has fallen upon all earthly things, when will you drink this wondrous soul – when, well of eternity, you brighter, more terrible

noontide-abyss! When will you drink my soul back into yourself? (*TSZ*, IV, 'At Noontide')

When Zarathustra falls into the well of eternity, time flies away and the world becomes perfect – but it is a happiness that stings his heart. The world becomes perfect through rapture – a plenitude of light, too immediate an affirmation of the sacred. Reflecting again the intensity one infuses into things, the will is completely externalized. There is only becoming, only transport at every moment. Art and *physis* do not exist independently of the differential relation by which they are eternally becoming other. As Bataille writes:

Ecstasy is *communication* between terms (these terms aren't necessarily defined), and communication possesses a value the terms didn't have: it annihilates them. Similarly, the light of a star (slowly) annihilates the star itself.[12]

This excitation is too swift or too diffuse or too intense to enter consciousness as an item of experience, yet without being actualized something is communicated. And the danger is that the machine might explode.

The genius – in work, in deed – is necessarily a squanderer: *that he expends himself* is his greatness.... The instinct for self-preservation is suspended, so to speak; the overwhelming pressure of the energies streaming out forbids him any such care or caution [....] He flows out, he overflows, he expends himself, he does not spare himself – fatally, fatefully, involuntarily, just as a river overflows its banks involuntarily. (*TI* 'Expeditions...', 44)

Schopenhauer endorses the gratuitous nature of genius – to be useless and unprofitable is one of its characteristics – but this extends beyond the works to everyday experience: 'the individual so gifted becomes more or less useless for life' (*WWV*, II, 508, *WWR*, II, #31, 389). The danger is that this abnormally enhanced power of knowledge will occasionally direct its attention to the business of the will only to apprehend its misfortunes too vividly, seeing everything in 'colours too dazzling, too bright a light and monstrously exaggerated' (ibid.). In this way the individual 'falls into extremes' (ibid.). We can truly say that 'Apollo has struck.'

In December 1888 both Nietzsche and Van Gogh began to succumb to the vertigo of acute mental illness. According to Bataille, at this time Van Gogh liberated the sun from its depiction as form and lent it the power of movement, of violent force. It is as though this giant and boiling star is summoning the incandescent lava from the earth's depths and the human world becomes the tormented threshold of their mutual conflagration. The bright pigments writhe as though on the point of blossoming with fire.

> At that moment all of his painting finally became *radiation, explosion, flame*, and himself, lost in ecstasy before a source of *radiant* life, *exploding, inflamed*. When this solar dance began, all at once nature itself was shaken, plants burst into flame, and the earth rippled like a swift sea, or burst; of the stability at the foundation of things nothing remained.[13]

Very little is known for certain about Nietzsche's creative output after his mental collapse. There is agreement however that music was one of his lasting pleasures. He would spend much time playing the piano, improvising for hour after hour. One visitor to the Nietzsche household in 1900 spoke of 'the deep sad star eyes, which roam in the distance and seem to look inward', eyes which radiated a powerful effect, an intellectual aura no sensitive nature could resist.[14] However, when the piano was struck up, the mighty tones 'seized the patient as if with magic power and quivered through his organism like an electric spark. Blissful rapture transfigured his features, his whole body quivered with feverish excitement – and behold new life flowed through his transparent lame hands. They broke the fetters of paralysis and moved toward one another as a sign of applause. He could not have enough of this manifestation of joy.'[15] It is also reputed that in the night in which he was conveyed to the Jena sanatorium accompanied by Franz Overbeck, he repeatedly woke up and sang loud songs, among them the beautiful gondola song in which he likens his soul to a stringed instrument trembling with all the colours of bliss. Rhythms of excitement or despair; there is an artist here yet, trembling with the fibres of a body which remembers its primordial joy.

Genius is an explosive power, one which fires a corporeal consciousness with countless subtle shudders and shivers. What is alerted in this rapturous state is a vitality which is *of* the body yet not owned, a glimpse in life of that which is in excess of life. Yet such extraordinary awareness emerges in virtue of our collapse and not in spite of it. To surrender to becoming may mean to resign the human condition but to do so is to realize '*in oneself* the eternal joy of becoming – that joy which also includes *joy in destruction*' [*TI* 'What I Owe to the Ancients', 5]. The lure of this joy is intoxicating. To know it is to burn, to break, to increase the power to live.

5
A General Theory of Collapse

> The most spiritual human beings, assuming that they are
> the most courageous, also experience by far the most
> painful tragedies: but that is exactly why they honour life,
> because it brings against them its greatest adversaries.
>
> *(TI* 'Expeditions...', 17)

The emergence within life of something that exceeds life lends to
each of its moments a mad and uneasy tension. It is not simply that
the desire for truth, traversing the border of coherence, leaves the
thinker perplexed, nor even that philosophy – like catastrophe – has
a tendency to *unhinge*. The problem is one of ruinous excess, excess
which has ceased to exceed anything determinable and which persists *uncontainably*. According to Schopenhauer, the genius is fated to
suffer from an 'abnormal' proclivity for perceiving the world 'objectively'. Having extended one's horizon far beyond personal experience in the intuition of Ideas, one is obliged to translate the fruits of
this inhuman encounter into discursive form. Yet discourse from
'out there' is of an unusual kind, eluding formulation in the language of identity.[1] If the voyage beyond life is tenable *within* life it is
questionable whether its percipient can ever return as 'the same'.

Deleuze and Guattari suggest that through 'having seen Life in
the living or Living in the lived' (through having reached the
percept as the 'sacred source') the artist 'returns' to life 'breathless
and with bloodshot eyes' (*WIP* 172). What the novelist or painter
now cultivate are forces of becoming that are not their own, visions
that are composed of 'that moment' when lived perceptions are

shattered 'into a sort of cubism, a sort of simultaneism' – an embrace of life with that which threatens it (*WIP* 171). Creativity of this order does not so much heighten life as dissolve and liberate its robust forms. In this respect, Deleuze and Guattari say, artists are like philosophers:

> What little health they possess is often too fragile, not because of their illnesses or neuroses but because they have seen something in life that is too much for anyone, too much for themselves, and that has put on them the quiet mark of death. But this something is also the source or breath that supports them through the illnesses of the lived (what Nietzsche called health). (*WIP* 172–3)

Nietzsche writes in the 'Physiology of Art' notes that 'it is exceptional states which condition the artist – all of them profoundly related to and grown together with morbid phenomena, so that it seems impossible to be an artist and not to be sick' (*WP* 811). Sickness is not necessarily the consequence of organic weakness; on the contrary, it may constitute a strange kind of homeopathic excess. We are told that physiological states which flourish in the person of the artist also reside in human beings in general but what may be morbidity for 'us' signals a 'full and blossoming life' for the artist (*WP* 812). Furthermore, the fact that 'genius' might be considered as a 'form of neurosis' is 'an objection to "today", not to "artists"' (ibid.). The imperative is to ask *of what* certain physiological tendencies are symptomatic, indeed, it is in this sense that aesthetics is 'applied physiology'. Extravagant powers of understanding *appear* to be the by-product of hysterical and histrionic states which one might insist are themselves the progeny of impoverishment or depletion of health. However, Nietzsche contends that these hyperaesthetic conditions may also spring from inner plenitude:

> *Excess* of sap and force can bring with it symptoms of partial constraint, of sensory hallucinations, refined susceptibility to suggestion, just as well as impoverished life....The stimulus is differently conditioned, the effect remains the same.... (*WP* 812)

Nietzsche's diagnosis of Greek tragedy as the product of an ecstatic and 'blossoming body' overflowing with life is to be recalled at this point (*BT* 'Attempt...', 4). In the preface to *The Birth of Tragedy* he comments that this analysis was formulated during a period of 'convalescence' in which pessimism as an inevitable sign of weakness, decay and weary instincts was called into question. That there might in fact be a 'pessimism of *strength*' – a predilection for the hard, gruesome, evil and problematic aspects of existence – and that this might be spawned by well-being and overflowing health – is a proposition hazarded for the first time (*BT* 'Attempt...', 1). The Greek craving for tragedy signifies for Nietzsche that it is possible to suffer from a plenitude of health and well-being, from *too much life*:

> And what is the meaning, then, physiologically speaking, of that madness out of which tragic and comic art grew – the Dionysian madness? What? Is madness perhaps not necessarily the symptom of degeneration, of decline, of a culture past its peak? Are there perhaps – a question for psychiatrists – neuroses of *health*? (*BT* 'Attempt...', 4)

Nietzsche rejects the notion of health and sickness as an antithesis, commenting instead that 'it is a matter of degree' (*WP* 812). This said, health and sickness do not mark out a graduated scale or continuum. Gradation thus conceptualized would connote 'measure' – a form of identity – but as we have seen in Chapter 2, Nietzsche thinks of vital rhythms or bodily tempo in terms of immanent differentials. What conditions the stimulus will determine the *value* of the effect. This bears on the question of measure because it could be argued that the notion of quantifying health and sickness is itself the product of an 'impoverished body'. This means that 'excess' – understood in relation to a superabundant physiology – is not a quantifiable term, nor even a paradoxical 'supplement'. It is, perhaps, a name for the 'boundless' yet it coexists with that which attains form, just as the Apollinian cuts itself out from the Dionysian swell with which it remains eternally continuous. Taken to the limit, neuroses of health would surely exhilarate us to death. But Nietzsche suggests that a limit is *internally generated* in these excessive states, calling into question the constitutive role of 'form'.

If it is legitimate to claim that humanist values of 'the same' continue to dominate so much contemporary thinking then sickness will generally be identified as a deviation from the 'normative' baseline of health, while madness will be regarded as a matter of mistaken belief or perception. Perhaps the legacy of Enlightenment rationalism is such that the mad person is regarded as one who sees something that is not really there or believes something that is not really true but in each case it is not the *form* of their cognition which is held to be at fault, simply the content. What happens should this holding pattern also collapse is a question which Nietzsche pursues in his exploration of ecstasy as aesthetic sensibility. In 'The Physiology of Art' notes, he advances the thought that form has an aesthetic rather than a moral or epistemological significance, an orientation which sharply conflicts with the hylomorphic model of the form/matter relation:

> One is an artist at the cost of experiencing [*empfindet*] all that non-artists call 'form' as *content*, as 'the matter [*Sache*] itself'. With that, of course, one belongs in an *inverted* world: for henceforth content becomes something merely formal – our life included. (*WP* 818).

Nietzsche challenges the role accorded to form as the lawful or 'given' boundary of experience. On his interpretation, 'form' is that which is materially produced and which is immanent to the 'content' of matter. Vying with the ideal forms of experience which seem to promise coherence, albeit of a kind which is necessarily lacking (transcendent), Nietzsche's artistic notion of form implies that order is emergent. What for the non-artist is constitutive of experience, ensuring re-cognition of 'the same', the artist experiences as the fluid matter of creativity – the flux of material forces. Life becomes the site of transformation and experiment, a non-human becoming. Perhaps, as in tragic *pathos* we feel the 'excess of innumerable forms of existence which press and push one another into life'; we incarnate the thought that everything that comes into being must pass away (*BT* 17). Yet since *formally speaking* this is an unmasterable thought it is always in excess of its own realization – a formulation of the formless at odds with 'the matter itself'. In endeavouring to give form beyond the form that is 'given' the artist is liable to collapse – at least from the perspective of 'common sense'.

For example, Blanchot says of Hölderlin that he struggled with sovereign determination to 'raise to poetic form – to expression in its highest and most masterfully controlled sense – what he had grasped, which is beneath any form and lies short of all expression' (*MPE* 115). This endeavour is contemporaneous with the development of his mental illness, tempting one to say that it is the impossibility of representing lived intensities which is shattering. The fact that so many fine thinkers, writers and artists exhibit this tendency towards collapse leads one to wonder at the contiguity of greatness and sickness. There is something painfully raw and indescribably delicate about the expression of 'sensitive knowing' cut free from any anchoring in the comfort of a human world. Such superlative works communicate an excitement and unease which reflect the enigma of a contact which refracts the possibility of reciprocity. But even if it is self-defeating to rationalize madness or even to speculate why artists such as Hölderlin or Van Gogh disturb and delight, the failure of a certain kind of intersubjectivity may be instructive *in its own terms*. If rapture excites the state that creates art it may be that the ruin of recognition could be cultivated as a positive force philosophically.

Such an 'understanding' of collapse would be aesthetic rather than epistemological. In a post-romantic age, it is often said that artistic greatness transcends aberration. According to Bergson, illness is not *inherently* creative, it is simply that certain morbid and abnormal states 'seem to introduce into the mind certain new ways of feeling and thinking' (*MPFR* 44). If illness inhibits certain functions that in the normal state prevent others from having their full effect, this tells us nothing yet about the link between madness and creativity.[2] The problem is that to 'explain' in this context is to triumph over the phenomenon in question – knowledge is victorious at the price of vanquishing its object. Similarly, to attribute causal factors to unusual behaviours is to invoke the validity of transcendent cognitive principles. Delivered over to sanity, the mysterious ceases to mystify (we know how it works but it ceases to move). Such, for Nietzsche, is the mortician's touch which characterizes 'reason' in philosophy (*TI* ' Reason...', 1). Nietzsche insists that in spite of this 'will to know' understanding can be conducted further than explanation. From *The Birth of Tragedy* onwards, he seems to seek the path of thinking that will evoke as a force that which will not abide as a form. In the latter text, he proposes that the 'sublime metaphysical illusion' that thought can 'know being' accompanies knowledge as an instinct which leads it 'again and again to its limits at which it must turn into *art – which is really the aim [abgesehn ist] of this mechanism*' (*BT* 15). In this formulation, art emerges as the consequence of knowledge driven to its limit, as if creativity erupts at the very point where 'natural cognition' is surpassed. In a similar vein, Blanchot declares that the extreme limit 'is not only the end of comprehension, its moment of closure, but also its opening moment, the point at which it illuminates itself against a background of darkness which it has brought to light' (*MPE* 112). At the extreme limit of accessibility, madness dazzles in a darkness which it preserves in its obscurity. It is not that some 'essential truth' is made luminous, rather, its irreducibility is made manifest. Such a thought calls to mind the notion that in sublime experience we are forced to see what it is impossible to see. Madness is glimpsed according to its own lights, perhaps. As Blanchot suggests of the occasion of Jaspers' meeting with Van Gogh:

> On confronting Van Gogh he felt, more clearly although no doubt less physically, what he had felt when coming face to face with certain schizophrenics. It is as if an ultimate source of existence made itself momentarily visible, as if hidden reasons for our being were here immediately and fully in force. (Ibid.)

Nothing is made clear but everything is communicated. The question is – how is this possible?

The guiding clue seems to be that confrontation with otherness is registered affectively and profoundly, not grasped intellectually in terms of familiar codes of thought. This encounter is simultaneously fascinating and disturbing, the intrusion of the unpredictable, the unassimilable, the ineluctably alien. Everything is communicated here at the level of affect; indeed madness – like art – appears to have both an aesthetic impact and an aesthetic impetus. Blanchot likens the tendency of certain schizophrenics to live 'more passionately, more unconditionally, in an unbridled way' to a *demonic* tendency of existence 'to surpass itself eternally' – an experience which he suggests is muted in the healthy man who organizes his life according to goals and projects (*MPE* 116–17). Although he does not draw the salient links here between the thought of eternal return and the Freudian repetition compulsion – both of which are identified with the demonic[3] – it is clear that for Blanchot there is a monstrous moment at which a 'breakthrough' occurs and which compels existence to assert itself relentlessly with regard to the absolute: 'Everything transpires as if in the lives of these beings something manifested itself briefly which exposed them to shuddering dread and ravishment'(*MPE* 116). This 'something' which is 'too much' for anyone to bear becomes the object of a new relation to existence. One might say that the goal becomes the desire to surpass the goal eternally, that desire becomes so excessive that it exceeds itself – a thought which philosophy is unable to contain.

Were we to say that in the artist receptivity to the perceptual richness of the world is appropriated by illness, yielding the possibility for stranger dimensions of experience, perhaps it could be claimed that the attempt to 'give form' to such experiences *exacerbates* the sickness, reconfiguring its material conditions once again. Blanchot implies that schizophrenia is the condition which enables the artist to raise 'the opening of the depths' to an 'objective form' but he also suggests that this process is 'the development which leads to collapse'; that is, to the breakdown of the artist as a conscious subject (*MPE* 117). It is the *form of the self*, the ego, which is annihilated. If it is sickness which comes to intensify art rather than to initiate it, it quickly becomes art which intensifies sickness because the shattered subject now strives to give form to the extreme. Arguably, this is the 'demonic' element that traverses creativity – the rebounding, escalating repetition of the urge to surpass. Collapse takes on 'poetic meaning' and thinking is reformulated from the black heart of alterity. For Blanchot, it is not that the poet has the power to communicate the incommunicable but in him the incommunicable becomes what makes communication possible:

> ...schizophrenia seems to be just the projection of that life at a certain moment and on a certain plane, the point of the trajectory where the truth of existence in its entirety, having become sheer poetic affirmation, sacrifices the normal conditions of possibility, and continues to reverberate from the deep of the impossible as pure language, the nearest to the undetermined and yet the most elevated – language unfounded, founded on the abyss – which is announced also by this fact: that the world is destroyed. (*MPE* 120)

This is the Dionysian madness of which Nietzsche speaks when he describes the ecstatic self-abnegation of the lyric poet whose voice shudders and vibrates from the abyss of being (*BT* 5). With the sacrifice of the 'normal conditions of possibility' experience is *of me* without being *mine*. A wealth of psychiatric literature affirms that psychotic discourse is typically marked by use of this third person or 'neuter' voice. One could also add that it is not dissimilar to the Kantian account of disinterested reflective aesthetic judgement, affectively stimulated yet typically expressed in the third person ('this is beautiful' rather than 'it pleases me').

This emergence within human experience of excessive, non-human becomings is not simply a question of language but a matter of life. Blanchot's essay is traced through with a Heideggerian thematic of truth as 'unconcealment' and as the 'happening' of the artwork but arguably this is to address the collapse of subjectivity ontologically rather than aesthetically. It could be said that madness approached aesthetically demands a rethinking of the affective and the physiological, not because illness is to be located aetiologically in the organic, but because the crisis of thought impacts on the body and the crisis of the body in turn impacts on thought. The pathways that thought can take when the ideal forms of communication break down suggest that ideas can materialize in ways that circumvent the sayable. As Kant and Schopenhauer demonstrate, the inspired genius no more knows how he came by his ideas than the recipient of them knows why they delight yet there is a circuit of communication operative here that bypasses conceptual determination entirely. In the 'Physiology of Art' notes Nietzsche relates this issue of communication to the multiplicity of sensitive powers which ecstastic carnality triggers into life. The 'feeling of rapture' corresponds to an exalted sensation of power and transfiguration. This condition produces a 'superabundance of means of communication' (*WP* 809), a 'quite different sign language' (*WP* 811), new 'pigments, colours and forms, above all, new movements, new rhythms' (*WP* 808) and even 'new organs, new accomplishments' (*WP* 800). Moreover, he goes on to assert that in the state of rapture a range of new perceptual powers is acquired:

> ... the sensations of space and time are altered: tremendous [*ungeheure*] distances are surveyed and are, as it were, for the first time

perceptible; the *expansion* of vision over greater amounts and expanses; the *refinement of organs* for the perception of much that is extremely small and fleeting; *divination*, the power of understanding with only the least assistance, at the slightest suggestion: "intelligent" *sensuality*.... (*WP* 800)

In rapture, thought becomes ex-centric, unassimilable within the forms of common sense. What ecstasy reveals is the pre-eminent power of the physiological to communicate another kind of thinking, a sensitive knowing of a non-human-centred kind. The potential of this ecstatic thinking for philosophy is enormously rich, particularly because it suggests a very different way of considering those elements of life which fail to make sense yet which have an immense affective yield. It will become increasingly clear in the course of our inquiry how these rapturous mutations of the body are prerequisites for encountering the thought of eternal return.

The 'art' of sickness

It is well documented in medical, psychiatric and neurological literature that the temporal and spatial patterns of experiencing the world may undergo profound modification. In cerebral paroxysms such as migraine and epilepsy, in psychotic and toxic states, but most interestingly, in states of dream and intoxication, the way in which the brain constructs 'space' and 'time' may exhibit significant variation. We have already noted the different 'speeds' of perception which Nietzsche associates with the Apollinian and Dionysian. A related set of observations are made by Oliver Sacks, who describes the changing qualities of the human perceptual landscape exemplified in cases of severe migraine.[4] We are told that size/distance constancy may vary with gradual or abrupt micropsia and macropsia – terms which do not simply denote the apparent diminution or enlargement in the size of objects but their seeming approach or recession. This account calls to mind Van Gogh's images of looming stars and it is notable that Sacks uses 'painterly' rather than 'pathological' terms to describe what one might insist were *merely* physiological aberrations. For example, he employs the phrase 'mosaic vision' to refer to 'the fracture of the visual image into irregular, crystalline, polygonal facets, dovetailed together' (a state which he suggests is scaled from the 'crystalline iridescence' of a pointilliste painting to the much larger components of a cubist image).[5] One thinks of the shattered perception, the 'sort of cubism' that Deleuze and Guattari associate with the percept. Sacks' term 'cinemato-graphic vision' is reserved for visual experience where the illusion of motion has been lost, creating the effect of rapidly flickering 'stills' (a state which may accelerate to 'normal' during the course of an 'aura' but which may also be continuously modulated). These 'aesthetic' descriptions of what might seem to be 'morbid' physiological experi-ences serve to remind us of the power of 'genius' to give expression to deviant sensations. The point seems to be that this articulation exacerbates the abnormality, complicating its aetiology. Creativity induces collapse of 'necessary' forms and this collapse induces cre-ativity *once again*. In 'The Physiology of Art' notes, Nietzsche indi-cates that the power to perceive the most delicate reliefs, the finest gradations of colour, line and timbre is not simply facilitated by rapture but provokes rapture in return.

> The artist gradually loves for their own sake the means which dis-close a condition of rapture: the extreme fineness and splendour of colour, the clarity of line, the nuance of *tone*: *distinctness*, where otherwise, under normal conditions, all distinction is lacking: – All distinct things, all nuances, insofar as they recall [*erinnern*] the extreme intensifications of strength that rapture produces, retrospectively awaken [*wecken rückwärts*] this feeling of rapture: – the effect of art works is the *excitation of the state that creates art*, rapture.... (*WP* 821)

Ecstasy opens thought to a wider reservoir of times and spaces beyond the limits of normal perception. As Sacks notes, Hildegard of Bingen (1098–1180), the mystic of exceptional intellectual and literary powers, experienced countless 'visions' which appear to have been induced by migraine, recording them in narrative and pictorial form. She reports seeing points of light which shimmer and move in a wave-like manner, often appearing as stars or flaming eyes but she insists that such visions are not beheld with carnal eyes but with 'the eyes of the spirit'.[6] What she gives shape and consis-tency to are non-formal, energetic, 'cosmic' intensities – the non-human becomings which we have identified with the 'percept'.

Deleuze and Guattari argue that whereas romantic philosophy still appeals to a formal synthetic identity (*a priori* synthesis) which renders matter intelligible, modern philosophy tends to elaborate 'a material of thought' in order to capture forces that are not thinkable in themselves (*TP* 342). The forces to be harnessed are not those of the earth ('a great expressive Form') but 'molecularized matter', nonvisible forces (ibid.). They maintain that 'the essential thing is no longer forms and matters, or themes, but forces, densities, intensities' (*TP* 343). It is the thermal, magnetic and germinal forces in which world and self co-evolve that are seen but seen in a visionary way – as a form of '*divination*'.

In conjunction with these aesthetic and mystical dimensions, rapture also discloses the excessive powers of 'intelligent *sensuality*'. In this connection it is worth noting that Wilhelm Reich characterizes the effects of what he calls the 'atmospheric orgone' in terms of expanding and contracting dots of light and the cinematographic shuttering of the sky:

> The flickering of the sky, which some physicists ascribe to terrestrial magnetism, and the glimmering of stars on clear dry nights, are direct expressions of the movement of the atmospheric orgone. The 'electric storms' of the atmosphere which disturb electrical equipment during intensified sun-spot activity are, as can be experimentally demonstrated, an effect of the atmospheric orgone energy.[7]

Reich contends that the colour of orgone energy is *blue* or *blue-grey*, that it contains three kinds of rays (blue-grey, foglike vapours, deep blue-violet expanding and contracting dots of light and white-yellow, rapidly moving rays of dots and streaks) and that the blue colour of the sky and the blue-grey of atmospheric haze on hot summer days are reflections of the atmospheric orgone.[8] Reich has been much ridiculed for his exotic ideas about intra-atomic energy but is it so strange to align sexuality with electrical storms, the atmospheric haze and sun-spot activity? Can we be sure that the enormous rush of the sublime has nothing to do with cosmic libido? Once again, we are entitled to ask what triggers 'visionary' insights once the body as an ideal form of the same has collapsed. Did Reich go mad looking at the sky? Or did the sky become frenzied looking at him? He saw something in life that was too much for him, he *saw* too much, perhaps.

Madmen, like artists and philosophers, are often depicted as sky-gazers. If they fail to learn from experience, 'falling again and again into the same ditch', this may be because the 'ceaseless blue stare' of the heavens lures them to 'heights, far, far above the human' (*TL* 2; SS 105). It is as if something is being communicated at the limit of vision, in excess of the senses which strain to unite the manifold. According to Reich's theory, orgone energy produces 'differences in potential or intensities distributed on the body considered from a molecular viewpoint' which is associated with a 'mechanics of fluids in this same body considered from a molar viewpoint'.[9] From the perspective of flows of orgone rather than from the concept of bio-logical finality, the body emerges as an open, fluid system sensitive to minute fluctuations in its cosmic and microcosmic environments. We might say that the organic body experiences itself as a 'stellar body' when ecstatic, that is, when viewed dynamically (as energetic materiality) and libidinally (as 'highly charged'). Star clusters, galax-ies, weather-patterns and clouds are complex and variable forma-tions that resonate with non-organic bodily processes, attesting to Nietzsche's claim that there are multiple processes within which the material flows of the body are implicated and of which conscious-ness is oblivious. In fact, Nietzsche was convinced that the vast majority of his own protracted migraines and gastric discomfort could be attributed to meteorological influences, particularly the electrical patterns in the cloud cover and the effects of the winds.[10] In his letters he expresses longing for an 'eternally clear sky' but his landscape is perpetually overshadowed by highly charged clouds, his brain agitated, oscillating – at times prompting 'a sensation closely akin to seasickness' (*SB* 6, 96, 3). And yet, extraordinarily, Nietzsche declares that in spite of this: 'As a whole, I am happier now than I have ever been in my life' (*SB* 6, 3).

There is something quite curious about this affirmation, which is repeated constantly in his published works. Where one might have anticipated a malcontent's litany of medical complaints, Nietzsche's works are marked by gratitude for suffering. He says that for a typi-cally healthy person being sick can be an 'energetic *stimulus* for life, for living more' (*EH* 'Why I am so Wise , 2) that he owes 'indescrib-ably more' to his illness than to his health, that he *owes his philoso-*

phy to it (*KSA* 6, 436). Nietzsche makes it clear in these passages that sickness is not something to be stoically endured but actively affirmed as a positive force; 'one should not only bear it, one should *love* it: *Amor fati*: that is my inner nature' (ibid.). As ever in Nietzsche's philosophy, the notion of monstrous love assumes an uncanny prominence. The peculiar addiction to suffering, more ferocious and extreme than any simple masochism, seems to achieve in intensity what it lacks in clarity: it wills to be more than itself.

In his notebooks, Nietzsche transcribes a segment from one of Dostoyevsky's novels which might be characterized as a thought of *amor fati* if not eternal return itself. The 'brain storms' of epileptic seizures, which seem to play a central role in liberating the human subject from a familiar relation to the forms of intuition and the categories of experience, are explored by Dostoyevsky in a way which impels the thought that illness should be embraced and intensified rather than eradicated. In his novels *The Idiot* and *The Devils*, Dostoevsky vividly presents the moment of 'epileptic clarity' as a vision of 'eternal harmony' (*DV* 586) and 'the most direct sensation of one's existence to the most intense degree' (*I* 244). The infinite happiness felt in these moments is such that one feels moved to exclaim: 'Yes, I could give my whole life for this moment' (*I* 244).We are told that the hero of *The Idiot*, Prince Myshkin, reflecting on this experience afterwards when 'he was well again' would remind himself that these flashes of the 'highest mode of existence' were 'nothing but a disease, a departure from the normal condition, and, if so, it was not at all the highest mode of existence, but, on the contrary, must be considered to be the lowest' (*I* 243). Yet he would then feel compelled to ask himself whether it mattered that it was a 'disease':

> What does it matter that it is an abnormal tension, if the result, if the moment of the sensation, remembered and analysed in a state of health, turns out to be harmony and beauty brought to their highest point of perfection, and gives a feeling, undivined and undreamt of till then, of completeness, proportion, reconciliation, and an ecstatic and prayerful fusion in the highest synthesis of life? (Ibid.)

Taking this and our other examples together as a whole, it could be argued that certain experiences of sickness present a genuine

challenge to received notions about 'abnormality' but it is important to stress that this is not an empirical point. The 'art' of sickness
is bound up with a movement of overcoming. Sickness as an energetic stimulus to life is to be thought of as a will to transcend forms
which inspire conformities.[11] The impetus is to make sickness creative by exploring and redirecting its effects, assembling percepts,
mystic insights, new philosophical 'truths'. In all these cases the
physiological breakdown or cognitive dissonance is *real* – it is registered affectively – but its artistic actualization has no merely biological referent. If the material conditions for renewing philosophy are
inhibited by sclerotic forms of thought the impetus for a genuinely
exploratory philosophy is to promote a kind of convalescence.
'Healing' the body may mean to make it more obviously 'sick' but
this is not simply because the 'impoverished' physiological perspective of anthropocentric thought will inevitably regard it this way.
The transformation of thought entails more than an exchange of
'forms', it is born out of the collapse of forms which for Nietzsche
commands an active nihilism.

Creating new organs

The 'death of God' – the overcoming of metaphysics – means for
Nietzsche the collapse of the form of identity in all its guises. It is not
simply the transcendent ideas of the true and the good that must be
overcome, it is the values which they embody. That subjectivity
might be a *moral* construct is a provocation that thinkers after
Nietzsche have certainly considered but that time, space, and the categories of understanding might equally be *moral forms* is an argument that philosophy has been less swift to assess. As Gilles Deleuze
has argued, the 'dogmatic' or rationalist image of thought is one
which presupposes a *common sense* as 'the norm of identity from the
point of view of the pure Self and the form of the unspecified object
which corresponds to it', while *good sense* is the 'norm of distribution
from the point of view of the empirical selves and the objects
qualified as this or that kind of thing' (*DR* 133–4). The subjective
identity of the self and its faculties and the objective identity of the
thing which the faculties 'recognize' as 'common' comprise a model
of thought which commutes difference to sameness, aberration to
normality and chaos to order. The possibility of philosophizing
outside this paradigm is constantly hampered by methodologies

which are shored up by these values, irrespective of anti-rationalist commitments. To see how it might be possible to think difference in its own terms we shall now consider a text of intense philosophical interest, the full value of which has yet to be appreciated.

Between 1884 and his death in 1911, Daniel Paul Schreber (a prominent jurist from the kingdom of Saxony), spent approximately thirteen years in mental asylums, detailing his experiences in a set of memoirs which subsequently became the classical locus for the study of schizophrenia. In *Memoirs of my Nervous Illness* Schreber details a philosophy of sensitive knowing which is intricately located in a transpersonal physiology. For reasons 'contrary to the Order of the World' (which he is at pains to understand) the boundaries of his body have become neuronally extended into a vast network of connection beyond all familiar spatio-temporal coordinates and across categorial divides as fundamental as self and other, male and female and life and death.

> I do not deny that a conception according to which one has to think of my body on our earth as connected to other celestial bodies by stretched out nerves is almost impossible for people to grasp considering the tremendous [*ungeheuren*] distances concerned. Nevertheless, as a result of the daily experiences that I have undergone over the last six years there can be no doubt as to the objective reality of this relation. (*DNK* 92, *MNI* 118–19)

Soberly analytical in tone throughout, the *Memoirs* chart the course of Schreber's passage into an amazing world of visions, miracles and supernatural intrigue in which he becomes the 'greatest spirit seer of all *millennia*' (*DNK* 57, *MNI* 88). Among the first symptoms of his nervous illness is acute insomnia which brings on an unbearable intensification of awareness. Initially this manifests itself in terms of an augmentation of the power of the senses such that he is able to *hear* the most minute vibrations in the atmosphere (such as 'crackling' noises in the walls of his bedroom). As the illness progresses, Schreber's 'organs' become so refined that he is able to engage in 'nerve contact' with dead souls, 'miracled birds' and with 'God's omnipotence itself'. We learn that in the normal course of things regular contact between God and human beings occurs only after death, although in special circumstances, He will communicate via the nerves of highly gifted individuals, particularly poets, in order to bless them with ideas about the beyond. Nerve language, which has an inner vibratory, repetitive quality, is something of which 'the healthy human being is as a rule unaware' although Schreber offers the analogy of somatically encoding a poem or speech one is trying to learn by silently going over the words (*DNK* 34, *MNI* 69). However, divine inspiration through nerve language is not allowed to become the rule because the nerves of living human beings have such power of attraction for God, particularly when in a 'state of *high-grade excitation*' that He risks fusing with them, endangering His own existence (*DNK* 8, *MNI* 48). This is because, in the 'Order of Things' God approaches corpses to 'draw up their nerves' to 'the forecourts of heaven' (*DNK* 9, *MNI* 49) where souls enter a highly sexualized state of Blessedness [*Seligkeit*] and become one with Him. Ascension to grace takes this unusual form because, according to Schreber, 'the human soul is contained in the nerves of the body' and God 'is only nerve, not body, and somewhat akin therefore to the human soul' (*DNK* 5, 6, *MNI* 45, 46). Nerves from corpses have to be purified by God according to the variable condition of the respective human souls, hence there are 'various *grades* of Blessedness' which determine the longevity of contact with the divine (*DNK* 10, *MNI* 49). However, souls are not accorded a personal immortality even though they attain an eternal existence: they merge into indeterminate aggregates and live a continued life with a different awareness. This may be explained by the fact that '*the soul is not purely spiritual, but is based on a material substrate, the nerves*' (*DNK* 251, *MNI* 244). Since God is nothing but 'nerve' and is far from omniscient (having no understanding of the living) He is rather different from the supreme deity of monotheist metaphysics. Rather than a transcendent being extrinsically presiding over the process of transmigration, He is a fluctuating assemblage of departed souls (active 'dead' matter). In short, God is a principle of *material becoming*, composed by the system of which He is Himself a part.

The sharpness of the senses, the extreme urge to communicate and the susceptibility to suggestion which Nietzsche identifies with rapturous creativity could scarcely find a more perfect exponent than Schreber, whose experiences of God and the transmigrating souls demonstrate the extent to which the body may be thought of as a pathway or fortuitous constellation of forces. For Schreber, it is not so much the case that 'God is dead' but that God *is* death – the principle of the collapse of identity or essential unity. God does not represent the 'One', for He is made up of multiple migrant yet indeterminate souls. Nor does He symbolize phallic identity (the *only* culturally determined *form* of subjectivity according to Irigaray) because the ecstatic Blessedness of which He is composed is explicitly feminized. Schreber explains that as part of everlasting Blessedness, 'voluptuousness' or 'bliss' is granted to souls in perpetuity and as an end in itself but to human beings solely as a means for the preservation of the species. Interestingly, although *female bliss* is said to consist mainly in the 'uninterrupted feeling of voluptuousness' and hence is inferior to male bliss, it is female bliss which is definitive of God and immortality (*DNK* 13, *MNI* 52). Moreover, Schreber succeeds in transforming his considerable suffering into a source of affirmation by 'becoming-woman'. It seems that as an indirect consequence of Schreber's nervous illness, a 'crisis' has occurred in the Order of Things in which God, irresistibly attracted to Schreber's overcharged nervous system, has become melded in a dangerous neuronal alliance with him, inhibiting dead souls from attaining Blessedness via their usual route. Unable to understand the needs of the living and in a bid to free Himself, God inadvertently torments Schreber by straining to 'draw up' his nerves. Schreber reasons that appeasement for God can only be won by providing what is relinquished through their unfortunate fusion, namely the state of Blessedness for nerve-souls. Initially traumatized by their 'indecent assaults', Schreber's task is greatly alleviated when his body becomes suffused with 'nerves of feminine voluptuousness'. Explaining that he must 'cultivate voluptuousness' as much as possible in order to please God, Schreber sees it as his destiny to tirelessly indulge in the kind of corporeal excitation he assumes to be the sole preserve of women. In fact it is only when Schreber submits to the liquidation of the *form* of phallic identity and gluts himself on *jouissance* that he is able to appreciate the pleasures of tactility, proximity, fluidity – principal elements of the female sexual imaginary. Like Irigaray's 'woman' Schreber has '*sex organs more or less everywhere*' (*CS* 28, *TS* 28).

Thanks to his 'nervous illness' Schreber comes to experience physiology as ever renewing, materially 'intelligent' and hyperadaptive. This is a virtual world of immanent, innovative becoming in which 'form' is continually developed and reformatted. In addition to an ever-changing sense of spatial location (including existing as a miniature colony of Schrebers on another planet), Schreber encounters mutant temporalities. While he slavishly records the dates of moves between asylums, he experiences centuries of world history in a single night, journeys to the centre of the earth and recapitulates the whole of human history backwards, discovers that he has already existed as a replicant – and still does, and feels that all the clocks of the world are 'running out'. He also learns that the end of the world is imminent – or already past – and that all will return except himself and a Jesuit priest. This is a logic that cannot be commuted to oneness, to the form of 'common sense'. Indeed, Schreber shows what it is to live in and through a world that cannot be represented, a world in which identity mutates with every new physiological encounter and which is conceptually impervious to mapping. Not only is 'God' not a unitary term, He is associated with both 'the forecourts of heaven' and with a realm prior to them; He has posterior realms further subdivided into a lower God Ariman and an upper God Ormuzd, the former of which is subsequently identified with the sun and the latter with a pin dot on the inner nerve lining of Schreber's head. The same could be said of the psychiatrist Flechsig who in Schreber's cosmology exists both as a living being and as a soul, the latter being variously composed of different nerve-clusters, sometimes of between forty and sixty parts, sometimes conjoined in hybrids with other souls (e.g. the joint Flechsig – von W. soul) and once as a bulky soul of wadding or cobweb which Schreber in a gesture of sympathy expels through his mouth despite its foul taste.

The point here is that the *form* of Schreber's world is constantly re-contoured with every new connection in the nerve network and the terms of this universe do not pre-exist their relations. It may be helpful to think of the composition of Schreber's neurocosmos in terms of Bergson's philosophy of creative evolution which develops the notion of a heterogeneous or continuous multiplicity as an affective continuum (*TFW* 75). Bergson suggests that mathematics tends to deal with discontinuous multiplicities, that is, relations between elements of determinate magnitude that can be spatially distinguished, juxtaposed and enumerated. By contrast, he attempts to think of duration in terms of an immanent multiplicity which is defined in terms of elements which interpenetrate and are *indeterminate*. Since this cannot be represented in conceptual terms (units) it is scarcely fortuitous that Bergson should use aesthetic criteria to exemplify continuous multiplicities.[12] It would seem that Schreber's cosmos is composed of elements (such as the grades of Blessedness) which are irreducible to an abstract or *a priori* unity. The nervous composition is variable and eventful, a constantly mutating multiplicity of elements that exceeds even the most baroque archictectonic. Every connection changes the whole to the extent that all the souls are connected at various degrees of intensity.

Uncannily, Nietzsche likens increased powers of aesthetic communication to contact with the souls of others, a thought which resonates with Schreber's experiences once again:

> *Empathy* [*sich hineinleben*] *with other souls* is originally nothing moral but a physiological susceptibility to suggestion: 'sympathy' or what is called 'altruism' is merely a form of that spiritually inclined psychomotor rapport (induction psycho-motrice thinks Charles Féré). One never communicates thoughts: one communicates movements, mimetic signs, which are *read back* to our thoughts. (*WP* 809)

Considered aesthetically rather than epistemologically, Schreber's madness attests to the power of ecstasy as a conduit for transversal communication between heightened physiologies. Again in 'The Physiology of Art' notes, Nietzsche speaks of the power of the 'contagious example' – the divination and immediate enactment of states through the power of suggestion, by-passing consciousness entirely (*WP* 811). Naturally, one thinks of the Dionysian throng and the demonic transmission of affects but Schreber seems uninspired by such phenomena. Despite 'soul storms', 'fluttering of radiant divine rays', and 'tying to celestial bodies' he remains fascinated by railway travel and its revolutionary effect on human communications. Ironically, having 'reached the stars' it is terrestrial transport that becomes the object of his dreams.

In an early essay, 'Dreams of a Spirit-Seer Elucidated by Dreams of Metaphysics' (1766), Kant argues that all life rests on the inner capacity 'to determine itself *voluntarily*' and that the principle of life is to be found in something in the world which 'seems to be of an immaterial nature' (*TG* 934, *DSS* 315). Kant rejects the idea that the soul might be material in nature on the grounds that one would be unable to distinguish it with any certainty from 'the raw elementary matter of corporeal natures' (*TG* 934, *DSS* 314). He contends that the 'thinking "I"'would be subject to the common fate of material natures: 'Just as it had been drawn by chance from the chaos of all the elements in order to animate an animal machine, why should it not in the future, after the chance combination has been dissolved, return to it once again?' (Ibid.). Kant sagely concludes that it is sometimes necessary to warn the thinker to pay more attention to the principles 'by means of which he has allowed himself to be carried along as if in a dream' (ibid.). And yet what a dream. Once liberated from a hylomorphic model which consigns matter to inertia and life to spirit, the notion of the vagrant, fortuitous self materializes as the threat of alien possession. The demonic tendency of existence to surpass itself erupts into thought at the point where the form of identity is annulled. As we shall see somewhat later in our explorations, the dream of an eternal return of the self as *other* is premised upon the collapse of the principle of identity. In Schreber's world it is already realized.

In another pre-Critical piece, 'Diseases of the Head', Kant describes the madman as the dreamer who remains awake.[13] His thought is that the madman is unable to distinguish fantasy from reality but there is another, non-epistemological sense in which we might understand the nature of the waking dreamer – the one who takes delight in form. There are numerous examples in the *Memoirs* which indicate that Schreber is only too aware of how fanciful his narrative sounds from the perspective of common sense yet he insists on attributing reality to it on its own terms. One *could* say that he seems to be aware of the phenomenal aspect of his experiences and does not confuse them with 'objective reality' but this formulation is still too overdetermined by the forms of 'common sense' and 'good sense'. Much like Nietzsche's account of Apollinian rapture in *The Birth of Tragedy*, Schreber's experiences display an ability to sense illusion *as* illusion. We might say that the will to know has been taken to the limit at which it turns into art. Indeed, it is a world of creative becoming that is intuited and affirmed as real, material force. We recall Nietzsche's remark that 'nervous disorders' have the capacity to understand a wholly new sign language and to create one. On this note, Blanchot says of Hölderlin that he 'dwells in the world which he creates, a world closer to myth' (*MPE* 115). The same could be said of Schreber, who displays what it might mean to live in a mythically inspired universe where anything is possible at any moment. Schreber asserts that he was in no sense a poet or a believer in the supernatural, and yet during his 'holy times' of nerve contact with God his soul was immensely inspired by supernatural things. Indeed, he comments that the impressions which 'rushed in' upon him were 'such a wonderful mixture of natural events and happenings of a supernatural nature', that it was extremely difficult to distinguish mere dream visions from experiences in a waking state (*DNK* 48, *MNI* 81). Having acknowledged this, Schreber remarks that some visions have a 'plastic clarity and photographic accuracy' that surpasses anything experienced when well and, using a phrase evocative of mystic experience, he reports again and again that he saw these visions with his 'mind's eye' (*DNK* 49, 116, *MNI* 81, 137). He comments too that it is as if the body is illuminated from the inside by divine 'rays' projected on his nervous system (*DNK* 116, *MNI* 137). Clearly, Schreber was no stranger to atmospheric orgone.

In a Kaufmannesque footnote in the *Memoirs*, Schreber mentions that he has consulted Kraepelin's *Textbook of Psychiatry*, which deals with the phenomenon of hearing voices and suffering hallucinations and readily agrees that in many cases the patients in question are patently deluded; nevertheless, he speculates that a considerable number may have been 'genuine spirit seers' owing to their reports of the exceptional vividness of their visions (*DNK* 58–9, *MNI* 89–90). However, he disputes Kraepelin's claim that the criterion for determining whether a patient is deluded or not rests on the patient's inability to use earlier experiences to correct newly acquired ideas. This criterion is one which Schopenhauer also endorses, his theory being that mad people suffer from a broken thread of memory and are unable to establish any coherent connection with past experiences (*WWV* I, 283, *WWR* #36, 192). In an interesting reversal of this logic Schreber protests: 'I believe that I have proved that I am not only not "controlled by the memory of fixed chains of thought and previously formed ideas" but that I also possess in complete acuity the "capacity to critically amend the content of consciousness with the help of judgement and deduction"' (*DNK* 58, *MNI*

89–90). Schreber goes on to take Kraepelin to task for his narrow Enlightenment rationalism which he coolly remarks has been superseded in the approaches of most theologians, philosophers and scientists. In effect, Schreber eschews the view that thought should conform to pre-given categories. In a will to understand so acute that it constantly goes beyond itself, dissolving forms of thought and developing them anew, Schreber indicates what happens when thought connects with the 'real' rather than with an image of thought (the concept or object). In his ecstatic transcendence of the functional body he encounters the unknown – the concrete plenitude of the sensible. In this sense it is transcendentality that is transcended. New faculties, new sense organs are created as a result of his hyper-receptivity to affective force, without ever stabilizing into anything more than a temporary holding pattern. Indeed, Schreber's world is particularly resistant to universalizing abstractions. For Schreber, empirical actuality is given in a receptivity that grasps what comes to it from the outside, not from concepts; indeed, nervous magnitude is the empirical condition of conceptual determination. It is the abstract which has to be accounted for because it is derived from real experience and then projected backwards to create the impression of being the prior condition of experience.

In summary, what Schreber's *Memoirs* exemplify is the activity which Kant calls non-determinative synthesis, synthesis not controlled by the pre-given categories of the understanding. As we have seen, according to Kant's Analytic of the Sublime, when confronted with a manifold that it is unable to synthesize, consciousness is threatened – a traumatic experience which produces the feeling of a momentary inhibition of vital force (the sublime is an 'abyss' in which the imagination is afraid to lose itself). However, the collapse of understanding – the failure of cognitive synthesis – ushers in the awareness that what we can do is not limited to what we can know; in other words, the power of synthesis can function otherwise than as a servant to the understanding. Such an experience brings on an overwhelming feeling of bliss, for we glimpse an alternative to the codes of the understanding, but it is important to acknowledge that this only occurs through straining the will to know to its limit – the point at which it becomes something else. In this regard, it is essential to remember that Schreber is no stranger to ecstasy. The turning-point in his illness occurs when he submits to soul-voluptuousness and reflects that the considerable pleasure that this affords him is the prize of relinquishing the desire to be master of his own head.

The sublime is one example which Kant gives of a faculty coming up against its limit, encountering what it cannot recognize, provoked by raw nature in its ruleless disarray to transcend its own rules. In sublime experience synthesis can attain autonomy precisely because it emerges from the collapse of imagination and the imposition of the Ideas of reason, Ideas that can be thought but cannot be imagined or 'known'. Deleuze sees in this discordant harmony between reason and imagination a disjunctive functioning of the faculties, a relation in which the differences between the faculties are not subsumed to the law of the same: 'There is, therefore, something which is communicated from one faculty to another, but it is metamorphosed and does not form a common sense' (*DR* 146). Perhaps what this reveals is the possibility of an aesthetics of innovation, a glimpse of the infinite possibilities of life. This may be the consequence of collapse but as in sublime experience, the intensification of our ruination gives rise to an unprecedented joy. Suffering and sickness are no objections to life, they are its stimulus.

Living experimentally

In a particularly candid passage in *Ecce Homo* Nietzsche writes:

> Never have I felt happier with myself than in the sickest and most painful periods of my life: one only need look at *Daybreak* or perhaps *The Wanderer and his Shadow* to comprehend what this 'return to *myself*' meant – a supreme kind of *convalescence*! ... The other kind merely followed from this. (*EH* 'Human all too Human', 4)

The unusual notion of 'convalescence' is curiously introduced in *Thus Spoke Zarathustra* to depict the aftermath of Zarathustra's nausea and collapse, brought on by the attempt to embody the thought of eternal return. The notion of convalescence dominates the series of new prefaces which Nietzsche composed for his earlier works in the year after finishing this text and it is noticeable that they all share a concern with recovery and *return*. For example, in *The Gay Science* preface he describes himself as the 'resurrected one', in *Human all too Human* as one drawing near to life again after a long sickness, and in the *Daybreak* preface he says 'for I have returned, I have come back from it' (*D* Preface, 2). Like Zarathustra, returning to himself after his death-like coma, Nietzsche presents himself as one in the process of *becoming man again*. He claims that he has attempted to convalesce from his entire life hitherto, that he took sides *against* himself and *for* everything painful precisely for him: 'thus I again found my way to that courageous pessimism that is the opposite of all romantic mendacity, and also, as it seems to me today, the way to 'myself', to *my* task' (*HH* II, Preface, 4). Effectively, Nietzsche prescribes for himself a process of estrangement which is itself an intensification of pain and suffering. He speaks of waging a war *with himself* and against the pessimism of weariness with life in order to return to himself *once again*.

This is to exhibit 'demonic existence' – the tendency of life to surpass itself eternally. By pushing thinking to its limit, by making pain the object of an affirmation, a different possibility of life emerges. We repeat in order to liberate ourselves from the form of 'the same'. In 'The Convalescent' chapter of *Thus Spoke Zarathustra*, the teacher is presented as one 'returning to himself' after choking with disgust at the prospect of the eternal return of all that is lowly and reactive. The unmasterable task of 'representing' a thought that can only be felt and literally incorporated now falls to 'art' and particularly the art of beautiful illusion. Zarathustra's animals insist that 'convalescents should sing' and the text concludes with sacred songs of affirmation to his soul, to life and to eternity (*TSZ* III, 'The Convalescent'). If 'knowledge chokes' it would seem that it is only through art that recovery will take place.

The exacerbation of pessimism is not a dialectical passage of opposites into one another. To exacerbate pessimism means to deny all that was previously cherished, to enact rather than merely enunciate scepticism in relation to every fundamental conviction. In place of truth, Nietzsche speaks in the prefaces of cultivating a truthfulness – an excess of honesty – which means to go beyond merely 'suspending' the *form* of belief and to take the nihilistic will to know to its limit. It is only by means of this escape from all that is human that the convalescent is able to 'live experimentally'. Finally, drawing near to life again, the convalescent sees the world anew:

> [W]here *had* he been? These near and nearest things: how changed they seem! What bloom and magic they have acquired! He looks back gratefully – grateful to his wandering, to his hardness and self-alienation, to his viewing of far distances and bird flights in cold heights [....] He had been *outside* himself no doubt of that. (*HH* I, Preface, 5)

The free spirit draws near to life again as if returning from death. Indeed, what else could the liberation from one's entire hitherto signify? Nietzsche's convalescence marks the experience of sacrifice of self – an ecstatic annihilation greatly reminiscent of the downgoing of the tragic Dionysian hero. But this does not mean that one returns to the self one has left as if having momentarily taken leave of one's senses. One senses the world quite otherwise, as if having acquired new perceptive organs. In drawing near to life the convalescent literally re-encounters existence anew for *everything* is transfigured including the one who experiences it. The gratitude expressed for this painful self-estrangement indicates how, paradoxically, affirmation of sickness is crucial to its overcoming.

In Dostoyevsky's *The Idiot*, Prince Myshkin's epileptic fit is finally brought on when the brooding storm-cloud that had covered the sky bursts in torrents. He lets out a dreadful scream, his face becomes distorted and spasms and convulsions seize his entire body. Dostoyevsky writes that in that scream 'everything human seems suddenly to be obliterated' and one gets the impression that there is someone inside the man who is screaming (*I* 252). The horror – and the 'blinding *inner* light' that floods his soul – 'has something mystical about it' (ibid.). Similarly, the shepherd in 'Of the Vision and the Riddle', after the horror and convulsions of choking on the snake and biting off its head, springs up 'a transformed being, surrounded with light' laughing with a laughter which is 'not human' (*TSZ* III, 'Of The Vision and the Riddle').

That Nietzsche was captivated by the transfiguring, 'mystic' power of 'epileptic insight' is indicated by his inclusion of the whole of Kirilov's speech from Dostoyevsky's *The Devils* in his private note-book. What is so fascinating about this speech is the intimation that affirmation of the whole is so intensely joyful it is unbearable. One would have to *undergo a physical change to bear it*:

> There are seconds – they come five or six at a time – then you suddenly feel the presence of eternal harmony in all its fullness. Man in his mortal frame cannot endure it; he must either physi-cally transform himself or die. It is a lucid and ineffable feeling. You seem to be in contact with the whole of nature and you say: 'Yes, this is true!' God, when He created the world, said at the end of each day: 'Yes, it is true, it is good.' It is not emotion, it is joy. You forgive nothing because there is nothing to forgive. Nor do you really love anything – oh, this feeling is much higher than love! The most terrible thing is the horrific *certainty* with which it expresses itself and the joy with which it fills one. If it lasted longer the soul could not endure it, it would have to disap-pear – In these five seconds I would live the whole of human existence, I would give my life for it, the price would not be too high. In order to bear this any longer one would have to trans-form oneself physically. (*KSA* 13/11[337])

One must become embodied otherwise to survive this unbearable joy. To live the whole of human existence would be to bear the weight of transversal, transhuman connections on a cosmic scale. We recall the demon's words: 'If this thought possessed you it would change you as you are or perhaps crush you' (*GS* 341). Perhaps to think eternal return we have to develop 'new organs', to sharpen and multiply the senses beyond those privileged in cogni-tion. We need a sense for the tragic, a sense for climate, for electric-ity, for new forces, new philosophical problems. What eternal return will be for us is a matter of what we will be for it – what we shall be capable of embodying. Our philosophy of ecstasy seeks to cultivate these conditions for new thoughts, to discover the organs for new affects. Like the genius who has seen too much, like the madman who senses the whole in the moment, one would feel oneself to be a part of a fluctuating, mutating order that is unmasterable, unknowable. Yet, in the words of Schreber: 'In all these matters, the human being must attempt to disregard their petty and, so to speak, in-bred, geocentric ideas and consider the matter from the lofty viewpoint of eternity' (*DNK* 38–9, *MNI* 73).

If Scheber's lavish cosmic encounters and Dostoyevsky's vision of 'eternal harmony' retain an air of the mysticism of the 'other-worldlings', it must be remembered that the 'divine' forces accessed by these psychonauts are of 'this' world. The collapse of what are after all only the most *common* forms of thinking and sensing need not consign philosophy to mute inspection of the ineffable. Indeed, aesthetics considered as applied physiology indicates something monstrously sacred and far more dangerous.

6
The Night of Unknowing

> ...to put it mystically, the path to one's own heaven always
> leads through the voluptuousness of one's own hell.
>
> *(The Gay Science* 338)

The insolence of an existence that we are unqualified to master may
tempt us either to philosophy or to mysticism, the first to convince
us of the transcendence of human spirit, the second to transcend
even this conviction. If knowledge functions to shield us from the
firestorms of extra-human experience, mystic *unknowing* is the fate
of an all-too-brilliant lucidity. According to Nietzsche, the prejudice
that life is *explicable*, even 'correctible' is the monstrous legacy of
Socrates – who physiologically speaking 'might be described as typically *non-mystic*' (*BT* 13). The 'opponent' of tragic art and the sacred
rites of the Dionysian, Socrates is presented by Nietzsche as the
supreme antithesis of the hierophant, rivalling the excessive
'instinctual wisdom' of the latter through an irrepressible faith in
the power of reason. Yet it is by means of this belief and not in spite
of it that Nietzsche sees a new possibility of thinking emerge. It is by
conducting the Socratic 'will to know' to its self-annihilating limit
that he envisages a rebirth of myth – 'the necessary prerequisite of
every religion' (*BT* 18). The question is how the 'one great Cyclops
eye of Socrates' that has never glowed with artistic enthusiasm, has
never known the pleasures of gazing into the Dionysian abyss,
might be turned back upon its own desire to illuminate what eludes
it (*BT* 14). This is not simply so that it would welcome myth and
mystery as a cure for vision 'damaged by gruesome night' for the

curious aspect about this remedy is its failure to 'redeem' (*BT* 9). The 'tragic cure' – Apollinian *Schein* – ceases to veil and comes to *reflect* life's gratuitous expenditure (nature's 'contrapurposivity'). If the becoming-ecstatic of philosophy involves a reintensification of nihilism it seems that suffering is to be made creative *once again*.

It is scarcely a contentious point to acknowledge that Platonic-Christian thinking has enjoyed a monopoly on the spiritualization of suffering unrivalled by any other cultural force in two millennia. According to Nietzsche, the greatest triumph of the 'ascetic ideal' has been to lend a meaning to affliction – one inspired by the Socratic evaluation of existence as fundamentally perverse and reprehensible. The claim that Christianity stands opposed to 'the tonic affects which heighten the energy of the feeling of life [*Lebensgefühl*]' is one of the most insistent in Nietzsche's philosophy (*A* 7). The 'ill-constituted' who pose as the 'healthy', slander existence for its unintelligibility and arrant indifference to the needs of the human, then prosecute their *ressentiment* in their nihilistic moral values. Yet Nietzsche never looks to other-worldly analgesia as a recompense for the vicissitudes of fate, nor does he regard suffering as an argument against existence. To the extent that the relation between adversity and philosophy is approached here in terms of *value for life*, physical torment, including the self-cruelty of asceticism, is never regarded as self-evidently objectionable. Indeed, Nietzsche indicates that tragic wisdom is the prism through which the consecration of suffering is ultimately to be realized. In identifying esoteric Mystery rites of sacrifice as the well-spring of tragedy, he affirms the eternal sanctification of pain (*TI*, 'What I Owe to the Ancients', 4; *BT*, 10).

Whereas the 'ill-constituted' narrow the ambit of spirituality to moral revenge, the supremely healthy are capable of 'experiencing [*empfinden*] a kind of *deification of the body* in themselves and are as distant as possible from the ascetic philosophy of the proposition "God is a spirit"' (*WP* 1051). It would not be inappropriate to cite Schreber as a somewhat exotic exemplar of this tendency, particularly if we recall Nietzsche's genealogical criteria for great health. Health in this context is not opposed to sickness: it is figured in terms of '*how much of the sickly it can take on and overcome*' (*WP* 1013). As a 'convalescent,' Nietzsche depicts himself as one destined to 'be sicker than any other kind of individual' for this is to 'know the way to a *new* health' (*HH* II, Preface, 6). This is a knowledge of a 'carnal' kind (as hazardous and unscriptable as any erotic initiation). Indeed, it is via a spiritualization of the passions that Nietzsche anticipates using the energy of asceticism against itself, just as he sees the intensification of the Socratic thirst for knowledge as having transformative effects. Voiced as an attempt to '*overcome* everything Christian through something supraChristian and not merely to dismiss it', Nietzsche announces a reappropriation of the sacred for philosophy (*WP* 1051).

It is notable that for Nietzsche this reappropriation is an aesthetic endeavour. The exacerbation of nihilism, in both its metaphysical and monotheological guises, leads to artistic concerns or what more generally we might term 'sensitive knowing'. In 'The Physiology of Art' notes, he lists the 'ecstasy of religious feeling' as one of the sovereign states in which 'we infuse a *transfiguration and fullness* into things and poetize about them until they reflect back our own fullness and joy with life' (*WP* 801). Religious feeling of this order is aligned with the 'tonic affects' of art and its life-enhancing power: 'art is essentially *affirmation, blessing, deification* [**Vergöttlichung**] *of existence...*' (*WP* 821). Since the exalted feeling of intoxication refines, multiplies and augments the senses – and is rekindled by expressions of its potency to new expressions of itself – it is symptomatic of the fecundity of life as such. Indeed, not only do these excitations reproduce themselves (furthering the 'feeling of life') they simultaneously cross-fertilize, provoking internal resonances across the affective plenum:

> All these elevated moments of life mutually stimulate one another; the world of images and ideas of one is sufficiently suggestive for the others... to such an extent that finally states grow into one another which might have reason to remain foreign. For example: the religious feeling of ecstasy [*das religiöse Rauschgefühl*] and sexual excitation (two profound feelings miraculously almost practically co-ordinated...). (*WP* 800)

In a similar vein, Bataille writes that the saint turns from the voluptuary in alarm: 'she does not know that his unacknowledged passions and her own are really one' (*E* 7). In juxtaposing the mystical with the erotic, Bataille describes his philosophy as one that 'reveals the co-ordination of these potentialities' and which without identifying them with one another, seeks to locate 'the point where they might converge beyond their mutual exclusiveness' (ibid.). In this regard there are deep affinities between the respective inquiries of Bataille and Nietzsche. Both identify 'the sacred' as a site of affirmation of the primary prodigality of nature, and both see sexuality as its most potent symbol. For Nietzsche this is expressed in tragedy,[1] for Bataille in eroticism more generally. In describing the 'concept of the mystic' as 'one who has enough, who has too much of his own happiness and seeks a language for his happiness – out of a desire *to give it away*' (KSA 11/79/25[258]), Nietzsche associates sacred affectivity with the fundamental tendency of life to squander its riches – a process that Bataille makes central to his own theory of non-productive expenditure. Furthermore, the Dionysian affirmation of 'this world' is seen by Nietzsche as a celebration of life – not simply as eternal fruitfulness and recurrence but as torment, destruction and annihilation, themes which again Bataille echoes in his examination of eroticism and 'ferocious religion' (*WP* 1052; *VE* 179). Indeed, Nietzsche tells us that the striving of the Dionysian worldview for expression (a striving which 'lives on' in the Mysteries) manifests itself in the 'most miraculous metamorphoses and degenerations' – phenomena which hold a devastating allure for Bataille (*BT* 17). However, it is significant that Nietzsche's question to this 'striving' should imply a desire for its sublimation: 'Will it not some day rise once again out of its mystic depths as art?' (ibid.). This is where the profound similarities cease and the divergence between the two thinkers begins to emerge.

Unlike Bataille, Nietzsche appears to locate the transformative potential of religious affectivity within the dimension of the aesthetic rather than in the more orthodox sites of spirituality, thereby calling into question the extent to which the overcoming of Christianity through something supraChristian is to be attempted. The affirmative reappropriation of Christian mysticism, particularly of the *unio mystica*, is a possibility seemingly rejected by Nietzsche, but it is not clear whether this is on account of the 'slave' values associated with individuality, with unity or with God, or indeed with all three. In *On the Genealogy of Morals*, Nietzsche likens 'mystical union' with deep sleep and hypnosis (*GM* III, 17) and declares that 'the longing for a *unio mystica* with God is the longing of the

Buddhist for nothingness, Nirvana – and no more!' (*GM* I, 6). Given that it is in this context that his remarks concerning the 'spiritual disturbances' exhibited by mystics are discussed, it is reasonable to assume that the 'auditory and visual hallucinations' and the 'voluptuous outpourings and ecstasies of sensuality (the case of Saint Teresa),' which are mentioned here, are to be counted as mere outcrops of Christian nihilism – symptoms of an *anaesthetic* physiological regime designed to 'reduce the feeling of life in general to the lowest point' (*GM* III, 17). This said, Nietzsche does acknowledge that Saint Teresa of Ávila is exemplary of those natures that love danger, adventure, opposition – indeed everything that induces *self-risk* as a means of heightening the feeling of power (*KSA* 12/569/10[188]). Yet if the mystical way is passed over all too fleetingly, this may be because the 'unitive life' is seen as too conceptually overdetermined by ascetic ideals or, more controversially, because of a failure to see the subversive philosophical potential of *feminine* eroticism. Perhaps it is not so difficult to see why the prospect of 'melting into God' would make the writer of *The Anti-Christ* wince but the pursuit of a philosophy of ecstasy may yet find intriguing resources in this most unexpected of sites.

Becoming divine

In a text from 1939, Bataille writes that mystical and ecstatic states cannot do without certain extremes against the self: 'To give up my sexual habits,' he complains, 'would mean I'd have to discover some other means of tormenting myself' (*G* 22). In splintered prose of excruciating beauty, Bataille's atheological writings present a sustained meditation on the *experience* of ecstasy. Despite linking art to sacred expenditure, Bataille does not develop the relation between *the mystical* and the aesthetic, rejecting poetic discourse as a substitute for 'actual ecstasies'.[2] Choosing instead to mine the rich seam of religious eroticism pursued by Christian saints, martyrs and visionaries, he announces in *Inner Experience* an inner necessity to challenge everything without permissible rest, an ardent thirst to 'voyage to the end of the possible of man' (*IE* 7). In the hope of letting experience lead where it will rather than to some end-point given in advance, Bataille seeks to go beyond the limits of knowing, to 'emerge through project from the realm of project' (*IE* 46).

Striving for insight, when taken to this limit, has strangely inflammatory effects.

> Determination is necessary if a person is to endure a light so blinding, if you're not to experience empty understanding [....] To remain a man in the light requires the courage of demented incomprehension; it means being set on fire, letting go with screams of joy, waiting for death, acting in a realization of some presence you don't and can't know. It means becoming love and blind light, yourself, and attaining the perfect incomprehension of the sun. (*G* 20)

Cleaving to life with steely resolution while succumbing to the searing implosions of *incomprehending vision* describes a very different kind of philosophical 'method', one which seeks to allow an experience of intensity to flare up in thought. This process must proceed through a paradoxical determination, a determination to 'surrender' the habits which would protect us from confronting the unknown. While of the view that 'philosophy is often pointless, an unpleasant way of employing minor talents', Bataille approves of its destabilizing tendencies, its passion for sacred (non-utile) quests (*G* 128). Moreover, he believes that reason alone has the power to undo its work, 'to hurl down what it has built up' (*IE* 46). Pushed beyond its limited powers of illumination, the philosophical will to know yields to the harsh incandescence of mystic unknowing. Philosophy, it would seem, is the very last means of tormenting himself that Bataille is prepared to relinquish.

In exploring the effects of 'experience laid bare' Bataille continues to refine a philosophy of unknowing commenced in the conscientious researches of early Christian mysticism. Dedicating themselves absolutely to the cause of communicating God's grace, the intrepid pioneers of this movement submitted their minds and bodies to agonizing experiment, meticulously recording the affective traumas induced by contact with the divine. The 'undoing' of the 'normative' body which plays such a central role in Nietzsche's thinking of ecstasy is detailed in these mystical testimonies in ways which point far beyond the ascetic values of self-negation and spiritual redemption. What appears to typify an otherwise heterogeneous group of accounts is the accent placed upon the sacrifice of self-knowledge as

a precursor to the 'unitive life'. This ranges from a carefully cultivated contemplative autism (in which external stimuli, particularly
the *visual*, are systematically screened out) to violent paroxysms of
self-annihilation in which every vestige of will, reason and understanding are ruthlessly crushed. While it is entirely plausible to
follow Nietzsche's suggestion in *On the Genealogy of Morals* that
these are symptoms of a will to nothingness, the thirst for sacrifice
may equally flow from an affirmation of life, as the Dionysian
Mysteries clearly demonstrate.

That the 'blinding' and abasement of self should yield both
insight and beatitude is one of the enduring enigmas of mystical
experience. It is precisely through the abdication of knowledge,
through the liquidation of its conditions of possibility, that 'divinity' is touched. Like Hildegard of Bingen, mystics such as Saint
Teresa frequently speak about that which cannot be 'pictured' by
the imagination or 'bodily eye' but this is no more the absence of
knowledge than night is the absence of day. What the 'bodily eye'
fails to perceive it arguably fails to 'know' – at least this would seem
to be the case in a predominantly 'scopic' economy. Yet mystic
'unknowing' inaugurates a philosophical trajectory which bypasses
the logic of self-reflexive subjectivity, plunging representational
thought into the vortex of night. What appears to be stammering
for expression in the beguiling simplicity of mystic utterance is the
thought that contact with the divine is *inhuman*. The 'night of
unknowing' is not a clouded reason. It is a passage into a realm of
the *unconditioned unknown* which reason can do nothing but cloud.

It was noted at the outset that for Nietzsche knowing and becoming exclude one another (*WP* 517). Because philosophy is unable to
adequately articulate the 'continuity of life' in its available concepts
('formulas for that which remains the same'), epistemology in its
various configurations remains of necessity a discourse about
'beings'. In posing the question of how a 'subject' comes to know an
'object', a relation of self-present 'knower' to given 'known' is
instantiated and the question of the *production* of each systematically evaded. In transcendental philosophy the supposition that
objects exist ontologically prior to the thinking which constitutes
them is submitted to critique, yet Kant's noumenon – a darkness
which theoretical cognition is unable to illuminate – remains in
principle an unknown 'object' in default of representation. So long

as the unknown is conditioned by the known, mystical awareness of 'God' must be thought of privatively, a limit point for knowing. As Bataille maintains, the intellectual apprehension of God is an obstacle in the encounter with the *unknown* for it captures divinity within the mirror of ego-identification – the order of the object:

> If I say decisively: 'I have seen God', that which I see would change. Instead of the inconceivable unknown – wildly free before me, leaving me wild and free before it – there would be a dead object and the thing of the theologian – to which the unknown would be subjugated .... (*IE* 4)

If what impacts in mystic *unknowing* is refractory to categories of the understanding, it must be thought beyond the terms of the subject–object relation. Yet this is problematic for any understanding of mystical experience which seems to presuppose precisely such a condition. Even if the fusion of self and Other in the 'oneness' of religious ecstasy signals the defeat of representational thinking, it is still, by definition, bound by it and thinkable only in its terms. But perhaps the potency of mystic *communication* lies in its illegibility within the discourse of human knowing. The question is whether it is possible to understand contact with alterity in the absence of an *image* of thought.

In her philosophical exploration of female mysticism, Irigaray succeeds in evading the presuppositions of speculative thinking by 'mimicking' or *repeating* its gestures. Inspired by the confessional writings of figures such as Saint Teresa, she explores the thought that rapturous delight or *jouissance* marks the subtraction of representable unity from the self–other relation and a *return* of the base materiality of the unknown. Although she is deeply sceptical of the values underpinning Nietzsche's imagery of ecstasy,[3] there are surprising parallels between themes in her 1974 essay 'La Mystérique' and Nietzsche's reflections on an affirmative yet inhuman[4] *feeling of life*. According to Irigaray, mystical experience is one of the rare sites in patriarchal history in which women's activity is more publicly recognized and highly prized than that of men. As a locus for tracking the migration of the self–other relation from philosophy it is of particular interest because it exposes the limitations of 'deconstructive' gestures for a philosophy of ecstasy. Irigaray contends that any theory of subjectivity 'has always been appropriated by the "masculine"' so one might assume that this *includes* theories of ego-loss to the extent that they presuppose the masculine subject which they foresake (*SA* 165, *SW* 133). Given that the 'feminine' is already 'outside' this economy, the ecstasy of the female mystic might now be read as flight from identity to the second power and not as a necessary stage on a path towards its redefinition. This is at least implied by Irigaray's suggestion that the mystic blazes a trail for thinking which is defined purely through its own movement, 'tending towards no perceptible end' (*SA* 241, *SW* 194). In the name of female mysticism, Irigaray conducts philosophical discourse to its own heart of darkness: an abyss appears at the point where the omnipotence of 'phallocentrism' is to be confirmed in the supremacy of God as self-reflecting ego-ideal. In this 'dark night' consciousness, understanding, form and reason have little worth and actually constitute obstacles to *jouissance* (*SA* 238, *SW* 191). A semiotics of subjectivity gives way to a libidinal energetics of desire. Philosophy submits to autocritique, begins to smoulder.

Reminiscent of Nietzsche's remarks about the 'coarse organs' of perception, Irigaray suggests that the mystic's gaze is all too accustomed to seeing reflections of her cultural milieu and that her eye 'actually hides what she is seeking' (*SA* 240, *SW* 193). Since the eye is 'already guardian to reason' the mystic's first imperative is to 'get away unseen' from the 'matrix of speculation' (*SA* 239, *SW* 192). She wanders randomly and in darkness, with no map or compass points to guide her.

It is *the very shadow of her gaze* that must now be looked at [*reparcourir*]. Night [again] for all sensible vision, [again] for all solar vision, through a bedazzlement that would condemn this star itself to repent its sufficiency. Night [again], above all, for all intelligible speculation, for all theoretical contemplation, even that upon Being itself. (*SA* 240, *SW* 193)

Night is looked upon but not *seen* so long as it exists as an *object* of speculation – so long as it is captured in the telescopic lens of inquiry. Much the same could be said of the 'feminine' so long as it is viewed as a background for projections of 'masculinity'. As is well

known, Irigaray contends that the construction of masculine subjectivity is dependent upon imaging the feminine as its negative *alter
ego* and hence that the feminine functions as a 'mirror' which
confirms the social and sexual identity of masculinity as 'self-
sufficient'. One of Irigaray's abiding preoccupations is to challenge
the *oculocentric* bias of the Western philosophical tradition and to
expose the 'invisibility' of the feminine (the 'dark continent')
within its optics.[5] Such a project resonates with Heideggerian
themes (the forgetting of difference) but it has a more Nietzschean
dimension in its *mystical aspect* which is thought here in terms of a
repetition of escape. Rather than seeking to illuminate the 'blind
spot' in a philosophical symbolics (in which woman represents the
horror of 'nothing to be seen') Irigaray's strategy is to *intensify* its
darkness. Reluctant to confine woman as *other-to-the-same* within its
specular logic she invokes an *other* mirror for thinking, one no
longer implicated within the dialogics of resemblance.

In a strategy which bears comparison with Nietzsche's reintensification of nihilism, Irigaray proposes that the mystic submit
herself to 'obscurity' once again. Deprived of any focal point for her
gaze, whether of *telos*, Godhead or self, the only possibility that she
has is to 'advance further into the night until it becomes a transver-
berating beam of light, a luminous shadow' (*SA* 240, *SW* 193). She
pushes onward 'into a *touch* that opens the "soul" again to divine
contact' and to the wounding impact of searing light (ibid.). To feel
a luminosity beyond the clarity of day she must sink into the night,
plunge into the starless pool with such abandon that it eclipses
itself: night *appears*. Beyond a dialectic of presence and absence, too
neatly required by the dictates of signification, night emerges as an
active principle. In Irigaray's lexicon this willful submission to the
'night' is tantamount to '*crossing back through the mirror that subtends
all speculation*' (*CS* 75, *TS* 77). Instead of fighting for an autonomy
historically denied to her, the mystic deepens and augments her
'feminine role'. This means to 'resubmit herself – inasmuch as she is
aligned with the side of the "perceptible," of "matter" – to "ideas,"
in particular to ideas about herself, that are elaborated in/by masculine logic' in order to 'make visible' through 'repetition', what was
supposed to remain invisible: the '*elsewhere of "matter"*' (*CS* 74,
TS 76). Mimicking the association of the feminine with matter,
Irigaray seeks to problematize the terrain upon which speculations

about the subject are erected. As she says, 'mother-matter-nature must go on forever nourishing speculation' yet in so far as 'man' forms his *alter ego* out of matter, woman-as-matter remains in excess of any particular fashioning: 'this resource is also rejected as the refuse of reflection, cast outside as what resists it: like madness' (*CS* 74, *TS* 77). Intriguingly, many female mystics actually identify themselves with refuse and waste matter. For example, Saint Teresa frequently refers to herself as 'muddy water', a 'sea of wickedness', 'a foul and stinking dunghill' – in short a vile creature mired in the elemental (*LST* 130, 125, 75). Yet Irigaray's argument is that to 'deliberately assume' the role of the feminine is 'already to convert subordination into affirmation and by that fact to begin to thwart it' (*CS* 73–4, *TS* 76). In short, through this *productive repetition* the materiality of thought is re-engaged and re-activated. The lifeless 'matter' that had been frozen into phallomorphic *imagos* is liquefied once more.

> That *'elsewhere' of female pleasure* might [..] be sought in the place where it sustains ek-stasy in the transcendental. The place where it serves as backing for a narcissism extrapolated into the 'God' of men. (*CS* 74, *TS* 74)

Crossing back through the mirror, cutting through its tain, 'would allow woman to rediscover the place of her "self-affection." Of her "god," we might say'. (*CS* 75, *TS* 75)

Implicit within this cryptic remark is the thought that the touch that opens the 'soul' again to contact with divine force marks a *returning*: not a return *to* the base matter of the 'sex which is not one' but a returning *of* the conditions of its emergence. In this essay and in her work more generally, Irigaray explores the dynamic of female auto-affection as auto-eroticism, an idea which serves to reconfigure the corporeal coordinates of 'knowing'. In rethinking the transcendental as 'sensible' she takes the 'matter' of femininity as formative for thought. The autoerotic retouching (*retouche*) of the 'two lips' of feminine sexuality describes a libidinal experience of 'return': ' "she" also turns upon herself', 'she knows how to re-turn (upon herself)', (*SA* 167, *SW* 134). The 'encore' – the 'again and again' of feminine orgasmic bliss – is offered as a non-unitary, non-unifying 'model' for thought, one which she insists is resistant to the phallic forms of identity. This idea invites a comparison with Nietzsche's depiction of the Dionysian lyricist who is 'without any images, utter primordial pain and its primordial reverberation' (*BT* 5). Arguably, the difference between primordial pleasure and primordial pain in these respective contexts is not a decisive one (as we shall shortly see, Irigaray situates female mysticism within a savage eroticism of burning, wounding and laceration). This begs the question as to what extent ideas can be gendered rather than simply sexualized once an image of thought is relinquished. How is it possible – or indeed *is* it possible – to find another 'mirror' for thinking without falling prey to 'the dogmatic image of thought'? Everything now hinges on how *the experience of ecstasy as a sacred eroticism* is to materialize itself in philosophy.

The burning glass

In the 'Physiology of Art' notes Nietzsche writes that *love* is the most astonishing 'proof' of how far the 'transfiguring power of rapture' can reach (*WP* 808). Here, ecstasy has 'had done with reality' to such an extent that the 'cause' is extinguished and something else takes its place – 'a vibration and a gleaming of all the magic mirrors of Circe' (ibid.). He goes on to add that 'love, even the love of God, the saintly love of "redeemed souls"remains one in its roots: a fever that has grounds to transfigure itself, a rapture that does well to lie about itself' (ibid.). Again, he insists that what one encounters in love, even in the most angelic instinct, is '*art* as an organic function'. One does not merely seem 'more perfect', one becomes more perfect. In linking the transformative power of sacred 'love' to art, Nietzsche emphasizes an unconscious creativity, an affirmative will to power. This is an association echoed by Bergson who identifies mystic experience as *creative emotion*, a position also endorsed by Deleuze.[6] However, it could be argued that Irigaray and Bataille are able to explore the transfigurative potential of mystic ecstasy somewhat further than any of these thinkers because they seek to reappropriate Christianity from within its own cloisters and do so without making the move to art. Beyond exposing the libidinal affectivity that allows the contiguity between 'holy rapture' and sacred excitation to be remarked, Nietzsche does not see Christianity as offering a site for productive repetition and intensification. While exacerbating the nihilism of 'Socrates the non-mystic' points towards an artistic or tragic mysticism, such destructive intensification is promised but not fully realized in relation to Christian mysticism. Yet the latter, in its specificity, adds new elements to a philosophy of ecstasy. Irigaray and Bataille exploit the fact that the mystic way tends to pass through a number of stages from 'awakening' through 'purification' and 'illumination' to the 'dark night' which may precede the 'unitive life'. As a result, they are able to deepen the possibilities of *unknowing* as a potential *philosophical* trajectory.

Having awoken to the awareness of God, the mystic may experience a bewildering experience of estrangement from the 'social world' and, not unlike the genius or the schizophrenic, may find it increasingly difficult to 'reconnect' at this level. Unlike the latter, the exacerbation of this estrangement appears far more wilful, involving extreme acts of 'self-mortification'. The prelude to this process may take the form of an uncanny shutdown of the senses – a 'dark rapture'. Saint Teresa declares that in this state 'the faculties of the soul are asleep, not entirely lost nor yet entirely conscious of how they are working' (*LST* 112). The intellect is of 'no value' here, none of the faculties 'dare even to stir' and, if the will understands, 'it does not understand how it understands' (*LST* 113, 127). Irigaray evokes the mystic experience of 'expectant expectancy' and passive waiting in which no decision or project may obtrude (*SA* 242, *SW* 194). Yet this is also a time of extreme torment which bears all the hallmarks of a futile, unrequited passion. In the words of Saint Teresa:

> Ordain that I may have no part in the affairs of this world or take it from me entirely. This servant of Yours, O Lord, can no longer suffer such trials as come when it sees itself without You. If she must live, she wants no rest in this life – so give her none. The soul longs to be free. Eating is killing it, sleep brings it anguish. It sees itself wasting the hours of this life in comforts, though nothing can comfort it now but You. It seems to be living unnaturally, since now its desire is to live not in itself but in You. (*LST* 114)

Unbearable longing for the divine prompts the mystic to expend without reserve, severing all ties with the persons, properties and proprieties which populate her daylight. All worldly charm must be cast aside; indeed, everything that binds her to the brute laws of human preservation must be jettisoned. Wanton self-destruction becomes so inextricably bound up with desire that the boundaries between pleasure and pain become hopelessly blurred as each takes on the appearance of the other, reflecting back its features. 'Passive purgation' is consummated in a violent enucleation of the self. Indeed, to please God 'she would gladly have had herself cut to pieces, body and soul, to show the joy that she felt in that pain' (*LST* 113).

An anonymous fourteenth-century work of Christian mysticism, *The Cloud of Unknowing*, informs us that God is utterly beyond the scope of human understanding but He can be reached and 'known' through *love* (*CU* 63). Yet this is desire of an alien dimension. Without any love object *in view* the lover drifts free of all narcissistic identifications. As Irigaray remarks, this is 'a jouissance so extreme, a love so incomprehensible, an illumination so unbounded that un-knowledge (*nescience*) becomes desire' (*SA* 242, *SW* 194–5). Indeed, everything now depends on the strength of 'desire' since God 'is a jealous lover, and will brook no rival' (*CU* 60). Should one attempt to behold God intellectually, failure is guaranteed. In order to be a 'perfect lover' one must 'trample' down all knowledge and feeling of anything less than God and strive to forget not only the lures and distractions of daily life but to *forget oneself entirely* (*CU* 110).

> So crush all knowledge and experience of all forms of created things, and of yourself above all. For it is on your own self-knowledge and experience that the knowledge and experience of everything else depend. Alongside this self-regard everything else is quickly forgotten. For if you will take the trouble to test it, you will find that when all other things and activities have been forgotten (even your own) there still remains between you and God the stark awareness of your own existence. And this awareness, too, must go, before you experience contemplation in its perfection. (*CU* 111)

When one gazes into the abyss of night, its terrifying vacancy fatally rebounds. As Bataille acknowledges, in the spark of ecstasy the necessary subject/object terminals are consumed: 'This means that as the subject is destroyed in meditation, the object (god or God) is also a dying victim' (*G* 45). When both self and other are annihilated in ecstatic bliss, 'each becomes the other in consumption, the nothing of the other in consummation' (*SA* 244, *SW* 196). Yet for Irigaray, this fusion of the mystic with God is 'a more abyssal unity than the still, already, speculative unity that subtends the sense of these wrenching contradictions' (ibid.). Both *la mystérique* and God are in *excess* of representation, their intercourse a 'marriage of the unknowable'. This is not a sublation of contraries (nor a variant of negative theology) but an autoerotic touching, a *jouissance* of a 'soul' to which '"God" alone descends when he has renounced modes and attributes' (ibid.).

How Irigaray's thought of sacred ecstasy resists a metaphysical or dialectical moment of unity now begins to emerge. By exacerbating the 'lacking', negative 'abyssal' role accorded to her, the mystic succeeds in liberating a primary plenitude – 'a sweet unrest' which 'cannot contain itself' (*LST* 113). Her sex which is 'not one' (deficient, 'castrated') is made the site of a limitless eroticism (not 'one' but multiple). In this sense, both Irigaray and Nietzsche succeed in thinking 'from the abyss of being'. In the absence of an image of thought, Irigaray's libidinal dynamic marks the upsurge of a primary differentiation akin to Nietzsche's figuration of Dionysian intensities. The immersion of the divine into feminine matter is experienced as an extreme eroticism within which the castrated 'non-sex' of woman retouches the primary productivity of base materiality. The beginnings of a feminine libidinal erotics takes the form of a primary return, returning *on itself* to make a difference materialize. The mystic's fusion with 'God' – thought carnally as a feminine self-reflection/affection – is no more a union of 'beings' or a becoming-One than is the Dionysian. Her ecstasy marks a libidinal returning of the indetermination of 'dark matter' – a process utterly inassimilable to idealist formulation. In this sense her retouching rebounds in an *other* mirror, a 'living mirror' which 'reflects' in its darkness, the embrace of her sex with itself, already one and two: lips in intimate caress (*SA* 245, *SW* 245). No externalization in Apollinian clarity is envisaged – although again, it could be said that the notion of 'illumination from within' constitutes a sympathetic parallel.

Perhaps it suffices to invoke the sexual ambiguity of the Dionysian to reinforce these affinities between Irigaray and

Nietzsche. Yet for Irigaray, to conflate their ideas would be to conceal the otherness of the feminine within Western thought. Arguably, she offers a different thought of the 'outside' and renders the invisibility of the feminine a *tangible* force in its own right. In this, she does far more than merely mark the intrusion of feminine matter into thought, she makes it proliferate and reproduce itself. The burning passion of the mystic for her 'God' is deemed unaccountable within the guarded discourse of representational philosophy which reduces 'ones' to 'One' and fails to register 'zero' but Irigaray intimates that the mystic's 'light' warms rather than illuminates and that this light is suited 'to the lone mirror, *and* its virtual reduplication' (*SA* 247, *SW* 197). Perhaps this is why 'woman' takes pleasure from the 'incompleteness of form of her sex' which allows her 'to touch herself over and over again, indefinitely' (*CS* 26, *TS* 26). Perhaps too this is why in the blackest of nights the mystic intensifies her abjection, her non-being, in order to make her absence palpable. According to Irigaray, the female mystic will take on the most servile of tasks, abase herself 'over and again' until finally she is 'purified' – 'having dared to repeat to the extreme point this abjection, this disgust, this horror to which she was condemned and to which mimetically she condemned herself' (*SA* 248, *SW* 199). In her 'return' to 'matter' *she passes through zero*. The wound of her 'castrated' sex communicates with the 'gaping slit' in the body of the lacerated Son who in his crucifixion opens up a path of redemption to her in her fallen state (*SA* 249, *SW* 200). To 'know' her 'God' Irigaray claims she only needs to feel the touch of those 'lips' that wordlessly bind her in His love. Is this not to succeed in 'deifying the body in itself', to recall Nietzsche's phrase? In the mystic the word is *made flesh* in order to enable her to become God in her *jouissance*. And thus, like Saint Teresa, she calls out for the dart which, while piercing through her body, will with the same stroke tear out her entrails. She is divinely transfigured in her love, not through the perfection and enhancement of life but through the sanctification of imperfections – which in their indeterminacy and incompletion mark the opening of philosophy to an *other* outside.

The burning eye

For Bataille, the excessive libidinal outpourings of mystic ecstasy express a 'love so rapturous only torment could fuel it', the sweet ecstasy of becoming inhuman to which Saint Teresa became so monstrously addicted (*G* 11). The erotic imagery of piercing, penetrating and violating threads through the discourse of medieval mysticism like a mainline artery, binding a community of self-abusers in common. Even when the author of *The Cloud of Unknowing* recommends a coyness on the part of God's suitor, eschewing the 'violence of emotional reaction', it is with a view to tying 'the spiritual knot of burning love' between self and God (*CU* 116). Ultimately, whether flagellated to distraction or mortified into insensate pulp, the tributaries of the mystic way flow into the same river of death. For vitality finds its essential unity with fatality in its orgasmic death throes, the only 'point' at which contact may be made. Both Irigaray and Bataille invoke the mystic experience of 'dying from not dying' – the torment of a protracted anticipation and unconsummated desire in which death is tasted again and again.[7] As Saint Teresa expresses it:

> Nothing gave me satisfaction, and I could not contain myself; I really felt as if my soul were being torn from me. O supreme cunning of the Lord, with what delicate skill did You work on Your miserable slave! You hid Yourself from me, and out of Your love You afflicted me with so delectable a death that my soul desired it never to cease. (*LST* 208)

To die *incessantly* is to taste the deep communion of sacred love which opens like a wound in being. For this is a love which binds only by wrenching the conditions of 'unity' asunder. Such a notion might be thought of as the dissolution of representable unity – the passage from the determination of the 'One' to the indeterminacy of 'zero' or pre-unitary intensity. Yet far from the haemorrhaging of 'originary' subjectivity, what the 'returning of' matter signifies is the renewed production of the lunge towards dissolution. On the brink of collapse, the soul is plunged into 'death-like yearnings' and 'is like a person with a rope round his neck, who is strangling but tries to take breath' (*LST* 140, 141). Asphyxiating on the absolute, Saint Teresa begs her lover to exacerbate her torture: 'I long to suffer like this for the rest of my life, although the pain is so extreme as to be nearly unbearable' (*LST* 140). Life overcomes itself in its thanatropic urges, differentiates itself in its perpetually reintensified drive towards the lips of the abyss. Divine contact enters like death through this 'wound' and love emerges as the 'overlapping of two lacerations' (*G* 30). Perhaps this is why the mystic must unmake herself, become a 'dirty pool', a 'sea of wickedness', and in her raptures, which vary in intensity, attain once again a blissful undoing, peaking like a wave which already affects itself in its upswell and undertow. Her imageless *jouissance* marks the perpetually re-intensified rebounding of inhuman desire, emerging 'again and again' from zero – the blind spot in the night of unknowing. In the ecstasy of holy union the mystic constitutes her own distance from herself as 'indefinitely other' (*CS* 28, *TS* 28). Alien yet continuous with itself, alterity is *touched*, skewered on the spit of a flaming spear.

As Irigaray's elaborations on the theme of female mysticism indicate, ecstasy is poorly interpreted from the perspective of the philosophy of representation. Any attempt to encapsulate ecstatic experience in discourse is inevitably a casualty of mystic night. For Irigaray, the 'feminine' is a question of felt proximity, not metaphoricity, indeed, any mediation would risk 'deferring the fleeting *moment*' of her rapture (*SA* 244, *SW* 195). Here, Irigaray is at her most distant from deconstructive philosophy and humanist concerns about representational politics. Famously, Lacan pontificates on Bernini's sculpture of Saint Teresa: 'You only have to go and look at Bernini's statue in Rome to understand immediately that she's coming'[8] – a remark which begs the question of whose desire is actually being talked about (*CS* 89, *TS* 91). For the Lacan of this remark to *see* is to *know* and to know is to seize the elusive [*insaisissable*] moment. Once ecstasy is caught in the voyeur's glass, it is already 'different and deferred', a re-presentation and (mis)recognition which renders the unknown spuriously intelligible once again.

Representational thinking petrifies mystic passion into a pillar of eternal presence, repressing its continuity with the opaque, feminine matter from which all cognitive discourse issues and returns. Yet as the testimony of the mystics avers, intellectual faculties are supererogatory in contact with the divine. Mystic ecstasy, in its purgatorial deviations from itself, resists the *stasis* that theoretical reason implies. Thus if 'knowledge' of the divine is possible, it is only attainable at the elusive moment of self-loss. In Bataille's meditations it is the *anguish* of unknowing which is experienced as the motor of intensification for this perpetual self-overcoming.

> If the proposition (non-knowledge lays bare) possesses a sense – appearing, then disappearing immediately thereafter – this is because it has the meaning: NON-KNOWLEDGE COMMUNI-CATES ECSTASY. Non-knowledge is ANGUISH before all else. In anguish, there appears a nudity which puts one into ecstasy. But ecstasy itself is elusive if anguish is elusive. Thus ecstasy only remains possible in the anguish of ecstasy, in this sense that it cannot be satisfaction, *grasped knowledge*. Obviously, ecstasy is *grasped knowledge* above all else, in particular in […] extreme sur-render [….] Barely have I known – entirely known – then surren-der in the realm of knowledge (where knowledge leaves me) is revealed, and anguish begins again. But anguish is the horror of surrender and the moment comes when, in audacity, surrender is loved, when I give myself to surrender: it is therefore the nudity which puts one into ecstasy. Then knowledge returns, satis-faction, once again anguish, I begin again, more quickly, right up to exhaustion [….] (*IE* 52)

Since for Bataille, ecstasy is experience 'laid bare, free of ties, even of an origin', the vertiginous spiralling and rebounding of unknow-ing is to be thought of as the unfounding of knowledge, rather than its privation (*IE* 3). Interpreted in this sense, the rebeginning of anguish does not mark the personal loss of self-knowledge but the impersonal knowledge of self–annihilation. Perhaps this is why the *return* of *la mystérique* to base matter never registers as the re-cognition of an origin ('she will never know it or herself *clearly*') but the exacerbation of departure, its reintensified return. The repetition of mystic abjection which Irigaray enunciates is echoed in Bataille's anguished recoil: 'I can only, I suppose, reach the extreme limit in repetition, for this reason, that I am never sure of having attained it, that I never will be sure' (*IE* 42).

Ecstasy is 'known' at the precise moment of knowledge's surren-der when experience is stripped of every remnant of self-intuiting subjectivity. As the author of *The Cloud of Unknowing* reminds us, only when personal existence has been thoroughly obliterated may

God's love be 'known'. As this utterly *inhuman* knowledge ebbs, anguish recommences but this does not signal a return *to* a former egoic state. Anguish constitutes *becoming inhuman once again*. In its tensile deviation from itself – dying from not dying – mystic ecstasy overcomes what it can only ever become in the night of unknowing. For if knowledge is 'grasped' in the elusive instant it is *night* which seizes it. It is unknowing which communicates ecstasy.

This is why the intercession of an intermediary defers the mystic voyage into the unknown. The spectator who speculates on divine *jouissance* inaugurates a self–other dialectic which effaces the primary impersonal self-differing of excruciating rapture. By contrast, for Bataille, 'full communication' is accessible only 'to the extent that existence successively strips itself of middle terms' (*IE* 116). Within the schema of epistemological positions, the 'I' gives a domesticated appearance to the universal, representing to itself the 'whole' in its own likeness whereas ecstasy is only 'possible' for the one who sacrifices the project of knowing. However, this anguished surrender of self is not a diffuse outflowing into an empty, indefinite expanse 'where everything is drowned' but an enigmatic *repetition of self-loss* which substitutes the object of knowledge for 'an object of a different nature' (*IE* 117, 120). Proposing that this object in experience is at first the projection of a 'dramatic loss of self' Bataille goes on to suggest that because the self 'leaves itself' in love it projects itself as a vertiginous point 'ostensibly containing inwardly that which the world harbours as heartrending' (*IE* 117, 118). This redoubling of self–loss lends to existence both its tormented and erotic character: 'Who amongst us does not dream of breaking open the gates of the mystical realm – who does not imagine himself to be "dying to die", to be pining away, to ruin himself in order to love?' (*IE* 120). Rather than figuring a self-reflective narcissism, this projected point of desire extinguishes itself in its own white-hot intensity. In the projection of the point, the inner movements have the role of the magnifying glass concentrating light into a very small incendiary site (*IE* 118). Like Irigaray's *la mystérique* what is at stake is not so much seeing as lighting, the submission to a night which nevertheless radiates like a sun: 'I adhere to this point and a deep love of what is in this point burns me to the point that I refuse to be alive for anything other than what is there' (*IE* 121).

Bataille writes that the remains of the point, even effaced, gives an 'optical form' to experience: 'As soon as it admits the existence of the point, *the mind is an eye*' (*IE* 118). Such a locution may appear to imply the restitution of the specular model of knowing which Irigaray's tactics subtly seek to displace. Yet Bataille's projected loss of self is a vanishing–point for knowledge, 'neither visible not tangible in any imaginable way' (*IE* 122). Ecstasy forces representational thinking to confront its own 'blind spot'. Whereas the blind spot of the eye is 'inconsequential', this blind spot in understanding absorbs one's attention: 'it is no longer the spot which loses itself in knowledge, but knowledge which loses itself in it' (*IE* 110).

> In this way existence closes the circle, but it couldn't do this without including the night from which it proceeds only in order to enter it again. Since it moved from the unknown to the known, it is necessary that it inverse itself at the summit and go back to the unknown. (*IE* 110–111)

The philosophy of representation institutes and reinforces the perceptual distance that demarcates the prohibition against contact: 'subject' and 'object' enter into a 'knowing' relation, safely shielded from the intense, wounding radiation of a sun which burns. But ecstasy is kindled in the incinerator of intellection, soaks into the void which gapes open within speculation itself. If unknowing were simply the yet-unknown it would be possible to explore this night: 'But no, it is night which explores me' (*IE* 111). Like the point on the retina in which vision is not experienced, unknowing is a dazzling darkness which dilates from within. Existence comes full circle to the extent that daylight is swallowed into the black hole of night, the blind spot of knowledge.

Although Bataille's account implies transcendence of the (masculine) self one might ask what would prevent this 'blind spot' from fulfilling the function of the 'other mirror' for thinking of which Irigaray so enigmatically speaks? Unable to generate an image it is – like the feminine – simultaneously the site where the power of vision is condensed. Moreover, it is this elusive 'point' which is intensified in repetition, dilated in the night of unknowing which pitches the longing to know into the chasm that subtends speculation. Like the sexuality of the mystic, this 'darkness' cannot be 'pictured' or in any sense visualized by the mind's eye/I. Since it cannot be *re*-presented to consciousness its reverberation is not to be confused with the self-defining circularity of masculine subjectivity. Night *appears* as a 'vision' that nothing resists, a gaze no bodily organ can limit. Such a thought seems to complement Irigaray's notion of a mirror untouched by any reflection *'like a pupil* [..] dilated to encompass the whole field of vision, and *mirroring itself'* (*SA* 410, *SW* 328)]. The pupil reflects nothing but its own void, 'the *hole* through which one reflects' (ibid.). Could this also function as the chasm through which the mystic finds her sexuality reflected, the speculum which fires and radiates the dark interior of her bodily sex? Perhaps this is what it means to say that her 'light' is suited to a lone mirror and its virtual reduplication. Her redoubling is never a return to Being, to presence, to a moment of self-certainty, but imageless repetition, the becoming of affect. Alterity impacts in a perpetual undoing, reflecting the brilliance of a universe in which the eye/I never ceases to be lost.

Despite all these similarities, Bataille's philosophy of unknowing makes no claims to think *through* the 'feminine' body. From the perspective of sexual politics the role of the feminine as love 'object' and 'victim' in *Eroticism* reveals an uncritical adherence to heterosexual norms which are deaf to the material conditions of their own cultural production. Bataille does appear to see the abasement of the feminine as the conduit to the sacred (*E* 20–21) but like Schreber's 'becoming-woman' this trajectory to the divine moves via the feminine whereas Irigaray's voyage begins there.

We might say that Nietzsche also divinizes the feminine yet in a rather different way. Nietzsche's attempt to overcome Christianity's depressive effects via the 'feeling of life' involves a sanctification of pain of a particular kind. Nietzsche contends that the *'sexual* symbol' was to the ancient Greeks 'the most venerable symbol as such' and that every element of 'the act of procreation, pregnancy, birth evoked the highest and most solemn [*feierlichsten*] feelings' (*TI*, 'What I Owe to the Ancients', 4). Indeed, 'in the doctrine of the Mysteries *pain* is sanctified: the woes of childbirth sanctify pain in general' (ibid.). In the context of his discussion of the *'mystery doctrine of tragedy'* in *The Birth of Tragedy* he makes reference to the myth of Demeter who, sunk in eternal sorrow, *'rejoices* again for the first time when she is told that she can give birth to Dionysus *once*

more' (*BT* 10). It is the 'feminine' power of fecundity that is celebrated in this paradoxical formulation, one which resonates with
Zarathustra's songs to life and eternity at the close of Book Three of
Thus Spoke Zarathustra (and it is instructive that both life and eternity are feminized). If 'life is a woman' the rebirth of life is the
sanctification of the power of creative suffering (*GS* 339). For
Nietzsche, 'Dionysus versus the Crucified' is not the expression of
an antithesis in relation to matyrdom but in relation to its meaning.
The God on the cross is a curse against life, Dionysus torn to pieces
is a promise of eternal rebirth of life (*WP* 1052). Indeed, the
Dionysian Mysteries embody the promise of the eternal return of
life. In a note from Summer 1883, Nietzsche writes: '*I have discovered
the essence of the Greeks* [**Griechenthum**]: they believed in the *eternal
return*! That is the *Mysteries-faith*!' (*KSA* 10, 340 / 8[15]). Moreover,
Nietzsche writes in *Twilight of the Idols*:

> For only in the Dionysian Mysteries, in the psychology of the
> Dionysian condition, is the *fundamental fact* of the Hellenic
> instinct expressed – its 'will to life'. *What* did the Hellene guaran-
> tee to himself with these Mysteries? *Eternal* life, the eternal recur-
> rence of life; the future promised and consecrated in the past; the
> triumphant yes to life beyond death and change; *true* life as col-
> lective living on through procreation, through the Mysteries of
> sexuality. (*TI* 'What I Owe to the Ancients', 4).

We already know that for Nietzsche the 'mysterious symbol of the
highest world-affirmation and transfiguration of existence' appears
when the Greek body and soul 'bloom' and overflow with life
(*WP*1051). In the same note Nietzsche also writes that in the most
supremely affirmative beings 'the most sensual routine functions are
finally transfigured by a symbol-intoxication of the highest spirituality' (*WP*1051). Could this be a reference to the sacred ritualization of
feminine fertility? If so, could it then be said that in the Dionysian
Mysteries the thought of eternal return emerges *from the body of the
feminine?* Does the most potent expression of life-affirmation
blossom as a feminine principle? In these various formulations,
Nietzsche presents the thought of eternal return as a doctrine that is
embodied in the sacred fecundity of life itself. The eternal return of
life is *felt* in sacred Dionysian ritual. Here existence celebrates its own

transfiguration. Life consecrates its own ever-renewing power of self-differing in the Mysteries, it blesses itself as that which must return eternally (*WP*1067). To access this 'feeling of life' one must feel the self-overcoming of life in oneself and this at bottom is what it means to affirm the Dionysian. Dionysus is the Greek name for the height of joy where the human feels altogether a deified form and self-justification of nature (*WP* 1051).

Yet in what sense is the celebration of productivity synonymous with a 'feeling of life'? Birth and rebirth *symbolize* creativity but arguably it is in non-productive, gratuitous expenditure that life's self-overcoming is experienced and made jubilant. Nietzsche's various references to the Mysteries as orgiastic practices and to the eroticism of both Dionysian and Apollinian drives suggests that the becoming-sacred of philosophy and the sanctification of pain bloom from the bodies of those who luxuriate in the pleasures of the body, not in its 'functionality' or finality. And while the eroticism of pregnancy is not to be denied, the myth of the *Urmutter* is one that coexists unproblematically with the most reactionary sexual politics and the most impoverished libidinal repertoire.

It could be said that Nietzsche repeats the fetishization of the feminine in his notion of sacred fecundity. For it is in rapture, in 'expenditure without accountability', that the transfiguring power of love is realized. Irigaray and Bataille both illustrate how the attempt to '*overcome* everything Christian through something supraChristian is enacted in mystic affirmation (*WP*1051). Irigaray makes female sexuality the site of the divine by exposing how its withholding from view has served to make masculine fantasies of transcendence possible. Because Irigaray does not so much seek to render female sexuality visible in its invisibility but palpable and communicable, she does not commute the feminine to a principle of reproduction. It is not rebirth but rebounding that marks her sexualized spirituality. The re-coming of life in its retouching is the site of infinite repetition. The abyss now becomes abyssal in the mystic herself who is no longer torn in contrary directions. She 'knows' that height and depth spawn and separate each other 'infinitely-indefinitely' (*SA* 250, *SW* 200).

And that one is in the other, and the other in me, matters little since it is in me that they are engendered in their ecstasy. *Outside of all self (as) same.* Never the same, always new. Never repeated nor repeatable in their raptures. Thus, uncountable as without determinate measure – indeed, eternal because immense. (*SA* 250, *SW* 200)

The re-coming of life in its retouching is the site of infinite repetition. Like the Dionysian this is thought as imageless and indeterminate. No 'one' returns. Mystic ecstasy is returning itself. The recoming of becoming is intensified *encore*.

If the inhuman emerges from the blind spot of thinking this is because it is a thought which is no longer able to think itself. Night floods into the unseeing eye, capturing the object of its gaze and the gaze itself, *reflecting it back*. The eye then sees *as night would see*, no longer anchored to a human subject. In the night of unknowing the eye becomes ex-orbitant. I traverse an empty depth and an empty depth traverses me. I become unknown to myself, 'two terms merge in a single wrenching' (*IE* 125). Rapture is not a window looking out on to the outside but a mirror, reflecting a perpetual self-abandon.

The ruination of God is the ruination of the principle of identity. As Saint Teresa testifies, one must fling all restraint aside and 'burn with the great fire of God' (*LST* 115). Engulfed in ecstasy one is thrown into the hearth, becomes a flame:

> It is not aware of itself, it is absorbed in its own unknown; in this unknown, it loses itself, annihilates itself. Without this thirst for non-knowledge, it would cease right away. The flame is God, but ruined in the negation of itself. (*IE* 127–8)

If all our blinded visionaries are fated to burn in the conflagration of intensities outside of representation, this by no means implies that what they access there is the 'same'. Such would be to reinscribe the rules of representation outside of representation. At the level of the concept, the difference between their thoughts of the outside cannot be registered: 'outside' is the realm of the homogeneous unknown. But from the perspective of the different libidinal tempos of these unspeakable ecstasies, affects spark and smoulder, spreading their heat and flame across ever-new reaches of transfigured phyiologies. It is not their visions as such that claim our wonder but the intimation of the immensity of the power that caused their visions to be.

7
Great Moments of Oblivion

> *The vehemence of my inner oscillations* has been terrifying, all
> through these past years; now that I must make the transi-
> tion to a new and more intense form, I need above all a
> new estrangement, a still more intense depersonalization.
> So it is of greatest importance what and who still remain to
> me. What age am I? I do not know – as little as I know how
> young I shall become...
> (Letter to Karl Fuchs, 14 December 1888)[1]

There is a libidinal tempo of the body and of the senses which is
concealed by the time of the subject and its faculties. A tool in the
service of a more expansive and subtle intellect, the conscious ego is
testimony to the fact that the body has evolved the means to disci-
pline and silence itself, abdicating its powers to a functionary. The
'self' which the body produces aspires to transcend its material conditions and would seek instead to govern them. Its success is measurable, ironically enough, by the extent to which the idea of the
self has *materialized*. Its construction is a simplification for practical
ends, a 'coarse organ', but one which nevertheless is *felt* to express a
supersensible freedom. Impervious to the flux of becoming, the self
represents the 'form' of the same, the determination of possible
experience and its spatio-temporal grammar. This idea perdures
despite the ebb and flood of forces immanent to consciousness and
despite the unconscious energies which periodically seep into
thought. According to Nietzsche 'the past flows on within us in a
hundred waves; we ourselves are, indeed, nothing other than that

which we feel at every moment [*Augenblick*] of this continued flowing' (*AOM* 223). The self is a product *of* this multiplicity but seeks to flow against its own current, and think itself in unitary terms. Consequently, when we desire to descend into 'the river of what seems to be our own most personal being' we encounter the truth of Heraclitus's famous dictum: 'one cannot step into the same river twice' (ibid.).

If to feel the ebb and flow of the past is to 'be' and yet never to be *the same*, what grants the limits of a human life? Must the self be transcendent ('outside itself') in order to confirm its enduring identity or is it possible to 'be' *at the same time as one becomes other* – a different kind of 'ecstasy'? Perhaps there is a sense in which the first of these possibilities functions by concealing the second. For example, the Cartesian philosophy of the 'subject' could be said to obscure a faultline separating the idea of a determining self from its undetermined conditions (both of which are *evaluated* from one side of the fissure, the perspective of ideality). According to Deleuze, it is with Kant that the excluded otherness within this model is made manifest (*DR* 85). On the grounds that it is impossible for determination to bear directly upon the undetermined, Kant introduces a third element, the form in which the undetermined is determinable by the 'I think': *time*. Time is the way in which we are internally affected by ourselves. This is because the active, universal 'I' which determines my experience can only determine it in time, that is, it can only be understood as 'the affection of a passive self which experiences its own thought' as if from an other (*DR* 86). Citing Rimbaud's formulation 'I is *an other*', Deleuze describes this paradox as the 'double derivation of the I and the Self in time', the Kantian fracture (*ECC* 30). Choosing the subtitle 'How One Becomes What One Is' ('*Wie man wird, was man ist*') for his own self testimony in *Ecce Homo* Nietzsche deepens the Kantian rift. How does one mark the limits of one's own life when 'I' *becomes* other? What would happen if 'becoming *what* one is' hollowed out the *who* of identity to the extent that becoming 'one' was refigured as never having been, and eternally embroiled in becoming? The clues are instructive. We are told that becoming what one is 'presupposes that one does not have the remotest idea *what* one is', that 'self-forgetting, self-*misunderstanding*' may have greater value than the Socratic *nosce te ipsum* ('know thyself') and that wanting anything to be other

than it is is a desire to which this authorial 'self' has never succumbed (*EH* , 'Why I am So Clever', 9). Becoming what one is
appears to follow a path of *unknowing*, the decommissioning of consciousness, a process Nietzsche also calls 'active forgetting' (*GM* II,1).

Active forgetting is not to be equated with immersion in 'pure
becoming' – as if the latter were somehow the inevitable consequence of suspending consciousness. In fact Nietzsche argues the
reverse: failing to forget condemns one to a Heraclitean nightmare
in which one would no longer believe in oneself at all (*UM* II,1). We
are told that forgetting is an indispensable component of any
action, but by this Nietzsche means that other drives come to
assume prominence, not that all conscious activity ceases. To think
of subjectivity in these fluid terms requires a tidal vocabulary of
peaks, troughs, currents and counter-currents, slipstreams and
rapids. Nietzsche never tires of insisting that the body is a constellation of commanding and commanded impulses, that 'consciousness' is the means through which non-conscious activity is
interpreted as 'knowledge' but perversely, according to impulses
which are less strong than those for which they speak. Developed as
a 'social organ', consciousness is rule-following become rule, the
most servile part of the organism yet the one to have gained current
ascendancy. Becoming what one is entails 'forgetting' this marker
for the 'self' but according to Nietzsche, this self is already the
product of an originary amnesia. Knowledge is only possible by 'forgetting' that one is an *artistically creating subject*. To 'know' is to
commit thought to the formulas of logical identity, of which the
'self' is a prime exemplar. Should this forgetting also be forgotten –
if only for a moment – 'self-consciousness would slip away immediately' (*TL* 1). If only it were possible to 'get out of the prison walls of
this faith,' Nietzsche sighs, as if to be human were to be in jail.

But to forget to forget is not yet to 'remember' for the origins of
the memory drive are different in kind. Nietzsche distinguishes
between an inability to forget and a will to remember. The first of
these is an indirect consequence of a negative evaluation of tran-
siency. One of Nietzsche's most uncompromising judgements is that
ressentiment against the passing of time is constitutive of the
human animal. Once the child has come to understand the phrase
'it was' it is forced to confront what its existence essentially is: 'an
imperfect tense that can never become a perfect one' (*UM* II,1).

Fated to be an incomplete being, the human suffers from its historical sense, the weight of the irredeemable past inhibiting its will to
draw its proper limits. The drive to impose one's will upon the
future can be read as a response to this sense of an ever-receding
horizon. While he acknowledges that there is a noble or 'sovereign'
reading of this drive, the construction of a memory for itself is one
of the aspects of the cultivation of human consciousness that
Nietzsche sees as spectacularly self-cruel (*GM* II,3). Bred as a certain
kind of animal to make promises, memory evolves as a wound and
remembering involves the harsh aggravation of the scar tissue – lest
we forget. Subjected to the gridirons of conformity – of form itself
– the human animal becomes calculable, regular and necessary and
everywhere perceives equivalences, identities and logical sameness.
The organs become coarse, their evaluations impoverished: 'Our
memory is based on seeing the *same* and taking to be the same:
thus on seeing *imprecisely*' (*KSA* 9/492/11[135]). A moral imperative
with respect to temporality is thereby instituted. One must ensure
continuity between past being and future being, abiding contractu-
ally to pay one's dues to existence despite the fact that 'base' continuity is precisely what 'continence' obscures. To express it
otherwise: in order to make a memory for itself the human being
must forget the aesthetic, subordinate becoming to being, regulate
its actions causally, and relate its present to its future. Yet, the body,
silenced and subordinated by the self that it supports, remains
untamed by it and given certain conditions will dissociate itself
from it. In a note from 1885, Nietzsche characterizes the human
body as that 'in which the most distant and recent past of all
organic becoming, becomes living and incarnate again [*wieder
lebendig und leibhaft wird*], through which and over and beyond
which an immense [*ungeheurer*] inaudible stream seems to flow'
(*WP* 659). In this astonishing image, Nietzsche depicts the body as a
confluence of remote and proximate processes, within which the
entire past of all organic becoming is latent or virtual and is capable
of being actualized *again*. Expressed thus, it might seem as if the
same forces could recombine to create the same physiological phenomena, but it is not certain, despite Nietzsche's interest in atavism,
that it is specific character traits or genetic dispositions that return
as such. If the body is thought as that in which the most distant and
most recent past of *all* organic becoming is reanimated and incar-

nated once again, then it would seem that it is the tendency of becoming to coexist with its recoming that literally 'embodies' the body. In other words, it is not 'the body' which is the reservoir of recurrence but recurrence which is the wellspring of the body. Such a thought is at odds with the idea of time as self affection. For it is not simply the inference that the past endures in the present that undermines the possibility of synthesizing representations as they progressively unfold in time but the fact that there is no interval between them. It seems that for Nietzsche the body that is identical with 'me' is not yet unified by the form of the 'I' and may pass out of phase with itself, exceed its bounds, or recreate the conditions by which it might 'know' itself.

We have gathered a series of clues thus far as to the way in which the ecstatic body might express itself in thought and they lead us once again to the aesthetic. The notion that art 'reminds us' of states of animal vigour, that art rekindles the libidinal drives that stimulate us to glorify existence, is a dominant theme throughout the 'Physiology of Art' notes. We are told that everything perfect and beautiful works as 'an unconscious reminder' of that 'amorous condition' of intoxicated intensity and 'awakes through contiguity aphrodisiac bliss' (*WP* 805). Indeed, Nietzsche goes further and suggests that there is a special kind of affective process that ecstasy ignites:

> All art works *tonically*, increases strength, inflames desire (i.e. the feeling of strength), stimulates all the more subtle recollections of rapture – there is a specific memory that pervades such states: a distant and fleeting world of sensations here comes back…. [*kehrt da zurück*] (*WP* 809)

Unlike the memory of the enslaved animal psychically branded by a thousand 'Thou shalt nots', this is a memory of the passions which answers to a rather different imperative. There is a compulsion at the level of sensations which lacks the determinacy of the moral law, indeed lacks the sense of self that would process intensity into intentionality. Moreover, this is a realm of action which does not enter consciousness. It is as if joy is contracted in the body – not a sacrificial contract but a contraction of sacred excitations, a pressure point of surplus pleasures. In the same note, Nietzsche speculates that art exercises a power of suggestion over the muscles and senses and speaks to a kind of 'subtle excitability' of the body. It could be said that art excites the state that creates art because it communicates the intensity *of* the body *to* the intensity of the body. It excites a transmission of energies, creating senses for itself.

These remarks on the subtle powers of the excitable body recall our earlier discussion of the self-intensifying powers of the Apollinian and Dionysian. It was suggested that both the Apollinian and the Dionysian are self-enhancing drives, furthering life and repeating the impulse to further life, respectively. It is worth noting in this connection that both the Apollinian and the Dionysian involve a process of forgetting. This is most apparent in relation to the Dionysian since it is defined in relation to the vanishing of everything subjective into complete oblivion, but the Apollinian, which is championed as the very embodiment of the maxims 'Know Thyself' and 'Nothing in Excess', is also a power which demands a forgetting: 'if we are to be able to dream with this inner joy in gazing, the day and its dreadful intrusiveness have to be completely forgotten' (*BT* 4). Perhaps it is the 'moral' self that has to be forgotten if the body is to 'remember'. At all events, when the demonic folk-song, the bewitching tones of the Dionysian festival and the sound of all of nature's excess in pleasure, grief and knowledge rang out in a serene Olympian world: 'The individual, with all his limits and measures, succumbed to the self-forgetfulness of the Dionysian states and forgot the precepts of Apollo' (*BT* 4). If the limits of a life can be so easily forgotten, one wonders what it is that ecstasy liberates. If Greek tragedy is born from the spirit of music, from the ecstasy of the enchanted throng, it is the *forces* that no longer conform to 'limits' that now break into thought.

The time of tragedy

For Nietzsche, to have a sense for the tragic means to consecrate one's life to something higher than itself. This entails an overcoming of a certain sense of self. Indeed, Nietzsche suggests that the spirit of tragedy provokes one to confront the 'terrible anxiety which death and time evoke in the individual' and thereby to overcome it (*UM* IV, 4). The joy which this tragic sense elicits is 'utterly transpersonal and universal' yet it is through the affects of the indi-

vidual that it is realized, or more precisely, through the transformation of *a* life: 'For in the slightest moment, the briefest atom of his
life's course, he may encounter something sacred that exuberantly
outweighs all his struggle and all his distress – this is what it means
to have a sense for the tragic' (ibid.). This glorious and monstrous
encounter opens up like a chasm in the familiar landscape of a life,
propelling the individual into a world in which he or she will be
perpetually other. The sense for the tragic is an intensity which wills
to create a body for itself, wills to liberate the body from the forces
which imprison it. Newly embodied, one rebegins life as if waking
from a dream, yet one no longer has the same orientation to this
reality which now seems strangely more dreamlike. To borrow from
Hölderlin, the beginning and the end no longer 'rhyme'.

In 'On the Difference of Poetic Modes', Hölderlin argues that the
tragic mode must be founded on an 'intellectual intuition' which
cannot be any other than that 'unity with every living thing which,
to be sure, is not felt by the limited soul, only intimated in its
highest aspirations, yet which can be recognized by the Spirit' (*H* 84,
FA 14: 370). The 'metaphor' of intellectual intuition does not illustrate the grounding of the identity of an individual; on the contrary
one gains an intimation of something transpersonal which is
unknowable for limited consciousness. Hölderlin's point, although
couched in the discourse of speculative philosophy, adds a further
clue to understanding Nietzsche's delineation of the Dionysian. The
'spirit' from which tragedy is born erupts as a force of nature in
the lyric poet who – in self-abandon and intoxication – recasts the
primal unity as music. In Hölderlin's remarks it is suggested that
through the greatest endeavours of the poet an intimacy with the
One is advanced, for in its 'harmonious alternation and progressive
striving' Spirit tends to 'reproduce itself within itself and others' but
like the One, Spirit is not directly available to the finite individual
(*H* 62, *FA* 14: 33). It is to be noted that it is only through the art-
work that the Spirit becomes manifest, yet the poet suffers the fate
of the Schopenhauerian genius who is unable to represent this
encounter in the mediated language of human knowing. In arguing
that the tragic mode reveals the insight that the Absolute can only
be presented indirectly as a 'sensuous unity', that is, according to
the mediating condition of human finitude (namely, *time*) Hölderlin
rehearses the Kantian paradox of inner sense. Yet he also intimates

something more: that tragedy *enacts* the crisis of becoming other, becoming boundless.

> The presentation of the tragic rests primarily on the fact that the monstrous [*das Ungeheure*] – how god and man couple, and how the power of nature and the innermost being of man boundlessly become as one in fury – is to be understood through the boundless becoming-one purifying itself through boundless separation. (*H* 107, *FA* 16: 257)

That which boundlessly becomes one through boundless separation is 'monstrous' – the terrifying and exhilarating moment in which the boundaries between mortal and divine are breached. The gravity of this event consists in the fact that in this coupling the human and the divine become momentarily undifferentiated. In terms of the *Oedipus* drama, this is presented as the hero's desire to *know himself* – a fatal incursion into the sphere of possibility reserved for the gods. In the 'Remarks on *Oedipus*', Hölderlin claims that in the monstrous union of god and man in tragedy, there is a forgetting of limits:

> At such moments man forgets himself and the god and turns around like a traitor, naturally in a holy manner. – In the utmost form of suffering, there exists nothing but the conditions of time and space. Inside it, man forgets himself because he exists entirely for the moment, the god [forgets himself] because he is nothing but time; and either one is unfaithful, time because it takes a categorial turn in such a moment, and in it beginning and end cannot be co-ordinated at all; man because he has to follow the categorial reversal and thus is entirely unable to resemble the beginning in what follows. (*H* 108, *FA* 16: 258)

In violating the boundaries of human reason and understanding, the tragic hero confronts the most extreme limit of suffering in which nothing exists save the 'conditions of time and space'. 'Man' is fated to suffer so unreservedly because unlike the god he is bound to the appearances of space and time and is stricken by the desire to know more than he can bear or contain. Following Kant, Deleuze notes that the activity of thought (time as the form of the determinable) applies to 'a receptive being, to a passive subject which represents that activity to itself rather than enacts it' (*DR* 86). It is to live the self as other. Unlike the self-grounding divinity, the human can only know itself as it appears, not as it is in itself. The tragic moment is both the collapsing of the boundaries that demarcate the human and the divine *and* their simultaneous 'turning away'. The human being forgets self at the limit because it exists entirely in the moment – a monstrous or *ungeheure* moment – and yet it is as a finite being that it enacts a becoming-divine. In contrast, at the extreme limit, the god who is nothing but time forgets himself in taking a 'categorial turn': time fails to give itself in itself because it is presented in a mediated form in the tragic mode – the divine is fated always to appear masked. Despite the specific technical and dialectical work that this transgression of bounds is intended to demonstrate (the confirmation of limits in their exceeding) perhaps this could also be read as the moment in which the transhuman emerges within the human as the other or virtual self – a moment of becoming other once again. Thus interpreted, tragedy reveals a boundless becoming-inhuman at the core of the human, the irruption of sensuous existence temporally unhinged. Having forgotten himself, the tragic hero cannot live with his excessive, inhuman knowledge because he is bound to the law of succession. Yet this monstrous moment 'wherein *transport* presents itself' is the moment at which the *punctuation* of a life dissolves (*H* 101, *BS* 730).

This moment is ecstatic, the opening of the boundless: 'tragic *transport* is actually empty and utterly unconstrained' (*H* 101–2, *BS* 730). Tragic ecstasy is the moment in which it is possible to cut loose from the prison of knowing, to encounter the unknown. Hölderlin refers to this in poetic terms as the 'counter-rhythmic rupture', the *caesura*.[2] For Hölderlin the caesura is the site of tragedy's recoil on itself, within which representation represents itself as such. This is the point at which an Apollinian delight is taken in show – in the illumination of the boundless, the communal soul of the Dionysian. Perhaps the reproductive power of the Spirit is communicated in this time of 'tragic transport': one senses the measureless 'not as individuals, but as *one living being*' (*BT* 17). The emptiness of tragic transport is the emptiness of an absolute *indetermination* – the horizon of the infinitive.

From this perspective, the 'whole of time' *is* the caesura. Since time is no longer subordinated to metrics, to cardinal points through which it must pass, it is liberated from the events which made up its content. It is no longer a container in which things unfold but is a pure and empty form, the unfolding of time itself. Again, Deleuze is illuminating:

> [T]ime is the most radical form of change, but the form of change does not change. The caesura, along with the before and after which it ordains once and for all, constitutes the fracture in the I (the caesura is exactly the point at which the fracture appears). (*DR* 89)

The caesura marks the undoing of time, its un-rhyming. Distributed on either side of the caesura, beginning and end no longer coincide. The counter-rhythmic fold at the heart of tragedy is catastrophic for the totality of time. According to Deleuze, it is Hölderlin who 'discovers the emptiness of pure time and, in this emptiness, simultaneously the continued diversion of the divine, the prolonged fracture of the I and the constitutive passion of the self' (*DR* 87). In the words of Beaufret, the pure and empty form of time marks the retreat of God 'such that he leaves man faced with the empty immensity of the endless sky'.[3] Like staring endlessly into lovely blueness, it is a *time of madness*. Deleuze claims that the retreat of the god marks the collapse of time: it means 'demented time or time outside the curve which gave it a god' (*DR* 88).

Striking a rather different note, Blanchot sees this dispossession as a mortal crisis and suggests that Hölderlin lives 'doubly in distress' because his time is 'the empty time when what he has to live is the double absence of the gods who are no longer *and* who are not yet' (*MPE* 123). He lives the 'empty time of absence' profoundly; he inhabits this double absence which is the most tragic instant yet also the union of the emptiness of the past and future which is the now of the 'breaking day', the 'irruption of the sacred' (*MPE* 122, 124). Yet, the empty form of time need not be heard simply as the lost time of the gods but as the full positivity of the death of God – the collapse of the principle of identity. Such an approach allows us to appreciate the collapse of time inhumanly and to view the 'movement causing error to blossom into truth' as becoming without negation, rather than the 'dialectic of derangement' that Blanchot proposes (*MPE* 123). Beyond the readings that would oblige us to see indeterminate being determined through the form of limitation, it is possible to see the undetermined as the virtual which is the real *a priori* condition of actuality. In this respect one might think of the Dionysian power of vagrant connection and communication as analogous to the reproductive power of poetic Spirit. In the absence of the divine the poets are 'like those holy priests of the wine-god who travelled from country to country in holy night' (Hölderlin, 'Bread and Wine').

To enact the process of becoming-other is to feel the tragic *pathos*, the feeling of life that is attained in Dionysian rapture. Within the caesura of time the human is forced to think what it is impossible to think: its self-affection by its *outside*. It is no longer the active synthetic identity which is encountered as other but the virtual – the silent stream of the most distant and most recent becomings. *It is of the body that tragedy speaks.* Against the Kantian view that the rule which governs the empirical necessity of time-consciousness is a 'pure original unchangeable consciousness' (*CPR* A107), the time of tragedy presupposes a corporeal consciousness at its core, the liberation of forces from the limits of the given.

Some further indications as to how this might be thought are supplied in Hölderlin's text 'Becoming in Dissolution'. Here, human experience and its self-understanding are broached in affective terms, primarily the *feeling* engendered by the perceived process of perpetual becoming and passing away. To the extent that the process is crystallized in art, particularly in tragic poetry, becoming in dissolution might be thought of as a 'frightful yet divine dream' (*H* 97, *FA*: 14, 174). Hölderlin explains that each moment of the temporal flow is to be thought in terms of becoming, decline and the 'moment' itself. As an existing actuality dissolves, it releases the potential for a new actualization and so the process goes on. However, because the conditions of experience are equally dissolvant – each moment perpetually overcoming the last – the possibility of marking the limits of the experience must simultaneously slip away. This will only be arrested if a point of recollection on that which has been dissolved is included in the process, enabling the synthesis of experience by 'a life'. Accordingly, Hölderlin marks a distinction between 'actual dissolution' and 'ideal dissolution' (which encompasses recollection) to distinguish the 'pure process' from its reflective comprehension as a 'reproductive act'.

> Thus dissolution as a necessity, from the viewpoint of ideal recol-
> lection, becomes as such the ideal object of newly developed life,
> a backward glance on the path that had to be taken [*zurückgelegt*],
> from the beginning of dissolution up to that point at which, in
> the new life, a recollection of the dissolved occurs, and from that,
> as explanation and unification of the gap and of the contrast
> occurring between the new and the past, recollection of dissolu-
> tion can ensue. (*H* 97, *FA* 14: 175)

Recollection enables the feeling of becoming and dissolution to be synthesized as experience. The constitution of an ideal object of a newly developed life implies the possibility of unifying intuitions in a manifold. In fact, the process of recollection invites a compari-son with Kant's account of the work done by the synthesis of reproduction in imagination in the Transcendental Deduction.[4] The comprehension of plurality in the unity of intuition is achieved by the unifying dynamic of the imagination which takes up the plurality of apprehensions which have run past, repeating the entire series and binding them into the unity of the present instant. An attempt is thus made to 'retain' the temporal flow. In an ideal sense linear continuity is established but at the expense of covering over the fearful chasm of time. Hölderlin goes on to develop the distinction between ideal and actual dissolution in terms of the act of reproduction and the feeling of life:

> The ideal dissolution is not to be feared. The beginning and end
> point is already posited, found, secured; therefore, this dissolu-
> tion is also more secure, more relentless, bolder, and it presents
> itself herewith as it really is, as a reproductive act, by means of
> which life runs through [*durchläuft*] all its points and in order to
> achieve the total sum, does not linger at any one, dissolves itself
> in each so as to produce itself in the next; except that the dissolu-
> tion becomes more ideal to the extent that it distances itself from
> its starting point, however, the production becomes more real to
> the extent that, finally, out of the sum of these feelings of decline
> and originating, which are infinitely run through in one

moment, there emerges a complete feeling of life [*ein ganzes Lebensgefühl*] (ibid.)

The ideal dissolution is presented as supplying continuity and coherence to the process of becoming and passing away in that it moves from moment to moment in a continuously determined manner. However, there is another level at which 'continuity' is experienced and this is in terms of the real – a feeling of life. This feeling might be thought of as the *idealization* of the actual dissolution, that is, as the intensification of the pure process which as a 'real nothing' is experienced in terms of pain and suffering. Hölderlin goes on to add that after this remembrance of the dissolved 'the individual is united with the infinite feeling of life [*unendlichen Lebensgefühl*] through the remembrance of dissolution' (ibid.). If we add these remarks to our reflections on tragedy it could be argued that Hölderlin gestures towards an immanent idealization, one which bears comparison to the emergence of the Dionysian through the prism of the Apollinian. The sense of 'oneness' which is felt in tragedy is not the Absolute but is a sense of an immanent outside. Recalling our earlier discussions in Chapters 2 and 3, we might now add that the Apollinian as a moment of idealization intensifies the 'frightful yet divine dream'. If it is legitimate to regard aesthetic 'reproduction' as different in kind from the synthesis of reproduction in imagination, then this 'vision' of imageless repetition (the Dionysian) may be blinding: what it shows is the collapse of time, the loss of the principle of identity. From the abyss of being, tragedy speaks of an otherness *beyond the auto-affection of time*. It is the other lives within which 'one' becomes which now are sensed as 'continuity' – something closer to Bataille's notion of the sacred. From the perspective of ecstasy, the newly developed life that emerges from the infinite feeling of life is always other to the life that recollects, is always other in this same life. The 'self' must ceaselessly be forgotten if the reproductive act is always exceeded anew. As we shall now see, it falls to the *body* to exhibit a different possibility of remembrance.

Infinite becoming

Among the cluster of notes that Nietzsche produced in the glorious aftermath of the Sils Maria ecstasy, there are a number which, both implicitly and explicitly, identify the thought of eternal return with a 'new manner of living'.[5] Prerequisites for this new way of living include *'dehumanization of nature'*, *'incorporation of experiences'*, detachment from the herd (*'the ultimate happiness of the Lonely One'*) and the desire to 'experience every thing again and eternally' (*'Annulus aeternitatis'*) (9/11[197/519–20). To this last point Nietzsche adds the coda: 'Incessant *transformation* – you must in a short period of time go through many individuals. The means is *ceaseless struggle'*. This strange imperative is illuminated somewhat if we consider the ecstatic transfiguration at the heart of tragedy. The *'dramatic* primal phenomenon' is entirely this: 'to see oneself transformed before one's own eyes and now to act as if one had actually entered into another body, another character' (*BT* 8). Lest it be thought that this is simply masquerade, Nietzsche adds that 'this phenomenon is encountered epidemically: a whole throng feels itself enchanted in this way' (ibid.). This process of becoming-other underscores the defeat of the human being as self-identical, self-reflective consciousness. Liberated from the forces which drive the subject together into a recognizable, responsible self, life celebrates its transfiguration and rebirth as art through the ecstatic bodies of the 'throng'.

This has yet to tell us anything about the dynamic of this metamorphosis. As we noted in Chapter 2, despite any superficial similarity, this becoming-other fails to commensurate with the cheerfully vacuous 'play of polyvalent identities' of postmodernist ideology. Nietzsche seeks to engage *affective* states (continuous multiplicities) not discrete states of affectation, to explore the streaming of subjectivity at the pre-individual level. This virulent transportation of thought outside itself describes a vector of loss which is epistemologically irrecuperable. It is not the signifier which shifts, *it is life*. A lateral transition is achieved between the participants of the tragic throng, marking out a zone of communication.

Inasmuch as this remains external to conscious processes this might be best understood in terms of entering a new affective rhythm. It might also be likened to the phenomenon of 'entrainment' – spontaneous phase-synchronization of different dynamical processes.[6] Rather than the movement of division that maintains identity, this is the movement of difference which differentiates itself. In this context it is worth recalling the ominous listing of 'the question of epidemic and contagion' in 'The Physiology of Art' plan (see the notes to Chapter 4). This thought is developed in connection with Nietzsche's notion that exceptional states condition the artist, one such being the 'compulsion to imitate' (*WP* 811). Nietzsche speaks here of 'an extreme irritability according to which a given example [*Vorbild*] is contagiously communicated – a state is immediately guessed and *enacted* on the basis of signs' (ibid.). This is an instance of the Dionysian 'facility of metamorphosis' the incapacity not to react (*TI*, 'Expeditions...', 10). Consciousness is not engaged but a feeling of life is touched – *transpersonally*.

This process may be clarified further if we recall Nietzsche's characterization of the body as a silent sea of becoming in which distant and recent processes return. Nietzsche seeks to think about 'becoming what one is' in terms of the very materiality that knowing consciousness must forget, the subtle excitable body. It is as if ecstasy were a sign of the body's auto-differentiation. The dance, song, laughter, music-making and erotic excesses that connect beating hearts and writhing limbs suggest a different order for thinking, one which has its own necessity. The 'infinite feeling of life' may be thought of in this context as a series of contagions of energy. In the beautiful words of Bataille:

> What you are stems from the activity which links the innumerable elements which constitute you to the intense communication of these elements among themselves. These are contagions of energy, of movement, of warmth, or transfers of elements, which constitute inevitably the life of your organized being. (*IE* 94)

Life is thought here as continual becoming in dissolution, never situated at any particular point. The flows of energy enter into relations which constitute phenomena but there is no point of stability: 'Thus, there where you would like to grasp your timeless substance, you encounter only the poorly co-ordinated play of your perishable elements' (ibid.).

Echoing Bataille, Klossowski argues that the body 'is the *same* body only insofar as a single *self* is able to and wills to be merged with it, with all its vicissitudes' (*NCV* 55, *NVC* 29). The cohesion of the body would *seem* to be that of the self since the self is an idea incorporated in and by the body. Moreover, the identity of the self along with its own body is 'inseparable from a direction or meaning

formed by the *irreversible* course of a human life' (ibid.). According
to Klossowski, the more Nietzsche listened to his body, 'the more he
came to distrust *the person the body supports*' (*NCV* 51, *NVC* 24).
Klossowski contends that Nietzsche's suffering – his valetudinary
states – contributed to an increasing rejection of the idea that the
body is a property of the self. In this respect his convalescence can
be regarded as an experiment with the body at the expense of the
self. It is in this sense that the thought of eternal return is born of a
state of high intensity ('a certain tonality of the soul'), the eruption
of corporealizing thought into philosophy.

   What is fundamental in Nietzsche's experience of the eternal
return is the transformative effect that it has on the one who thinks
it. The originality of Klossowski's interpretation of this experience is
his insistence on *forgetting* as both the source and 'the indispensable
condition' for the revelation of the thought of eternal return, resulting in the *sudden transformation of the identity* of the 'one' to whom
it is revealed (*NCV* 93, *NVC* 56). Klossowski argues that in the revelation of the thought that all returns eternally I learn that I have
been brought back to a moment of necessary revelation 'but at the
same time I learn that I was *other* than I am *now* for having forgotten this truth, and thus that I have become another by learning it'
(*NCV* 94, *NVC* 57). The revelation of eternal return must be forgotten if I am to return eternally to the point at which the revelation
would *be* a revelation. This means that if I become other through
the process of return then I am no longer able to affirm the self that
I now am and have been up to this moment. The revelation opens
as a caesura in the rhythm of a life. If I am to re-will the eternal
return of everything then this must include this empty time, this
dispossession. This is a thought 'so perfectly coherent that it
excludes me *at the very moment* I *think* it' (*NCV* 101, *NVC* 64). I am
compelled to re-will all experiences but not as mine. Since I will
forget this moment too the act of affirmation involves an
affirmation of all the other selves that I must pass through and must
forget in order to establish a fortuitous identity for myself. It now
seems as if the inevitable direction of a life's course (the 'arrow of
time') is lived by the self at the expense of the transverse continuity
of the body which flows in multiple channels.

   To 'become what one is' is to become other in this same life.
Ecstasy in the experience of eternal return signals the 'loss of a given

identity' and the opening of the soul to 'all its possible identities' (*NCV* 94, *NVC* 57). For Klossowski, the 'death of God' is the rebirth of metempsychosis. It assumes that an individual's capacity 'could never exhaust the differentiated richness of a single existence, that is to say, its affective potential' (*NCV* 108, *NVC* 70–71). The key point to stress here is that this 'immortality' is not specifically individual, nor does the reference to transmigration imply discrete identities that are exchanged. As Klossowski notes, the eternal return suppresses enduring identities. This means that the dissolved soul which passes through an 'entire series' is to be thought of in terms of its coexistence or interpenetration with other souls, a thought which Schreber's conceptualization of the grades of Blessedness appears to accommodate well. This 'dissolved soul' returns to '*that degree of the soul's tonality in which the law of the circle was revealed to it*' (*NVC* 108, *NVC* 71). It is here that 'the feeling of eternity and the eternalization of desire merge in a single moment', the dizzying joy of the '*same* life lived and experienced through its individual differences' (*NVC* 110, *NVC* 72).

Without the One – the 'I' – others continue to think in us. This is the nature of a universality born of a sentiment that is of me yet not mine. It can now be said that to become what one is, is to experience one's subjectivity materially, as fluctuations of intensity – an *embodied immortality*. Yet, if we consider the *memory* of the body that is condensed in its pleasures and excitations, a body that resists the conformity to the 'same' ritually bred into the human animal, a further reading is possible. The experience of one's life as so many vibrations of otherness could be likened to the rebounding effect encountered in rapture as one becomes with the world. As Nietzsche says, in lyric poetry we 'are astonished to feel our ownmost feelings again, to have them thrown back to us from other individuals' (*KSA* 7/54–5/2[25]). Perhaps the 'special memory' that pervades the aesthetic state is one that contracts a body out of synaesthetic resonances. Recurrence constellates the body as so many affective becomings, as so many moments prolonged into one another.

Great moments of remembrance

It is to be recalled that for Nietzsche, forgetting is indispensable to action. Failure to forget, taken to its extreme, would consign one to 'everywhere seeing becoming' (*UM* II, 1). Such a person 'would no longer believe in his own being', would 'see everything in moving points flowing into each other and would lose himself in this stream of becoming' (ibid.). Perhaps it is *failure to forget the dream state* rather than failure to forget *simpliciter*, which enables the body to perceive what cannot be seen: something in *a* life which exceeds it ('too much for anyone'). In Nietzsche's famous final letter, written to Jacob Burckhardt prior to his collapse in Turin in early January 1889, he declares that in the end 'he would much rather be a Basel professor than God' (*SB* 8, 578–9). He goes on to identify himself as Prado and the father of Prado, Count Robilant and the father of the same, Lesseps, Chambige, Antonelli and father of Umberto: 'at bottom, every name of history am I' (ibid.). It is as if the entire vital past vibrates within him and is condensed in one soul. Nietzsche also claims to have twice attended his funeral and to have been crucified the year before by German doctors. The collapse of distinctions between self and other, between life and death yields a strange euphoria, a bliss born of pain. Do the conditions of time and space remain at the extreme limits of pain as Hölderlin proclaims? Perhaps, in the crash of time, pain is taken to the limit at which point it becomes something else. We should not forget that in the 'condition of pleasure called rapture' the 'sensations of space and time are altered' (*WP* 800). We learn in a revised draft for the section of *Ecce Homo* entitled 'Why I am so Wise' that we are least related to our parents and that 'higher natures have their origins much, much farther back'.[7] The past that flows on within us in a hundred waves may *flow back,* swallowing the self-identical subject in its splashing foam. As Nietzsche argues in a note from 1884:

> We must change our ideas [*umlernen*] about memory: it is the quantity of all experiences of all organic life – vital, self-organizing, reciprocally forming, struggling with one another, simplifying, condensing and transforming in numerous unities. There must be an inner *process* which behaves like the *formation of concepts* from numerous individual cases: the emphasizing of ever new elements from the fundamental schema and the discarding of marginal traits. (*KSA* 11/175/26[94])

This concept of memory as the quantity of all experiences of all organic life may serve to further the claim that an individual life is the affective resonance of so many contagions of energy, coursing through a pre-personal physiology. Klossowski suggests that what the eternal return implies as a doctrine 'is neither more nor less than the insignificance of the *once and for all* of the principle of identity or non-contradiction, which lies at the base of the understanding' (*NCV* 315, *NVC* 217). The lived experience of the intensity of the circle – which is substituted for the 'once and for all' as a principle – is said to open itself up to 'a number of individualities through which it passes, until it returns to the only one to whom the Eternal Return was revealed....' (ibid.). On Klossowski's account, all would stop if I remembered a previous revelation for it would serve to keep me within myself and thus outside the teaching of the return (*NCV* 96, *NVC* 59). Yet what the body remembers may be at odds with such consciousness as Nietzsche's Turin days so poignantly testify.

In his essay 'Memory of the Present and False Recognition', Bergson describes a curious sensation in which one feels as if one is 'living again, down to the minutest details' some moments of one's past life (*MPFR* 36). In this state, known in the psychological literature as 'false recognition', one feels strangely detached from time as a form of inner sense. This is because the 'illusory memory' is never localized in a particular point in the past: 'it dwells in an indeterminate past – the past in general' (*MPFR* 37). Bergson explains that false recognition does not arise from the identification of an actual perception with a former one strongly resembling its content. On the contrary, the two experiences appear strictly identical and one feels as if one is living through the 'already lived'. This feeling is considered to illustrate certain essential elements about memory and consciousness that are ordinarily obscured owing to the fact that consciousness typically has a high *tension* or *tone* when engaged in its immediate projects. False recognition – although distinct from delirium, hallucination and obsession – is to be classed among the 'morbid and abnormal states which appear to add something to normal life and enrich it instead of impoverishing it' (*MPFR* 44). The prejudice that the dream state is merely an inchoate and fragmentary version of our waking state is rejected by Bergson at the outset. Insisting that the rich diffusion of psychological life is itself 'dreamlike', he argues that the waking state is gained by the limitation, concentration and tension of the latter (*MPFR* 46). Further, he claims that memory and perception exercised in the dream state are more 'natural' than those in the waking state for in the former, consciousness can disport itself in a non-teleological way whereas in the latter, care has to be taken for the action to be accomplished:

> To be awake means to will. Cease to will, detach yourself from life, disinterest yourself, and by that mere abstention you pass from the awake-self to the dream-self – less *tense* but more *extended*. The mechanism of the awake state is, then, the more complex, more delicate and more *positive* of the two, and it is the awake-state, rather than the dream-state, which requires explanation. (ibid.)

There is a distinctly Schopenhauerian tone to this passage, not simply because the cessation of willing is likened to disinterestedness but because the dream self is 'more *extended*'. The claim that in ecstasy we are released into a transpersonal physiology – with which the 'empirical' self is continuous – seems to be supported in this notion of differential tension. It is tempting to say that there is a difference of tempo between the two states. Furthermore, Bergson's view of memory formation shares with that of Nietzsche a crucial emphasis on the coexistence of the virtual past with the process of actualization. Contrary to the common conviction that memory is posterior to the formation of perception Bergson proposes that it is *contemporaneous* with it. Memory is said to appear 'as doubling perception at every instant', arising with it and developing itself simultaneously *(MPFR* 49). He suggests that the present unfolds itself at every instant, springing in two 'jets' towards the past and the future but it is only the forward-surge (perception) that occupies practical consciousness whereas the latter pulse (memory) is disregarded for we have no need of the memory of things while we are occupied with them. One thinks of a coiling wave that falls backwards as it mounts its advance. Memory is to perception as the image reflected in the mirror is to the object in front of it. Whereas the object is actual, manipulable and capable of causing effects, the mirror image is virtual, incapable of doing what the object does and merely resembles it:

> Each moment of our life offers two aspects: it is actual and virtual, perception on one side and memory on the other. It

splits as and when it is posited. Or rather, it consists in this very splitting, for the present instant, always running on, fleeting limit between the immediate past which is no more and the immediate future which is not yet, would be reduced to a simple abstraction if it were not precisely the moving mirror which unceasingly reflects perception in memory. *(MPFR 51)*

In 'false recognition', the mind becomes conscious of this doubling, perceiving at one and the same time the object and its reflection. Just as Nietzsche speaks of a *feeling* of the past which is not separated from a present by any interval, Bergson suggests that what we are actually living through is a *memory of the present* *(MPFR 52)*. It is not a repetition of the same perception, mental item or fact. It is a return of the moment in the moment itself. Moreover, what is perceived and remembered in each moment is *affective life as such*: 'What is doubled at each instant in perception and memory is the totality of what we are seeing, hearing and experiencing, all that we are with and all that surrounds us' *(MPFR 52)*. At each moment the past is newly engendered. It does not succeed a present that is no more, it coexists with the present it was.

Bergson invites us to suppose ourselves repeating mechanically something that we once knew by heart but have long forgotten. Every word that we pronounce we recognize at the moment we repeat it such that we feel that we possess it before uttering it 'and yet we only retrieve it when we pronounce it' *(MPFR 53)*. It is tempting to align this example of corporeal memory with the somatic encoding analogy Schreber uses to explain 'nerve language', for in the grip of false recognition we feel that we both act and are 'acted' (ibid.). As Bergson puts it: 'We feel that we choose and that we will, but that we are choosing what is imposed upon us and willing the inevitable' (ibid.). This description might serve equally well as an account of the compelling qualities of beauty and the sublime – judgements which seem to both claim and desert their agent at the moment when they are made. The sense that one's freedom is fated, is, says Bergson (citing Bourget), 'a kind of unanalysable feeling that reality is a dream' *(MPFR 59)*.

In a passage in *The Gay Science* Nietzsche relates the time of the dream to the continuity of life, that which Bergson might think of as continuous multiplicity. Once again, the boundaries of a life are enlarged only to be exceeded anew:

> *The consciousness of appearance.* – How wonderful and new and at the same time how dreadful and ironic I feel my position to be with respect to all of existence in light of my realization! I have *discovered* for myself that primeval human and animal kind, indeed, the whole primal age and past of all sensate being continues in me to poetize, to love, to hate and to conclude: I suddenly woke up in the middle of this dream but only to the consciousness that I am still dreaming and that I *must* continue dreaming so as not to perish – just as a sleepwalker must go on dreaming in order not to fall down. What is appearance [*Schein*] to me now! Certainly not the opposite of any essence: what could I say about any essence other than to name the predicates of its appearance! Certainly not a dead mask that one could lay over an unknown X and also remove. Appearance is for me that which is effective and living itself, that which goes so far in its own self mockery that it makes me feel that here there is appearance and will-o'-the-wisp and a dance of spirits and nothing more – that amidst all these dreamers, I too, the 'knower', am dancing my dance; that the knower is a means for prolonging the earthly dance and to that end belongs to the festive spirits of existence; and that the sublime consistency and interrelatedness of all knowledge perhaps is and will be the highest means of *maintaining* the commonality of dreaming and the mutual understanding of all these dreamers and therewith *the continuation of the dream.* (*GS* 54)

The continuation of the dream is achieved through ecstasy – the Apollinian rapture that furthers and intensifies itself. This passage presents an ardent appeal for the tragic sense, for living and knowing aesthetically. If 'reality' is *Schein*, Dionysian 'truth' must participate in Apollinian semblance, a 'depth' to a surface which enabled the Greeks to be superficial out of profundity. Indeed, it is the Dionysian which is dreamt here; more precisely, *the thought of eternal return as the embodied pathos of the Dionysian.* As this passage makes clear, it is *Schein* which is the ontological reality of commonality – the virtual *physis* which is sustained by the continuation of the dream. As we have already noted, Nietzsche claims that in lyric poetry the 'I' of the poet is not equivalent to that of the 'awake, empirically real man' because this self is surrendered in the rapturous becoming one with the primal unity: 'The image that now shows him his unity with the heart of the world is a dream scene that embodies the primordial contradiction and primordial pain together with the primordial pleasure of semblance' (*BT* 5). Nietzsche's remarkable text from *The Gay Science* exemplifies the reality of the virtual as the *a priori* condition of the actual. The 'I' which is actualized is distinguishable from the transpersonal *physis* with which it remains continuous. From this perspective – that of a terrifying yet divine dream – one accesses an infinite feeling of life. In intensifying it, the eternal return is touched.

According to Blanchot, as Hölderlin advances towards schizophrenia his work is less concerned with historical time 'for he dwells now in the world which he creates, a world closer to myth, where an immediate expression of the sacred reaches fulfilment and is expressed' (*MPE* 115). Perhaps those who live in a mythically inspired world are liberated from the given because – as in a dream – anything is possible at any moment. Euphoric in Turin, Nietzsche comes to feel the infinite happiness of a soul which continues the power of the dream. Were it possible to experience the history of humanity as one's own history, crowding every joy, hope, and sigh into 'a single feeling' one would experience a 'happiness that humanity has not known hitherto' (*GS* 337). This is a divine joy – 'a happiness of a god full of power and love, full of tears and full of laughter, a happiness that, like the sun in the evening, continuously squanders its inexhaustible riches into the ocean....' (ibid.).

8
The Sense of Eternity

'Towards New Seas'

There ahead I *will*: and I trust
In myself and my grip.
Open lies the sea, into the blue
I head my Genoese ship.

All shines for me, new and newer,
Noon sleeps upon space and time –:
Only *your* eye – monstrously
Stares at me, infinity!

(GS 'Songs...')

In the opening of *Civilization and its Discontents*, Freud makes reference to a 'peculiar feeling' which many have identified as the true source of religious sentiments. It is a feeling that one might call 'a sensation of "eternity", a feeling of something limitless, unbounded – as it were, "oceanic"' (*PFL* 12, 251). Freud suggests that the 'oneness with the universe' which constitutes the ideational content of this feeling sounds like a first attempt at a religious consolation, perhaps a way of disavowing the danger which the ego recognizes as threatening it from the outside world. Distrustful of this feeling and equally sceptical of related discourses of mystical revelations, trances and ecstasies, he claims that a feeling can only be a source of energy if it is the expression of a strong *need*. According to Freud, the sensation of boundlessness is itself bound by a pre-existent form – the desire for the restitution of a 'limitless narcissism'. In translating this affect into a sense of lack, he dismisses the oceanic feeling as nostalgic and infantile, its joy concealing a need for security and a fear of helplessness. Such a reading is symptomatic of the reflexivity of metaphysical Judaeo-Christian thinking, its reliance on reason's re-cognition of the world as a reflection of itself. Whether reason strives to refind itself dialectically in the structure of the world or to ground that structure transcendentally, its relationship to totality is narcissistic. But there is a more complex desire that these familiar codes conceal, a longing for the raging ocean in 'ruleless disarray'. *Contra* Freud, the oceanic feeling may be a sign of the emergence of ecstasy in thought, an expression of delirious excitement at the dissolution of the given. If the voyage into the horizon of the infinite fills us with a 'sacred thrill' this is because something is glimpsed here which is in excess of the human, something that is 'too much' for me. To think *from* the boundless is the challenge for philosophy after Nietzsche. It is to voyage into the eye of the maelstrom.

The swallowing horizon

Erupting as a moment of life in excess of 'the living', ecstasy communicates a thought that we might describe as 'inhuman' or beyond the human (*übermenschlich*). If it is legitimate to claim that the human animal lives at a certain steady tempo, 'keeps time' according to the form of the same, the insurgence of ecstasy in life is likely to be dismissed as an aberration or even denied. This tends to indicate that ecstasy cannot be assimilated to a pre-existing order of things – to the humanist values of need, preservation and form. The promise of unheard of joy, announced all at once as a thrill that passes through a body, is transformative for a life 'in its entirety'. The very notion of a 'life course' calls to mind a temporal logic predicated on the linear temporality that we have argued is allied with the index of identity marking the 'self'. However, we have suggested that the body of which the 'self' is a part may beat to rather different rhythms. To think the moment of ecstasy in this register is to acknowledge its 'oceanic' quality – for it is corporeally all-determining yet lacking in the determinacy that would render it available for thought at the level of signs. Perhaps it is also to acknowledge that it is not 'we' who have a philosophy of ecstasy. It is ecstasy that philosophizes through us.

An ecstatic moment of this grandeur is described by Mishima in *Sun and Steel*. He relates how as a boy he watched the young men parade a portable shrine through the streets at the local festival. Intoxicated with their labour they wore expressions of an 'indescribable abandon', staring up to the heavens with a wonderment that the child had scarcely been able to comprehend (*SS*13). It was only much later when participating in a similar festival that he gained insight into the nature of this 'intoxicating vision':

> They were simply looking at the sky. In their eyes there was no vision: only the reflection of the blue and absolute skies of early autumn. Those blue skies, though, were unusual skies such as I might never see again in my life: one moment strung up high aloft, the next plunged to the depths; constantly shifting, a strange compound of lucidity and madness. (*SS* 13)

In their shared physical labour and savouring of stress, the group collectively attain an ecstasy for which a 'type of privileged moment' is 'especially designed' (*SS* 15). At such a moment, individual sensibility is vanquished to reveal a 'universal sensibility' – the elucidation of a corporeal mystery somewhat akin to the 'process of acquiring erotic knowledge' (ibid.).

> [M]y eyes, in their meeting with the blue sky, had penetrated to the essential *pathos* of the doer. And in that swaying blue sky that, like a fierce bird of prey with wings outstretched, alternately swept down and soared upwards to infinity, I perceived the true nature of what I had long referred to as 'tragic'. (*SS* 14)

Once he had gazed upon this sky, Mishima says that he understood all kinds of things hitherto unclear to him. Such luminous, wavering blueness does not require a consciousness to illuminate it, nor even an eye to perceive it. This touching of the 'divine blue sky' is a contraction of energy: both a temporal concentration and a catching of the pathogen that claims individual bodies and retunes them to another frequency – to the inhuman ebb and flow of the waves of becoming. It is an Apollinian vision of a Dionysian sensation, a

de-individuating ecstasy. Indeed, the 'universal sensibility' –
strongly evocative of the Kantian 'feeling of life' – describes a
transpersonal affectivity which unites the intoxicated throng. It is a
sensitivity with which one becomes 'entrained' – a kind of erotic
pulse which ripples across the glistening muscles and pervades the
cloudless landscape. As in Greek tragedy, when one looks one sees
something that it is impossible to see, like the ocean eternally
reflecting the sky. In this lovely blueness, the unknown is touched.
As Mishima writes: 'At that moment, I participated in the tragedy of
all being' (*SS* 15).

Those moments in life which stretch beyond life – opening out
flight vectors into new and unexpected worlds – overflow the terms
by which they might be comprehended and contained. As in tragic
ecstasy, there is a forgetting of limits, the ground seems to give way
and nothing will ever be 'the same'. These immense, monstrous
moments are chasms which swallow up the temporal or existential
structures that are evoked to define 'a' life: they are the ruin of *unity*,
its undoing. We said in Chapter 2 that the Apollinian and
Dionysian 'do not heed the single unit' and that their ecstatic
tempos have no relation to a principle of identity. We might think
of these rhythms as becoming-slower or becoming-faster but not
becoming slower or faster *than*. In fact, Nietzsche suggests that this
thought should be extended to temporality as such. In a note from
1881 he writes:

> 'Time' does not decide between slower or more rapid motion. In
> absolute becoming, force can never rest, can *never* be nonforce:
> 'slow and rapid motion of the latter' *cannot* be measured on the
> basis of a unit, for the unit is not given. A continuum of force is
> *without succession* and *without contiguity* (for this too would pre-
> suppose both the human intellect and gaps between the things).
> (*KSA* 9/549/11[281])

The conception of time as ordered and successive presupposes a
prior faculty of space (and the ancillary notion of points in space). If
philosophy continues to conceive of time as *spacing*, the 'moment'
will be addressed in terms of unity even if it can be shown that this
unity is traced through with a constitutive absence. This is because
the human subject as recipient of and marker for 'differing and

deferring' is necessarily assumed – despite lacking sufficiently 'refined organs' to perceive the absolute flux of becoming. Yet Nietzsche insists that it is only succession that produces the representation of time and 'if we sensed not causes and effects but a continuum we would not believe in time' (ibid.). To be ecstatic – to be 'outside' the perspective of the self – is to sense the continuum and to dream *of the dream* as Nietzsche so poetically suggests (*GS* 54). To think of duration non-spatially is to conceive succession as a flow of qualitative changes which merge into one another without becoming externalized as distinct. As we have seen, this is how Bergson contrasts two notions of multiplicity – determinate multiplicity made up of discrete units which may be spatially juxtaposed (and enumerated) and virtual multiplicity which is continuous fusion and interpenetration. It is the latter which we have associated with the Dionysian excess and it is this multiplicity which is intensified in an Apollinian 'moment of *vision*' [*Augenblick*].

To think eternal return is to access this inhuman vision, this transpersonal feeling of life. It is to see the world through the eyes of the genius – the one who is liberated from goal-driven willing and is able to see 'non-human landscapes of nature'. As Zarathustra says as his abyssal thought of eternal return emerges from the landscape: "'Is seeing itself not – seeing abysses?"' (*TSZ* III, 'Of the Vision and the Riddle'). In his dialogue with the Spirit of Gravity, Zarathustra looks into the abyss: *he becomes the moment that he sees*. The 'gateway of "Moment [*Augenblick*]"' becomes *visible*, materializes in thought at the limit of what can be seen. The long lanes reaching eternally into the past and the future confront one another in this placeless place, this 'caesura'. In terms reminiscent of both Kant and Hölderlin in their remarks on time, Zarathustra describes how everything that 'runs' along these lanes is 'bound together' but these moments are not 'synthesized' in terms of a transcendental unity. As Zarathustra says to the dwarf: 'And are not all things knotted together so firmly that this moment draws after it *all* that is to come? *Therefore* – itself too?' (ibid.). Past and future arise – 'exist' – in each moment of becoming. This moment 'is' time – there is nothing else – but this moment 'is' *ecstatic*. To *be* this moment is to be outside oneself, to exceed and exceed that exceeding.

However, even to say that Nietzsche's thought of eternal return accounts for the synthesis of moments of becoming without any recourse to transcendental subjectivity tends to evoke an image of extensive magnitude at the very moment its 'transgression' is thought. Interpretations of eternal return are bedevilled by the tendency to regard the 'moment' as a punctual 'instant' within time but after the 'death of God' such an appeal to the unit or unitary is no longer available. The moment is not 'one' but nor is it a multiplicity of ones. Deleuze suggests that 'the synthetic relation of the moment to itself as present, past and future grounds its relation to other moments' (*NP* 48) but it is important that this is thought from within the gateway, not from the perspective of the dwarf. It is not insignificant that the gateway which emerges *as* a moment of vision *in* a moment of vision should again disappear. After Zarathustra has finished speaking to the dwarf, a series of disjointed, 'shuttering' events flash into view. These moments do not succeed one another so much as intensively condense into one another in a vertiginously spiralling depth, culminating in the incident with the shepherd to which we alluded in Chapter 5. Perhaps what frustrates philosophical attempts to render the thought of eternal return meaningful is the inhuman nature of this thought and, most importantly, what it would *feel* like to think it. We need a different vocabulary for thinking this thought – one which is already 'ecstatic'.

We noted in Chapter 4 that Zarathustra, staring at the sky, falls into the well of eternity where time is lost. Here, the sky becomes abyssal, the gaze acentred. To see in a *moment of vision – Augenblick –* is to look through the mirror that reflects back the familiar anthropic image, to look eternally: 'And when you gaze long into an abyss the abyss also gazes into you' (*BGE* 146). What Zarathustra encounters is an eternity in depth – a feeling of extreme *intensity* – rather than one of endless 'horizontal' duration. This sense of 'deep, deep eternity' aggresses against the tendency to regard the 'moment' as a moment in time or indeed to regard time as a dimension of its own description. In a note from the period of the Sils Maria revelation, Nietzsche writes:

> You think you have a long rest until rebirth – but do not deceive yourselves! Between the last moment [*Augenblick*] of consciousness and the first appearance [*Schein*] of new life lies 'no time' – it passes by as quick as lightning, even if living creatures were to

measure it in terms of billions of years or could not measure it at all. Timelessness and succession are compatible as soon as the intellect is gone. (*KSA* 9/564–5/11[318])

Ecstatic thought does not progress through a series of points or stages but as in the unconscious, follows a succession without mutual externality. It is in terms of a libidinal time of the body and the senses that it is possible to think of time outside the transcendental unity of experience. It could be added that this is to think of temporality aesthetically, to think form as 'the matter itself', beyond the grammar of the intellect.

We have suggested that in the sublime, the displeasure of our vital sense gives way to the pleasure of our interior sense. As we have noted earlier in our investigation, the violence inflicted on inner sense in the sublime is transformative. Inner sense gives way to interior sense in an instantaneous rush of the feeling of life for the '*whole determination* of the mind'. As Bataille so powerfully reminds us, on the edge of death one feels most alive. One thinks of Dostoevsky's Prince Myshkin on the brink of an epileptic fit:

> [H]is brain seemed to catch fire at brief moments, and with an extraordinary momentum his vital forces were strained to the utmost all at once. His sensation of being alive and his awareness increased tenfold in those moments which flashed by like lightning. (*I* 243)

The electric storm breaking overhead brings on a sensation of the most intense joy – an infinite happiness for which the Prince feels his whole life to be worthwhile: 'Yes, I could give my whole life for this moment' (*I* 244). His entire life unfolds as this sovereign affirmation, *as* this moment. When experienced from the perspective of ecstasy, eternity is *of* the moment, rather than the moment being *of* eternity. Here again, one thinks of the tragic transformation in which one ceases to identify with the hero but starts to feel the forces that give rise to its form – an inhuman excitation: 'at that moment the extraordinary saying that *there shall be time no longer* becomes somehow comprehensible' (ibid.).

Ruined time

We have already noted that in the sublime, time as a form of inner sense is cancelled. We are now in a position to reflect more deeply on the ecstatic nature of this collapse. It will be recalled from Chapter 3 that it is the reach beyond the boundaries of sense that Kant associates with sublimity. However, we also know that for Kant, it must be possible to comprehend sublimity in terms of 'unity' if it is to exhibit purposivity. The conflicting feelings of pleasure and pain must be felt to be purposively related to one another to the extent that it is possible for them to coexist in the same subject. One thinks here of Nietzsche's reflections on the economy of 'great health' in which health and sickness are considered not as opposites but coexisting forces in a relation of tension. A similar dynamic is at work in the sublime in which the displeasure felt by the imagination as it comes up against its own limit has the effect of disclosing the unlimited power of reason in the *same* subject. The vast starry sky and the raging ocean are contrapurposive for the imagination which struggles to 'comprehend' the colossal expanse, the more 'apprehension' progresses. We noted in Chapter 7 that the comprehension of plurality in the unity of intuition describes the work done by the synthesis of reproduction in imagination. However, the sublime feeling overwhelms us when the imagination *fails to identify time*. Kant tells us that when confronted by an immense object 'the eye needs some time' to complete the apprehension yet is unable to complete its task because some of the earlier parts are invariably extinguished in the imagination before it has taken up the later ones (*KU* 174, *CJ* #26, 108). The power of the imagination to comprehend encounters its limit – *at which point it becomes something else*. In an unprecedented reversal of its function of synthesizing the progressive flow of apprehensions in inner sense, the imagination institutes a regress, violating its own schemas.

Let us recall the precise terms of Kant's account of the regress from section 27 of the *Critique of Judgement*:

> Measurement of a space (as apprehension) is at the same time a description of it and so an objective movement in the imagination and a progression. On the other hand, the comprehension

of multiplicity in a unity, not of thought, but of intuition, and therefore the comprehension in *one* moment [*Augenblick*] of what is apprehended successively, is a regression which once again annuls [*aufhebt*] the time condition in the progression of the imagination and makes *coexistence* [*zugleichsein*] intuitable. (*KU* 182, *CJ* #27, 116)

As we have seen, the role of the imagination in the mathematical sublime differs from that offered in the Subjective Deduction (in which imagination in its reproductive aspect is shown to be a necessary condition for deriving a complete representation from temporally discrete parts). In the 'Analytic of the Sublime' Kant inflects his account of imagination as a mode of sensuous apprehension with an aesthetic dimension. Indeed, Kant claims that imagination is capable of establishing a measure for itself. In the mathematical sublime Kant indicates that the numerical estimation of magnitude presupposes an aesthetic measure. The unit by which numbers are defined mathematically cannot be determined numerically. As Makkreel puts it: 'The concept of number not only has a pure intuitive content produced by the imagination as the faculty of pure *a priori* intuition, but also presupposes a given intuitive measure or form as its standard' (*ITKS* 379). This form is not empty but is both sensuous and absolute. While numbers present relative magnitude by means of comparison, the intuitive measure presents magnitude absolutely, prior to any comparison. The imagination has the role of both apprehending a magnitude in temporal succession and in comprehending it as a whole. As Makkreel points out, it is difficult to reconcile Kant's claim that the regress of the imagination allows for both comprehension in an instant [*Augenblick*] and for the intuition of coexistence, especially if we recall that in the *Critique of Pure Reason* Kant tells us that an instant is insufficient to enable us to apprehend the manifold contained in a given intuition (*ITKS* 386). Makkreel argues that the regression of the imagination in sublime experience does not annihilate time as such, simply the mathematical or linear form of time. He further argues that for logical comprehension, the content of sense is regarded as a 'manifold' [*Mannigfaltigkeit*], that is, as a complex of temporally determined parts, whereas for aesthetic comprehension the content of sense is regarded as a multiplicity [*Vielheit*] of *indeterminate* parts of a whole:

'The unity of the former must be inferred through a concept and involves an objective progress of the imagination. The unity of the latter can be instantaneously comprehended in the subjective regress of the imagination' (*IIK* 75).

The suggestion that imaginative regress concerns aesthetic intuition of a multiplicity rather than logical comprehension of a manifold recalls our earlier discussion of Bergson's notion of heterogeneous multiplicity and the affective continuum. There we noted that for Bergson, elements in a multiplicity interpenetrate and cannot be divided into discrete elements. Makkreel marks a similar thought in Kant by noting that in the 'Anticipations of Perception' Kant had distinguished between an extensive magnitude (generated by a successive synthesis, proceeding from parts to a whole) and an intensive magnitude which is apprehended in an instant. Intensive magnitudes represent multiplicity in the content of sense as a degree. Makkreel argues that aesthetic prehension names the act of grasping the 'absolute unity of a sensation' and hence must have an intensity that instantaneously measures a degree of influence on sense. Hence, 'whereas aesthetic prehension has as its correlate intensive magnitude as a measure of *existence*, aesthetic comprehension provides the measure for *coexistence*' (*IIK* 77). Aesthetic comprehension 'intuits multiplicity as an indeterminate unity, which is to be conceived as a totality or continuum without discrete parts' (*ITKS* 388).

The temporal chain is broken and with it the form of the same. It is in this collapse of time that a second nature is glimpsed – an immanent transcendence of 'this world'. In the crash of time the world is 'renewed'. The second nature which surpasses the 'given' manifold of experience is intuited aesthetically according to a measure which is given to itself. It is life which affirms itself in this moment and the immense joy – the painful happiness of a self-perfecting world – is consecrated in the depths of sacred ecstasy. This is the tragic feeling of life – a feeling which is of me but not mine – a thought so coherent that it excludes me at the moment that it is thought. It is this life beyond life, this life in excess of life which continues in me to invent, to hope, to dream, to desire. For past and present are the same kind, they belong to the same multiplicity, with the present only the most contracted form of the past. Past and present coexist virtually but the past is actualized when it enters into relation with a perception image – a moment of

Apollinian vision. In the searing light of intoxicated reality co-existence becomes intuitable. All the names of history am I. Nietzsche, euphoric in Turin, affirms the bliss born of pain from the abyss of being.

Thinking ecstatically

We have been concerned to show that a philosophy of ecstasy throws into relief new powers of thinking. In the annihilation of the temporal condition of experience it is possible to think otherwise, to live otherwise. Kant in the Second Analogy insists upon the objective validity of the *a priori* concept of causality – otherwise our ideas about succession are mere fantasy – a 'mere dream' (*CPR* A202/B247). Yet we might now say that we find ourselves in the position of one who has woken up in the middle of a dream but only to the consciousness that one is still dreaming. In the regress of the imagination we are able to comprehend as a whole that which is normally successively perceived.[1] The *Augenblick* is a concentrated moment of vision which carries with it a 'a feeling of life's being furthered'. As an idealizing power it eternalizes the return of the new – the cancellation of the form of inner sense *once again.*

We have suggested that the eternal return is a feeling that the body is able to materialize in thought. This is not to suggest that the affects must be rendered up to consciousness and commuted to signs. The emergence of eternal return in thought does not take place through the herd values that shape philosophical reflection and render it propositional. Nor does it emerge through the intermediary of consciousness, a reactive reflex. The latter can only hear this thought in terms of its needs: How will it serve them? How can I invest this thought? Let us act *as if it were true* (this is apparently to be ethical). In any case, Nietzsche insists that every living being thinks continually without knowing it (*GS* 354). The question is how to make its affects potent forces, ones which will renew thinking. Nietzsche claims that the capacity for communication has steadily accumulated in the species and now waits for the heirs who might squander it: the artists (ibid.). The artist is the one who will squander the powers of communication by exceeding them, creating visions for eyes that we do not have, percepts for senses that have yet to evolve. Art weaves these affects, these virtual powers into the semblance of a body (*Schein-Leib*). It renders them material without making them conscious. This is the superlative power of rapture. It heightens the feeling of life, it stimulates it to become more perfect than itself. It incites it to create the signs and the senses through which to communicate itself. And it excites this state without engaging consciousness. This is the source of its mystery and its electrifying effects. What the artist creates is something that we feel before we recognize (*if* we recognize...). It is contact with the unknown – something mystical, some would say.

We catch consciousness off guard in these supreme moments. We sense that ecstasy is a sign of the body's experimentation with its own sensible possibilities. What the body creates when consciousness is idling – in dreams, in intoxications – is something that surpasses nature. And so one begins to see that the artist, the lover, the lunatic, the epileptic, the saint, are experimentation sites for new ways of thinking. In each case, the 'ever self-renewing drive' to artistic creation, to the bringing of 'new worlds into life', is affirmed as the *feeling of life* as such: 'that *which must overcome itself again and again*' (*TSZ* II, 'Of Self-Overcoming').

From beginning to end, Nietzsche's philosophy is punctuated by the words '*immer wieder*'. This is the motor of a genuinely exploratory philosophy. If Nietzsche remains mystified by his own thought of eternal return, refashioning it endlessly in his notes, this is because to repeat is to make different. It is return which 'gives' experience. If one moment 'is' every moment then as in a dream, anything is possible at each moment. This is why Dionysian ecstasy is ever again *anew* 'discharged' in an Apollinian world of images. The pulsation of the moment – its rise and fall – marks a necessary intermingling of flux and reflux which in the absence of 'ground' functions as the 'agent of meaning'. It is in this sense that we might understand Klossowski's remark that in order to be communicable an intensity 'must take itself as an object, and thus turn back on itself' (*NCV* 97, *NVC* 60). Furthermore, the repetitive impetus of this desire is profoundly erotic. Irigaray shows us how it is possible to think of a fundamental auto-eroticism beneath the structures of auto-affection which 'give' the subject. The body thinks beyond itself in orgasmic bliss, returning upon itself ever again anew. The abyss is sexualized as zero – which is 'not one' in the sense of being non-unitary (not one thing in particular nor nothing at all). The absence of God is thought positively as the sanctification of zero. As Irigaray shows, the *encore* is non-representable, non-representational, yet it is felt in tidal waves of pleasure and pain. Thus, when Kant speaks of being attracted and repelled 'ever again' [*immer wieder*] in sublime experience, or when Nietzsche speaks of the orgiastic movements of a people being eternalized in their music we might say that the eternal return is communicated in thought.

Above all else, it is the tragic feeling which remains the privileged site for thinking eternal return for it is here that life consecrates and blesses itself through the bodies of the sacred throng:

> We are really for a brief moment [*Augenblick*] primordial being itself, feeling its raging desire for existence and joy in existence; the struggle, the pain, the destruction of phenomena, now appear necessary to us, on account of the excess of forms which press and push one another into life [...] We are pierced by the maddening sting of these pains in the very same moment in which we become one, as it were, with the measureless primordial joy in existence and when we anticipate in Dionysian ecstasy the indestructibility and eternity of this joy. (*BT* 17)

As dreamer and as Bacchic reveller, the human is the sacred vessel through which life shines in its solar brilliance and flames in its dark libidinal heat. In the highest and most illustrious of human joys it is nature that 'celebrates its own transfiguration' (*WP* 1051). In Nietzsche's philosophy, ecstasy describes both the pulsions of desire in their tensional interplay and the molten core of erotic annihilation itself. In their intensely sexual conflict, the Apollinian and Dionysian seek to overcome one another, continually inciting each other to new and more powerful births. In their ultimate consummation in Greek tragedy Dionysian intensity is discharged ever again anew into an Apollinian world of images and each collectively attain their highest intensification. Not only does this account for Nietzsche's very clear tendency to demarcate the Apollinian as a differentiating moment within the Dionysian so that the latter comes to signify the relation as such, it also identifies an erotic and thanatropic rhythm in which the self is fatally imbricated. As a ruthless and implacable individuating power the Apollinian creates the tension against which the Dionysian will to destruction ever anew contends.

The temporal is the libidinal

As we have seen, the spatialized time of metrication with its units, instants or points is rejected by Nietzsche in favour of a non-identical or libidinal time of difference. For Nietzsche, time is not a measurable phenomenon thought on the basis of the presentness of the 'now', for as has been indicated, the tempo of becoming implies otherness without number or supervenient identity (the immanent transcendence of *physis*). Becoming is tensional and tendential. The indeterminate feeling of pleasure and pain encountered in rapture cannot be quantified in terms of a concept because what constitutes the sensations are virtual or intensive tendencies which are relationally determined and consequently inseparable. Whether this is the delight of the concentrated lingering gaze elicited by free beauty or the turbulent negative pleasure of the sublime, the feeling of life simply 'is' becoming. It is to *realize in oneself* the 'eternal joy in becoming – the joy which also encompasses *joy in destruction*' (*TI* 'What I Owe to the Ancients', 5). As Bergson notes, happiness modifies 'the shade of a thousand perceptions or memories, and [...] in this sense it penetrates them' (TFW9). The aesthetic feeling is composed libidinally – rhythmically – like a musical mood within which one discordant note damages the effect of the whole. In the continuous multiplicity which Bergson associates with duration, elements interpenetrate one another in such a way. This sentiment is at the core of Nietzsche's thought of eternal return as a philosophy of ecstasy:

> 'Did you ever say Yes to one joy? O my friends, then you said Yes to *all* woe as well. All things are interlinked and entwined together, all things are in love;
>   if ever you wanted one time twice, if ever you said: 'You please me, happiness, flashing instant, moment' you wanted *everything* back!
>   Everything anew [*Alles von neuem*], everything eternal, everything interlinked, entwined, in love, O thus did you *love* the world.
> (*TSZ* IV, 'The Night Wanderer's Song', 10)

While perception appears to rely on the intuition of the discrete, rapture discloses becoming or continuity at the level of affective awareness. If we are to take seriously the immanence of thought to life, and ourselves to time, a libidinal vocabulary recommends itself because transfer, flow and exchange of energy are not commuted to their representation *for us*. Libidinal flows give a *sense* of difference, a sense of that which can only be experienced affectively. The necessity that is felt is the expression of the interpenetration of multiple forces that cannot be otherwise.

To '*be oneself* the eternal joy in becoming, that joy which also encompasses *joy in destruction*' is to experience the 'overflowing feeling of life' that Nietzsche characterizes as 'tragic'. It is to experience eternal return. This is an unbearable pleasure, it is too much, too beautiful. It is the mystic agony of dying from not dying, avoiding too sudden a death from delight. Libidinal becoming can only recome since such becoming does not take place 'in' time but in itself. By diverging from itself perpetually, becoming rebounds on itself of necessity. In the ocean of becoming, its tempo is not thought of as flow but as *reflux*: 'I teach you release from the eternal flow; the stream flows back into itself again and again, and you enter the same stream again and again, as the Same' (*KSA* 10/205/5[1]161). This is why the affective account of eternal return is so important. One feels all the passions in passion, all the notes of a melody in one, each pulse of the blood music summoning senses yet to be born.

The swollen ache of erotic longing tells us more about eternal return than the cold prying tentacles of abstract reason. Like the god Dionysus, the thought of eternal return is born untimely and half-formed in Nietzsche's writings, prompting a generation of philosophers to puzzle through its crypto-logical implications. Yet Dionysus is reborn, this time from the monstrous fecundity of divine physiology. We have suggested that there is a latent genealogy of eternal return smouldering within the mute carnality of the deeper zones of the body and that this is pursued in Nietzsche's explorations of rapture. His voracious desire for voyages in ecstasy drives his expeditions from *The Birth of Tragedy* to 'The Physiology of Art' with an urgency no outcome, no insight, no disaster could slake.

All joy wants the eternity of all things, wants honey, wants scum, wants drunken midnight, wants graves, wants consolation of graves' tears, wants gilded sunsets –

> – *what* does joy not want! it is thirstier, warmer, hungrier, more frightful, more secret than all woe, it wants *itself*, it bites into *itself*, the will of the ring wrestles within it, –
> – it wants love, it wants hate, it is superabundant, it gives, throws away, begs for someone to take it, thanks the one who takes, it would like to be hated,–
> – joy is so rich that it thirsts for woe, for hell, for hatred, for shame, for the cripple, for the *world*, – for it knows this world, oh it knows it! [...]
> For all joy wants itself, thus it also wants heart's agony! [...]
> – joy wants the eternity of *all* things, *wants deep, deep, eternity*!
> (*TSZ* IV, 'The Night Wanderer's Song', 11)

In the delirium of erotic joy, the sacred thrill of sublimity, the fire of mystic visions, there is a glory that no concept can convey. This is a desire which stings as it seduces and every thrust deeper into paradise seems to pierce the soul. Tragedy is a word for a feeling of intimacy with collapse. One lives as if illuminated from the inside yet simultaneously hidden in the open. Superlatives fail in the incandescent glare of this fierce sensuality. This ardent longing for eternity, this deep primal lust for the ring of return is the highest feeling of life, life's supreme power. It will do us no good and yet we thirst for it, we are repelled and yet we like it all the more, it makes us sick and yet we would give our whole lives for it, the price would not be too high.

Perhaps it will be said of us some day that our fate was to be wrecked against infinity.

If I love the sea and everything that is sealike, and love it most when it angrily contradicts me:
if that joy in seeking is in me, that drives sails towards the undiscovered, if a seafarer's joy is in my joy:
if ever my rejoicing cried: 'The shore has faded away – now the last fetter drops from me,
the boundless roars around me, far out, space and time sparkle for me, well now! well! old heart!'

Oh how should I not lust for eternity [*nach die Ewigkeit brünstig sein*] and for the wedding ring of rings, the ring of return?
Never yet did I find the woman by whom I wanted children, unless it be this woman that I love: for I love you, O eternity!
For I love you, O eternity!

(TSZ III, 'The Seven Seals', 5)

Notes

1 In the Horizon of the Infinite

1. David Allison names Kierkegaard, Kojève, the surrealists, Bataille, Foucault, Lacan and Deleuze and Guattari as significant exemplars in 'Musical Psychodramatics: *Ecstasis* in Nietzsche' in Alan D. Schrift (ed.), *Why Nietzsche Still?: Reflections on Drama, Culture and Politics* (Berkeley: University of California Press, 2000), p. 67. It seems appropriate to add Heidegger to this list, given the wide-ranging and multifaceted treatment of ecstasy in both his earlier and later thinking in relation to temporality, language and the work of art.
2. Lingis, A. (1994), *Foreign Bodies*, p. 6.
3. If Sartre is right in his assertion that consciousness introduces a lack into the fullness of being, perhaps it could be argued that it is the life-negating perspective of the for-itself which conditions the value economy of modern thought whether overtly humanist or not. For example, as David Farrell Krell shows in *Daimon Life: Heidegger and Philosophy* (Bloomington & Indianapolis: Indiana Press, 1992) while Heidegger understands the disclosure of being as self-differing in non-negative terms, his discrimination of the human from the animal on the basis of the proper ek-sistence of man is premised upon a notion of the world poverty of 'mere life'. Similarly, it could be shown that the Derridean notion of *différance* encodes the negative within a logical syntax which implicitly reinforces the form of the same at the conceptual level albeit indefinitely deferred. Merleau-Ponty's fundamental conviction that the body is *of* the world – distinct yet not separate from it – provides an interesting contrast to this tendency and it is to be noted that his thought of 'wild being' registers a continuity that explicitly rejects the 'abyss' or ontological void between the 'for itself' and the 'in itself' (*V&I* 136–7). However, his commitment to phenomenological methodology provokes him into reinscribing a transcendental unity of apperception at the heart of the 'flesh'. In every case, it is language which is fetishized as the common ground for marking the 'groundless' but is it enough to note the failure of representational structures to avoid perpetuating their values? As Nietzsche famously said: 'I fear we are not getting rid of God because we still believe in grammar...' (*TI* 'Reason in Philosophy', 5).

2 The Tempo of Becoming

1. David Allison explores the theme of tonal anticipation in 'Musical Psychodramatics' (op. cit.) commenting how in musical psychoacoustics

resolution of dissonance yields a heightening of pleasure, a central component of Nietzsche's account of tragedy (72–3).
2. J. Sallis (p. 19), 'Apollo's Mimesis', *Journal of the British Society for Phenomenology*, vol. 15, no.1, January 1984, 16–21.
3. See Derrida's remarks in *Dissemination* (1972) translated by Barbara Johnson (London: Athlone, 1981), pp. 138–9. By contrast, for Deleuze the difference between a simulacrum and what it simulates is not to be thought in terms of an original identity. Although a resemblance to an original is implied it is derived as an effect of a primary difference. Deleuze argues that the will to eliminate simulacra has no motivation apart from the moral: 'What is condemned in the figure of simulacra is the state of free, oceanic differences, of nomadic distributions and crowned anarchy, along with all that malice which challenges both the notion of the model and that of the copy' (*DR* 265).
4. Note Schopenhauer's discussion of the folksong in similar terms in *The World as Will and Representation* I, # 51, 249; *WWV* I, 359: 'For to seize the mood of the moment [*Augenblick*] and embody it in song is the whole achievement of this kind of poetry'. It is worth noting that whereas Schopenhauer speaks of the 'constant recurrence' of the same sensations ('which exist as permanently as humanity itself') Nietzsche emphasizes the transformative power of their repetition.

3   A Feeling of Life

1. Y. Mishima, *Confessions of a Mask*, translated by Meredith Weatherby (London: Paladin, 1988), p. 5.
2. In *The Birth of Tragedy* and related writings of the period Nietzsche appears to endorse the Kantian notion of disinterestedness (see in particular *BT* 5) yet by the time of *On the Genealogy of Morals* he explicitly rejects the idea on the grounds that it introduces the concept of the spectator into the concept 'beautiful' and in Schopenhauer's case, is symptomatic of an ascetic desire to deny the role of carnality in experience of the beautiful (see 'Third Essay: What is the Meaning of Ascetic Ideals?'6). However, Nietzsche's objection in the latter text concerns the reactive value economy in which the experience is inscribed, which leaves open the possibility of reading disinterestedness as an affirmative wave of transcendental 'feeling'. The intricacies of Nietzsche's genealogical critique of Kant's theory of the beautiful and the sublime and its significance for a transcendental materialism is explored in a number of remarkable essays by Jim Urpeth including: 'A "Pessimism of Strength": Nietzsche and the Tragic Sublime' in J. Lippitt (ed.) *Nietzsche's Futures* (London: Macmillan Press – now Palgrave Macmillan, 1999), pp. 129–48; 'A "Sacred Thrill": Presentation and Affectivity in the Analytic of the Sublime' in A. Rehberg and R. Jones, *The Matter of Critique: Readings on Kant's Philosophy* (Manchester: Clinamen Press, 2000), pp. 61–78; 'The Vitalisation of Aesthetic Form: Kant, Nietzsche, Heidegger, Focillon' in

S. Brewster, J. Joughin, D. Owen, R. Walker (eds), *Inhuman Reflections* (Manchester: Manchester University Press, 2000), pp. 72–87.

3. Nick Land, 'Delighted to Death', *Pli: Warwick Journal of Philosophy*, vol. 3, no. 2 (1991), 83.

4. Jim Urpeth 'A "Sacred Thrill": Presentation and Affectivity in the Analytic of the Sublime' in A. Rehberg and R. Jones, *The Matter of Critique, op.cit.*, p. 71.

5. Gary Banham (pp. 160–1) 'Creating the Future: Legislation and Aesthetics' in J. Lippitt, op.cit., pp.149–66.

6. It is to be noted that Nietzsche quotes this section from Schopenhauer at length in section 16 of *The Birth of Tragedy* as a prelude to describing Dionysian art in terms of the eternal life beyond all phenomena.

7. For example, he writes in a short text, 'Music and Words', that all our language of feelings, emotions, sensations, willing are representations and cannot tell us about the essence of the 'indecipherable' will (*KSA* 7, 361). All degrees of pleasure and displeasure are expressions of this opaque yet universal 'subground' and it is this that Nietzsche calls 'will'. These sensations reverberate, they determinate each other in intensity but cannot be isolated and quantified. As Nietzsche says, our whole corporeality is related to this will. This will (an originary appearance form, not essence) signifies all becoming, including its 'scale of sensations of pleasure and displeasure' which is symbolically expressed in lyric and music (*KSA* 7, 362).

8. Nietzsche distinguishes three ways in which feelings can be known: through thought, gestural language and tonal language respectively. Conscious thought is least able to express representations conjoined with will owing to the inadequacy of conceptual language. Gestural language is more suited for the symbolism of unconscious feeling (representation) but it is tonal language that is best equipped to communicate the states of the will which it symbolizes in rhythm, dynamics and harmony, the latter signifying the 'pure essence' of the will (*KSA* 1, 574).

9. Such a genealogical analysis might be applied to Heidegger's account of aesthetic disinterestedness. In his commentary on Nietzsche's philosophy of art, Heidegger complains that Schopenhauer totally misunderstood Kantian disinterestedness (*N*, I, 100–102). The silencing of the will is seen as a call for indifference and apathy but arguably it is Schopenhauer's anti-humanism that needles Heidegger most. After all, Schopenhauer's recommendations for this silencing of the will (avoidance of alcohol and opium in favour of a cold bath and an early night) are ascetic regimes that Heidegger might endorse, especially given his rejection of rapture as an alcoholically induced state or indeed grand passion (*WWV*, II, 480, *WWR*, II, 368). Perhaps the idea that the body is already synthesizing its own drugs is thought to compromise the authenticity of *Dasein*.

10. Nick Land, 'Delighted to Death', 78.

4 Men of Fire

1. See Arthur Rimbaud, 'La Lettre du Voyant' in W.M. Frohock, *Rimbaud's Poetic Practice: Image and Theme in the Major Poems* (Massachusetts: Harvard University Press, 1963), p. 235.
2. Nietzsche also uses the phrase 'physiology of aesthetics' (in section 8 of the third essay of *On the Genealogy of Morals*). The relevant sections of *The Will to Power* are clustered in Chapter IV, 'The Will to Power as Art' (794–853). The plan below from 1888 indicates the scope of the projected investigation (*KSA* 13, 529–530/17[9]):
   Towards the Physiology of Art
   1. Rapture as prerequisite: causes of rapture
   2. Typical symptoms of rapture
   3. The *feeling* of power [*Kraft*] and plenitude in rapture: its *idealizing* effect
   4. The actual *increase* in force: its actual *beautification* [*Verschönerung*]. A consideration: the extent to which our value 'beautiful' is completely *anthropocentric*: on the biological prerequisites concerning growth and progress. Increase of force e.g. in the *dance* of the sexes. The pathological element in rapture; the physiological danger of art –
   5. The Apollinian, the Dionysian ... fundamental types: more extensive compared with our art specialisms
   6. Question: where architecture belongs
   7. The participation of artistic capacities in normal life, their tonic practice: conversely, the ugly
   8. The question of epidemic and contagion
   9. Problem of 'health' and 'hysteria' – genius = neurosis
   10. Art as suggestion, as means of communication, as the province of invention of the induction psycho-motrice
   11. The inartistic states: objectivity, mania for mirroring, neutrality. The impoverished *will*; loss of capital
   12. The inartistic states: Abstractness. The impoverished *senses*
   13. The inartistic states: emaciation, impoverishment, depletion, – will to nothingness. Christ, Buddhist, nihilist. The impoverished *body*.
   14. The inartistic states: idiosyncrasies (of the *weak*, of the *medium*). Fear of the senses, of power, of rapture (instinct of the *inferior* life forms)
   15. How is *tragic* art possible?
   16. The romantic type: ambiguous. Its consequence is 'naturalism'...
   17. Problem of the *actor* – 'dishonesty', the typical power of transformation as a *character flaw*...
   Lack of shame, the Hanswurst, the satyr, the buffo, the Gil Blas, the actor who plays the artist...
   18. Art as *rapture*, medically: Amnesty. tonic, complete and partial impotence
3. It is to be noted that Nietzsche frequently speaks *against* intoxication as a high or noble state and is often contemptuous of those given to ecsta-

tic trances and visionary pronouncements (e.g. *Daybreak* 14, 66, 50). Similarly, he speaks against the grand gestures of Romanticism. Perhaps it is Apollinian rapture which Nietzsche ultimately sees as the highest power. This might be understood as the *'calm of strength* which is essentially forbearance from reaction' as opposed to the *calm of exhaustion* which is 'rigidity to the point of anaesthesia' (*WP* 47). It is claimed that all philosophical and ascetic procedures aim at the second but really intend the former. Provoking the symptoms of derangement and ruin has been mistaken for becoming stronger, wiser, extra-human: 'Here the experience of *intoxication* proved misleading. This increases the feeling of power in the highest degree – therefore, naively judged, *power itself.* On the highest rung of power one placed *the most intoxicated,* the ecstatic. (– There are two sources of *intoxication*: the over-great fullness of life and a state of pathological nourishment of the brain.)' (*WP* 48). Further resources for regarding the Apollinian as the highest type are provided in the notes from *The Will to Power* which praise the strength to suspend activity and the capacity not to react (unlike the hysteric or Dionysiac) (*WP* 45). Other remarks concern misunderstanding rapture physiologically (*KSA* 13/253) or treating it as a means of getting over/ disavowing a fundamental poverty (*KSA* 10/660]).

4. The two contemporary philosophers whom I believe have done the most to challenge this conception of the body-subject are Pierre Klossowski and Gilles Deleuze. Klossowski suggests that 'the body, insofar as it is grasped by consciousness, *dissociates itself* from the impulses which flow through it', a thought provocatively elaborated in his account of a semiotic of impulses within which the self emerges as a fortuitous moment. See *Nietzsche and the Vicious Circle* (1969) translated by D. W. Smith (London: Athlone, 1997, pp. 27 ff.). Deleuze challenges the doctrine of the faculties as presented by Kant on the grounds that both a common object of knowledge and a common mode of knowing are presupposed by the claim that the faculties work in harmony with one another. See *Difference and Repetition* (1968), translated by Paul Patton (London: Athlone, 1994), especially Chapter 3.
5. *Hölderlin,* Selected verse edited and translated by Michael Hamburger, (Harmondsworth: Penguin, 1961), p. 247.
6. Ibid, p. xx.
7. Cited in A. M. & Renilde Hammacher, *Van Gogh* (London: Thames and Hudson 1982), p. 200.
8. Ibid.
9. Vincent Van Gogh, letter to Theo, Arles, mid-July 1888, cited in M. Roskill (ed.), *The Letters of Van Gogh* (Great Britain: Fontana, 1963) pp. 272–3.
10. 'A mood assails us. It comes neither from "outside" nor from "inside", but arises as a way of Being-in-the-world from out of itself' – Martin Heidegger, *Being and Time* (1927), translated by John Macquarrie and

Edward Robinson (Oxford: Blackwell, 1962), p. 176, *Sein und Zeit* (Tübingen: Max Niemeyer Verlag, 1986) p. 136.
11. Hammacher, op. cit., p. 174.
12. Georges Bataille, *Guilty* (1961), translated by Bruce Boone (USA: Lapis Press, 1988), p. 30.
13. Georges Bataille, 'Van Gogh as Prometheus', *October* 36, Spring 1986, MIT Press, p. 59.
14. Isabella von Ungern-Sternberg, cited in S.L. Gilman and D. Parent, *Conversations with Nietzsche: A Life in the Words of His Contemporaries* (Oxford: Oxford University Press, 1987), p. 259.
15. Ibid., p. 260.

5　A General Theory of Collapse

1. See Arthur Rimbaud, 'La Lettre du Voyant' in W. M. Frohock, *Rimbaud's Poetic Practice: Image and Theme in the Major Poems* (Massachusetts: Harvard University Press, 1963), pp. 235–6.
2. With respect to Bergson, Blanchot comments as follows: 'Normality is the abnormal surpassed. And the abnormal is an appearance of riches – in the most favourable cases – which indicates a real impoverishment (even from this point of view, it would seem more accurate to say only that madness is a kind of wealth which depends on an impoverishment, a lack)' (*MPE* 111). But can this be maintained? Doesn't Bergson insist on an originary plenitude when he designates states such as delirium, hallucination, obsession as positive facts (*MPFR* 44)? While certain phenomena (such as aphasia) are regarded by Bergson as merely impoverishments, mental illnesses are seen as frequently exhibiting an overplus. Indeed, with certain states 'we have to consider what they are and what they bring, instead of what they are not and what they take away' (*MPFR* 44). In claiming that illness may *inhibit certain inhibitory functions* it seems to me that Bergson regards it as positive *once again*. From this perspective, the question is not so much why individuals such as Van Gogh produce certain phenomena as why they are not found in the 'normal healthy mind'.
3. See the first communication of the eternal return in section 341 of *The Gay Science*. See also Freud (1920) 'Beyond the Pleasure Principle' in *On Metapsychology: The Theory of Psychoanalysis*, translated by James Strachey and Angela Richards (London: Pelican, 1984) p. 307. I offer some reflections on these 'demonic' overtones in 'Interminable Intensity: Nietzsche's Demonic Nihilism' in *Evil Spirits: Nihilism and the Fate of Modernity*, edited by Gary Banham and Charlie Blake (Manchester: Manchester University Press, 2000), pp. 72–88.
4. See Oliver Sacks (1971), *Migraine: Understanding a Common Disorder* (London: Duckworth, 1985, Second Edition).
5. Ibid., p. 85.

6. Ibid., p.106.
7. See Wilhelm Reich (1942), *The Function of the Orgasm: Sex-Economic Problems of Biological Energy*, translated by Vincent R. Carfagno (London: Souvenir Press, 1989), p. 384.
8. Ibid.
9. See Gilles Deleuze and Félix Guattari (1972), *Anti-Oedipus: Capitalism and Schizophrenia*, translated by Robert Hurley, Mark Seem and Helen R. Lane (London, Athlone, 1984), p. 291.
10. See David Farrell Krell and Donald L. Bates, *The Good European: Nietzsche's Work Sites in Word and Image* (Chicago: University of Chicago Press, 1997), pp. 148–9.
11. The phrase is Deleuze's. See *Difference and Repetition* (1968) translated by Paul Patton (London: Athlone, 1994), p.134.
12. Bergson gives the example of hearing a melody as a whole rather than as a sequence of distinctive notes. To dwell for too long on a singular note interrupts the rhythm and qualitatively distorts the whole of the musical phrase (*TFW* 100-1).
13. See 'Versuch über die Krankheiten des Kopfes', in *Immanuel Kant: Vorkritische Schriften bis 1768, 2 Werkausgabe Band II* , edited by Wilhelm Weischedel (Frankfurt: Surkamp, 1968), p.894.

6 The Night of Unknowing

1. According to Nietzsche, for the Greeks, the satyr is the 'archetype' of man, 'the expression of his strongest and highest excitations (*BT* 8): further he is a 'symbol of the sexual omnipotence of nature', an idea we are told that the Greeks used to contemplate with reverence (Ibid.)
2. See Bataille's remarks in the Preface to *On Nietzsche* (1945) translated by Sylvère Lotringer (New York: Paragon, 1992) in which he suggests that a recourse to the poetic may be to compromise extreme affective states. In this context he remarks that 'Nietzsche is far from having resolved this difficulty, since Zarathustra is a poet, in fact a literary fiction' (p. xxxii). This may also account for his claim that 'the work of Nietzsche hasn't a lot to do with investigations into mysticism' (p. 174). For a discussion of ecstasy as 'poetic intimacy with the world' in *Thus Spoke Zarathustra*, see Tyler T. Roberts, 'Ecstatic Philosophy', in *Nietzsche and the Divine*, edited by John Lippitt and Jim Urpeth (Manchester: Clinamen, 2000), pp. 200–225. Roberts notes how the closing sections of Book Three of *Thus Spoke Zarathustra* consist of love songs to life and to eternity and that the closing refrain 'Thus spoke Zarathustra' is absent from these passages, suggesting ecstatic dissolution and union with the cosmos (p. 204). As Roberts observes, the singing and dancing that end Book Three are explicitly 'Dionysian' expressions of ecstasy. What I would emphasize here is the erotic context of affirmation – a desire so strong that it annihilates the one who wills it. Again, in the 'Nightwanderer's Song' in Book

Four, eternity is loved, desired, adored and once more, it is a desire which is utterly transformative.

3. It may seem perverse to view Irigaray's exploration of female mysticism as consonant with Nietzsche's philosophy of ecstasy, especially given her concerted resistance to this theme in *Marine Lover of Friedrich Nietzsche* (1980), translated by Gillian C. Gill (New York: Columbia University Press, 1991). In the latter, Irigaray suggests that for Nietzsche ecstasy is flight from the body, that eternal return remains bound up in a masculinist model of the self-as-same and that for him there is no rapture of the deep. Some of her most beautiful formulations ('Yet is there any rapture greater than the sea?' (*ML* 13), 'And, for me, ebb and flow have always set the rhythm of time' (*ML*14)) strike me as extremely Nietzschean sentiments. However, to contest Irigaray's reading of Nietzsche in this way may be to mistake the nature of her 'amorous engagement' with him. I suggest that one of the issues at stake for Irigaray may well be the domestication of misogyny as exemplified by Derrida's *Spurs* (who wouldn't be irritated with all those sails and veils?) The productive question which her work poses is whether the *feeling* of eternal return is a gendered one. The anti-humanist position may seem by definition to reject this possibility but one must ask what will prevent anti-humanism from perpetuating masculinist 'monosexual' values.

4. It is perhaps fair to say that 'La Mystérique' occupies a point of tension in Irigaray's study of female subjectivity and sexuality in so far as it poses questions about the validity of any humanist politics. Andrea Rehberg provides an admirably lucid account of these issues in her discussion essay 'Feminism, Phenomenology, Writing', in *The Journal of the British Society for Phenomenology*, vol. 29, no. 3, (1998), 320–5.

5. One of Irigaray's chief interlocutors in *Speculum* is Freud, whose account of male psychosexual development hinges upon the occlusion of female sexual specificity and the construction of femininity as 'castrated'. It is at the moment at which the young boy *sees* the genitalia of a young girl that the 'reality' of the castration threat is realized, precipitating the relinquishment of Oedipal attachments and the genesis of social subjectivity. Irigaray argues that if this masculine ego is to be valuable some 'mirror' is required to reflect this image, a role which the 'lacking' feminine fulfils. Yet if an *other* image, an *other* mirror were to intervene, this would entail the risk of a 'mortal crisis' (*SA* 63, *SW* 54). Within Freud's theatre of representation, woman's sexuality presents the horror of 'nothing to be seen'.

6. In *Bergsonism* (1966) translated by Hugh Tomlinson and Barbara Habberjam (New York: Zone, 1988) Deleuze argues that access to 'the open creative totality' is achieved through action rather than contemplation: 'In philosophy itself, there is still too much alleged contemplation: Everything happens as if intelligence were already imbued with emotion, thus with intuition, but not sufficiently so for creating in conformity to this emotion. Thus the great souls – to a greater extent than philosophers – are those of artists and mystics (at least those of a Christian mysticism

that Bergson describes as being completely superabundant activity, action, creation)' (p. 112).
7. See Bataille's remarks in *Madame Edwarda* (1956) included in *My Mother, Madame Edwarda, The Dead Man* translated by Austryn Wainhouse (London: Marion Boyars, 1995), p. 141: 'The act whereby being – existence – is bestowed upon us is an *unbearable* surpassing of being, an act no less unbearable than that of dying. Since, in death, being is taken away from us at the same time it is given to us, we must seek it in those unbearable moments when it seems to us that we are dying because existence in us, during those interludes, exists through nothing but a sustaining and ruinous excess, when the fullness of horror and that of joy coincide'. See also *IE* 124 and *SA* 244, *SW* 196.
8. See Jacques Lacan, 'God and the *Jouissance* of The Woman (1972–73), cited in *Feminine Sexuality: Jacques Lacan and the École Freudienne*, edited by Juliet Mitchell and Jacqueline Rose, translated by Jacqueline Rose (London: Macmillan, 1982), p. 147.

7 Great Moments of Oblivion

1. See *SB* 8, 521.
2. Hölderlin writes as follows:

> Thereby, in the rhythmic sequence of the representations wherein *transport* presents itself, there becomes necessary *what in poetic metre is called caesura*, the pure word, the counter-rhythmic rupture; namely, in order to meet the onrushing change of representations at its highest point in such a manner that very soon there does not appear the change of representations but representation itself. (*H* 102)

3. Jean Beaufret cited by Ronald Bogue in his essay 'The Betrayal of God', in Mary Bryden (ed.), *Deleuze and Religion* (London: Routledge, 2001), p. 19.
4. See Kant's account of the three subjective syntheses in the A-Deduction in *The Critique of Pure Reason*. The first of these is the synthesis of apprehension in intuition. This makes it possible for multifarious impressions of sense to be apprehended as one manifold. Kant tells us that every intuition contains in itself a manifold which can be represented as a manifold only in so far as the mind distinguishes the time in the sequence of one impression upon another: 'for each representation, in so far *as it is contained in a single moment* [*Augenblick*], can never be anything other than absolute unity' (*KRV* 162, *CPR*, A 99, 131). In order that unity of intuition may arise out of a manifold it must first be 'run through [*Durchlaufen*]' and 'taken together [*Zusammennehmung*]' (*KRV* 163, *CPR*, A 99, 131). The synthesis of reproduction in imagination deals with the power of the imagination to reproduce past representations in the present (and their temporal progression). Consequently, 'the synthesis of apprehension is

inseparably bound up with the synthesis of reproduction' (*KRV* 165, *CPR*, A 102, 133). The synthesis of recognition in a concept provides the unity of complete representations. This is necessary because if we were not conscious that what we think is the same as what we thought a moment before, all reproduction in the series of representations would be in vain.

5. As is well known, Nietzsche claimed to have 'experienced' the thought of eternal return when out walking in Sils Maria in August 1881. Notes concerning a 'new manner of living' include: *KSA* 9/494/11[141]; 9/163[504]; 9/519/11[195]; 9/519/11[197].

6. See Manuel de Landa's discussion (p. 152), in his essay 'Nonorganic Life' in *Incorporations*, edited by J. Crary and S. Kwinter (New York: Zone, 1992), pp.129–67.

7. See page 84 of David Farrell Krell's illuminating discussion in 'Consultations with the Paternal Shadow: Gasché, Derrida and Klossowski on *Ecce Homo*', in *Exceedingly Nietzsche*, edited by David Farrell Krell and David Wood (London: Routledge, 1988) 80–94.

8 The Sense of Eternity

1. This is another way of thinking through the idea of 'contraction-memory' that Bergson discusses in *Matter and Memory*, which 'prolongs, one into another, a plurality of moments [...] contracting a number of external moments into a single internal moment'. (Cited in R. Durie (p. 161) 'Splitting Time: Bergson's Philosophical Legacy', *Philosophy Today*, vol. 44, no. 2/4, Summer 2000, 152–68).

Bibliography

Note on Translations

References to Nietzsche's published works are indicated by relevant *section* numbers. References to the *Nachlass* are from the Colli-Montinari *Kritische Studienausgabe*. My own translations of Nietzsche are indebted to the published translations listed below. For other foreign-language texts (e.g. Kant, Schopenhauer) references to both primary texts and relevant translations are supplied although translations have again been slightly modified. Where translations alone have been used this is indicated.

Editions of Nietzsche in German

[*KSA*] The edition used throughout is the *Friedrich Nietzsche – Sämtliche Werke, Kritische Studienausgabe*, Deutscher Taschenbuch Verlag, Walter de Gruyter, Berlin, edited by Giorgio Colli and Mazzino Montinari, 1967–77. References are by volume, page number and note number respectively.

[*SB*] *Friedrich Nietzsche – Sämtliche Briefe, Kritische Studienausgabe*, Deutscher Taschenbuch Verlag, Walter de Gruyter, Berlin, edited by Giorgio Colli and Mazzino Montinari, 1986.

English Translations of Nietzsche

[*BT*] *The Birth of Tragedy* (1872), translated by W. Kaufmann (New York: Vintage, 1967).

[*PTAG*] *Philosophy in the Tragic Age of the Greeks* (1873), translated by M. Cowan (Chicago: Gateway, 1962).

[*TL*] 'On Truth and Lies in a Non-Moral Sense' (1873), translated by D. Breazeale, *Philosophy and Truth: Selections from Nietzsche's Notebooks of the Early 1870's* (New Jersey: Humanities Paperback Library, 1979).

[*UM*] *Untimely Meditations* (1874), translated by R.J. Hollingdale (Cambridge: Cambridge University Press, 1983).

[*D*] *Daybreak* (1881), translated by R.J. Hollingdale (Cambridge: Cambridge University Press, 1982).

[*HH*] *Human all too Human* (1878), translated by R.J. Hollingdale (Cambridge: Cambridge University Press, 1986).

[*AOM*] *Assorted Opinions and Maxims* (1879), translated by R.J. Hollingdale (Cambridge: Cambridge University Press, 1986).

[*GS*] *The Gay Science* (1882), translated by Walter Kaufmann (New York: Vintage, 1974).

[*BGE*] *Beyond Good and Evil* (1886), translated by R.J. Hollingdale (Harmondsworth: Penguin, 1972).

[*GM*] *On the Genealogy of Morals* (1887), translated by Walter Kaufmann (New York: Vintage, 1969).

[*TI*] *Twilight of the Idols* (1888), translated by R.J. Hollingdale (Harmondsworth: Penguin, 1968).

[*A*] *The Anti-Christ* (1888), translated by R.J. Hollingdale (Harmondsworth: Penguin, 1968).

[*WP*] *The Will to Power* (1880s), translated by Walter Kaufmann and R.J. Hollingdale (New York: Vintage, 1968).

Works by Other Authors

Allison, David, 'Musical Psychodramatics: *Ecstasis* in Nietzsche', in Alan. D. Schrift (ed.), *Why Nietzsche Still?: Reflections on Drama, Culture and Politics* (Berkeley: University of California Press, 2000, pp. 66–78).

Banham, Gary, 'Creating the Future: Legislation and Aesthetics', in *Nietzsche's Futures*, edited by John Lippitt (London: Macmillan Press – now Palgrave Macmillan, 1999), pp. 149–66.

Banham, Gary and Blake, Charlie (eds), *Evil Spirits: Nihilism and the Fate of Modernity*, (Manchester: Manchester University Press, 2000).

[*VE*] Bataille, George, *Visions of Excess: Selected Writings 1927–39*, translated by Allan Stoekl (Manchester: Manchester University Press, 1985).

Bataille, Georges (1945) *On Nietzsche*, translated by Sylvère Lotringer (New York: Paragon, 1992).

[*IE*] Bataille, Georges (1954), *Inner Experience*, translated by Leslie Anne Boldt (Albany: SUNY Press, 1988).

[*ME*] Bataille, Georges (1956), *Madame Edwarda* included in *My Mother, Madame Edwarda, The Dead Man*, translated by Austryn Wainhouse (London: Marion Boyars, 1995).

[*E*] Bataille, Georges (1957), *Eroticism*, translated by Mary Dalwood (London: Marion Boyars, 1987).

[*G*] Bataille, Georges (1961), *Guilty*, translated by Bruce Boone (USA: The Lapis Press, 1988).

Bataille, Georges 'Van Gogh as Prometheus', *October* 36, Spring 1986 (Cambridge, MA: MIT Press 1986).

[*MPFR*] Bergson, Henri (1908), 'Memory of the Present and False Recognition', in Durie, Robin (ed.), *Time and the Instant: Essays in the Physics and Philosophy of Time* (Manchester: Clinamen, 2000), pp. 36–63.

[*TFW*] Bergson, Henri, *Time and Free Will*, translated by F.L. Pogson (London: Macmillan, 1910).

[*MPE*] Blanchot, Maurice (1951), 'Madness par excellence' in M. Holland (ed.), *The Blanchot Reader* (Oxford: Blackwell, 1995).

Bryden, Mary (ed.), *Deleuze and Religion* (London: Routledge, 2001).

de Landa, Manuel (1992), 'Nonorganic Life', in J. Crary and S. Kwinter (eds), *Incorporations* (New York: Zone, 1992).

Deleuze, Gilles (1966), *Bergsonism*, translated by Hugh Tomlinson and Barbara Habberjam (New York: Zone, 1988).

[*NP*] Deleuze, Gilles (1962), *Nietzsche and Philosophy*, translated by Hugh Tomlinson (London: Athlone, 1983).

[*ECC*] Deleuze, Gilles (1993), *Essays Critical and Clinical*, translated by Daniel W. Smith (London: Verso, 1998).

Deleuze, Gilles and Guattari, Félix (1972), *Anti-Oedipus: Capitalism and Schizophrenia*, translated by Robert Hurley, Mark Seem and Helen R. Lane, (London, Athlone, 1984).

[*TP*] Deleuze, Gilles and Guattari, Félix (1980), *A Thousand Plateaus*, translated by Brian Massumi (London: Athlone, 1988).

[*WIP*] Deleuze, Gilles and Guattari, Félix (1991), *What is Philosophy?*, translated by Graham Burchell and Hugh Tomlinson (London: Verso, 1994).

Derrida, Jacques (1972), *Dissemination*, translated by Barbara Johnson (London: Athlone, 1981).

[*I*] Dostoyevsky, Fyodor (1869), *The Idiot*, translated by David Magarshack (Harmondsworth: Penguin, 1955).

[*DV*] Dostoyevsky, Fyodor (1871), *The Devils*, translated by David Magarshack (Harmondsworth: Penguin, 1953).

Durie, Robin (ed.), *Time and the Instant: Essays in the Physics and Philosophy of Time* (Manchester: Clinamen, 2000).

Durie, Robin, 'Splitting Time: Bergson's Philosophical Legacy', *Philosophy Today*, vol. 44, no. 2/4, Summer 2000, 152–68.

[*PFL* 11] Freud, Sigmund (1920), 'Beyond the Pleasure Principle', in *On Metapsychology: the Theory of Psychoanalysis*, The Pelican Freud Library, vol. 11, translated by James Strachey and Angela Richards (Harmondsworth: Pelican, 1984).

[*PFL* 12] Freud, Sigmund (1930), 'Civilization and its Discontents', in *Civilization, Society and Religion: Group Psychology, Civilization and its Discontents and Other Works*, The Pelican Freud Library, vol. 12, translated by James Strachey (Harmondsworth: Pelican, 1985).

[*PFL* 2] Freud, Sigmund (1933), 'The Dissection of the Psychical Personality', in *New Introductory Lectures on Psychoanalysis*, The Pelican Freud Library, vol. 2, translated by James Strachey (Harmondsworth: Pelican, 1973).

Frohock, W.M., *Rimbaud's Poetic Practice: Image and Theme in the Major Poems* (Massachusetts: Harvard University Press, 1963).

Hamburger, Michael (ed.), *Hölderlin*, selected verse, edited and translated (Harmondsworth: Penguin, 1961).

Hammacher, A.M. and R. (eds), *Van Gogh* (London: Thames and Hudson, 1982).

[*B&T*] Heidegger, M. (1927), *Being and Time*, translated by J. Macquarrie and E. Robinson (Oxford: Blackwell, 1962).

[*N,I*] Heidegger, M. (1961), *Nietzsche: The Will to Power as Art*, translated by David Farrell Krell (London: Routledge & Kegan Paul, 1981).

[*SW*] Irigaray, Luce (1974), *Speculum of the Other Woman*, translated by Gillian C. Gill (New York: Cornell University, 1985). [*SA*] *Speculum de L'Autre Femme* (Paris: Les Éditions de Minuit, 1974).

[*TS*] Irigaray, Luce (1977), *This Sex Which Is Not One*, translated by Catherine Porter (New York: Cornell University Press, 1985). [*CS*] *Ce Sexe qui n'en est pas un* (Paris: Les Éditions de Minuit, 1977).

[*ML*] Irigaray, Luce (1980), *Marine Lover of Friedrich Nietzsche*, translated by Gillian C. Gill (New York: Columbia University Press, 1991). *Amante Marine: De Friedrich Nietzsche* (Paris: Minuit, 1980).

[*DSS*]Kant, Immanuel 'Dreams of a Spirit-Seer Elucidated by Dreams of Metaphysics', in *Immanuel Kant:Theoretical Philosophy 1755–70*, translated and edited by David Walford in collaboration with Ralf Meerbote (Cambridge: Cambridge University Press, 1992); [*TG*] 'Träume eines Geistersehers, erläutert durch Träume der Metaphysik', in *Immanuel Kant: Werkausgabe Band II: Vorkritische Schriften bis 1768*, edited by Wilhelm Weischedel (Frankfurt am Main: Suhrkamp, 1968).

[*CPR*] Kant, Immanuel (1781 and 1787), *Critique of Pure Reason*, translated by Norman Kemp Smith (London: Macmillan, 1933); [*KRV*] *Immanuel Kant: Werkausgabe Band III: Kritik der Reinen Vernunft I* & *Werkausgabe Band IV: Kritik der Reinen Vernunft II*, edited by Wilhelm Weischedel (Frankfurt am Main: Suhrkamp, 1968).

[*CJ*] Kant, Immanuel (1790), *Critique of Judgement*, translated by W.S. Pluhar (Indianapolis: Hackett, 1987). [*KU*] *Immanuel Kant: Werkausgabe Band X: Kritik der Urteilskraft*, edited by Wilhelm Weischedel (Frankfurt am Main: Suhrkamp, 1968).

[*AP*] Kant, Immanuel (1798), *Anthropologie in Pragmatischer Hinsicht*, *Immanuel Kant: Werkausgabe Band XI: Schriften zur Anthropologie, Gesichtsphilosophie, Politik und Pädagogik*, edited by Wilhelm Weischedel (Frankfurt am Main: Suhrkamp, 1968).

[*NVC*] Klossowski, Pierre (1969), *Nietzsche and the Vicious Circle*, translated by D.W. Smith (London: Athlone, 1997). [*NCV*] *Nietzsche et le cercle vicieux* (Paris: Mercure de France, 1969).

Krell, David Farrell, *Daimon Life: Heidegger and Life Philosophy* (Bloomington & Indianapolis: Indiana Press, 1992).

Krell, David Farrell 'Consultations with the Paternal Shadow: Gasché, Derrida and Klossowski on *Ecce Homo*' in *Exceedingly Nietzsche*, edited by David Farrell Krell and David Wood (London: Routledge, 1988) 80–94.

Krell, David Farrell and Bates, Donald L., *The Good European: Nietzsche's Work Sites in Word and Image* (Chicago: University of Chicago Press, 1997).

Land, Nick, 'Delighted to Death', *Pli: Warwick Journal of Philosophy*, vol. 3, no. 2, (1991) 76–88.

Lingis, Alphonso, *Foreign Bodies* (New York: Routledge, 1994).

Lippitt, John, (ed.), *Nietzsche's Futures* (London: Macmillan Press – now Palgrave Macmillan, 1999).

[*IIK*] Makkreel, Rudolf, *Imagination and Interpretation in Kant: The Hermeneutical Import of the 'Critique of Judgement'* (Chicago: University of Chicago Press, 1990).

[*ITKS*] Makkreel, Rudolf, 'Imagination and Temporality in Kant's Theory of the Sublime', *Immanuel Kant: Critical Assessments*, edited by R. Chadwick and C. Cazeaux, (London: Routledge, 1992), pp. 878–96.

[*PP*] Merleau-Ponty, Maurice (1945), *The Phenomenology of Perception*, translated by C. Smith (London: Routledge & Kegan Paul, 1962). [*PhP*] *Phénoménologie de la Perception* (Paris: Gallimard, 1945).

[*V&I*] Merleau-Ponty, Maurice (1964), *The Visible and the Invisible*, translated by A. Lingis (Evanston: Northwestern University Press, 1968).

Mishima, Yukio (1949), *Confessions of a Mask*, translated by Meredith Weatherby (London: Paladin, 1988).

[*SS*] Mishima, Yukio, *Sun and Steel*, translated by John Bester (Tokyo: Kodansha International, 1970).

Mitchell, Juliet and Rose, Jacqueline (eds), *Feminine Sexuality: Jacques Lacan and the École Freudienne*, translated by Jacqueline Rose (London: Macmillan, 1982).

Parent, D. and Gilman, S.L., *Conversations with Nietzsche: A Life in the Words of his Contemporaries* (Oxford: Oxford University Press, 1987).

[*H*] Pfau, Thomas (ed.), *Friedrich Hölderlin: Essays and Letters on Theory* (Albany: SUNY, 1988). [*FA*] Sattler, D.E. (ed.), *Friedrich Hölderlin: Sämtliche Werke (Frankfurter Ausgabe)* (Frankfurt: Roter Stern, 1978–92). [*BS*] Beissner, F. & Schmidt, J. (eds), *Friedrich Hölderlin: Werke und Briefe* (Frankfurt am Main: Insel, 1982).

Rehberg, Andrea 'Feminism, Phenomenology, Writing', in *The Journal of the British Society for Phenomenology*, vol. 29, no. 3, (1998), 320–25.

Reich, Wilhelm (1942), *The Function of the Orgasm: Sex-Economic Problems of Biological Energy*, translated by Vincent R. Carfagno (London: Souvenir Press, 1989).

Roberts, Tyler T. 'Ecstatic Philosophy' in *Nietzsche and the Divine*, edited by John Lippitt and Jim Urpeth (Manchester: Clinamen Press, 2000), pp. 200–25.

Roskill, Mark (ed.), *The Letters of Van Gogh* (London: Fontana, 1963).

Sallis, John 'Apollo's Mimesis', *Journal of the British Society for Phenomenology*, vol. 15, no. 1, January 1984, 16–21.

[*C*] Sallis, John, *Crossings: Nietzsche and the Space of Tragedy* (Chicago: University of Chicago Press, 1991).

[*WWR*, I] Schopenhauer, Arthur (1819), *The World as Will and Representation*, Volume One, translated by E.F. Payne (New York: Dover Publications, 1966). [*WWV*, I] *Die Welt als Wille und Vorstellung*, Band 1 (Stuttgart: Reclam, 1987).

[*WWR*, II] Schopenhauer, Arthur (1847), *The World as Will and Representation*, Volume Two, translated by E.F. Payne (New York: Dover Publications, 1966). [*WWV*, II] *Die Welt als Wille und Vorstellung*, Band 2 (Stuttgart: Reclam, 1987).

[*MNI*] Schreber, Daniel Paul (1903), *Memoirs of My Nervous Illness*, translated by Ida Macalpine and Richard A. Hunter (London: W. M. Dawson & Sons Ltd, 1955). [*DNK*] *Denkwürdigkeiten eines Nervenkranken* (Berlin: Kadmos Verlag, 1995).

Stone, I. & Stone, J. (eds), *Dear Theo: The Autobiography of Vincent Van Gogh* (London: Cassell, 1937).

[*LST*]Teresa of Ávila (1588), *The Life of Saint Teresa of Ávila by Herself*, translated by J.M. Cohen, (London: Penguin, 1975).

Urpeth, Jim, 'A "Pessimism of Strength": Nietzsche and the Tragic Sublime', in J. Lippitt (ed.), *Nietzsche's Futures* (London: Macmillan Press – now Palgrave Macmillan, 1999).

Urpeth, Jim, 'A "Sacred Thrill": Presentation and Affectivity in the Analytic of the Sublime', in A. Rehberg and R. Jones, *The Matter of Critique: Readings on Kant's Philosophy* (Manchester: Clinamen Press, 2000).

Urpeth, Jim, 'The Vitalisation of Aesthetic Form: Kant, Nietzsche, Heidegger, Focillon', in S. Brewster, J. Joughin, D. Owen, R. Walker (eds), *Inhuman Reflections* (Manchester: Manchester University Press, 2000).

[*CU*] Anonymous (c.1370) *The Cloud of Unknowing*, edited by C. Wolters (London: Penguin, 1961).

Index